STILL DIGGING

Other books by Sir Mortimer Wheeler

SEGONTIUM AND THE ROMAN OCCUPATION OF WALES
(Hon. Society of Cymmrodorion, 1924)

THE ROMAN FORT NEAR BRECON
(Hon. Society of Cymmrodorion, 1926)

PREHISTORIC AND ROMAN WALES
(Oxford University Press, 1926)

EXCAVATION OF THE PREHISTORIC, ROMAN, AND POST-ROMAN SITE IN
LYDNEY PARK, GLOUCESTERSHIRE
(with T. V. Wheeler: Society of Antiquaries of London, 1932)

VERULAMIUM: A BELGIC AND TWO ROMAN CITIES
(with T. V. Wheeler: Society of Antiquaries of London, 1936)

MAIDEN CASTLE, DORSET
(Society of Antiquaries of London, 1943)

FIVE THOUSAND YEARS OF PAKISTAN
(Christopher Johnson, 1950)

THE INDUS CIVILIZATION
(Cambridge University Press, 1953)

ARCHAEOLOGY FROM THE EARTH
(Clarendon Press, 1954)

ROME BEYOND THE IMPERIAL FRONTIERS
(Bell, 1954)

THE STANWICK FORTIFICATIONS, YORKSHIRE
(Society of Antiquaries of London, 1954)

PORTRAIT OF THE AUTHOR: VERULAMIUM, 1930

SIR MORTIMER WHEELER

STILL
DIGGING

*Interleaves from an
Antiquary's Notebook*

London
MICHAEL JOSEPH

First published by
MICHAEL JOSEPH LTD
*26 Bloomsbury Street
London, W.C.1*
1955

*Set and printed in Great Britain by Unwin Brothers Ltd., at the
Gresham Press, Woking, in Fournier type, eleven point, leaded,
on paper made by John Dickinson and bound by James Burn*

CONTENTS

ILLUSTRATIONS

PREFACE

TURNING out of Pall Mall, I was transfixed by the steely gaze of
Mr. Augustus John. 'Hullo, Rikki,' he said; 'still digging?' 'Hullo,
Augustus,' I replied; 'still sketching?' We both grunted and passed
on. A chance recollection of that momentous interchange has
solved my publisher's problem of a title for these pages. My own
choice, sequel to my last chapter, had been 'Twenty Years Asleep,'
but the eye of experience would have nothing of it. Sleep, it appears,
is not a marketable commodity. Digging for the past, on the other
hand, apparently is. *Pulvis et umbra* are news. The popular Press
has long found it profitable not merely to report but even to promote
archaeological excavation; so that the other day in Cincinnati I
scarcely gave the matter a second thought when I found the eminent
excavator of Troy at work in a comfortable study amidst the
machinery of the newspaper which is his generous patron. And now
radio follows suit and is, I understand, sponsoring a highly technical
archaeological enterprise in the Mediterranean. Yes, digging is
news, and I have no doubt that my publisher is wise in inscribing it
upon my title-page.

'Still digging' recalls by implication the considerable stretch of
time covered by this chronicle. In an unusual measure, the period
has been one of transition in the history of archaeological craftsmanship. During the years before the First World War archaeology was
still an unorganized discipline, its techniques were largely un-
evolved. Systematic training did not, and could not, exist, and
archaeological posts were in any case nearly non-existent. The past
had no future in it. Today the picture is of another kind. Most of
our universities now have chairs or lectureships in archaeology,
and every year some hundreds of our young men and women
receive instruction in the subject. The distant past is being combined, as never before, with the complexities of the present in a

lengthening perspective which at least provides a sort of working substitute for philosophy and at best a reassuring context for our own antics and absurdities. It is my present privilege to sit on Thursday evenings in an imposing chair at Burlington House and to listen to the latest news of human vicissitudes from any quarter of the globe and from any moment within the last half-million years. Not all of this stuff is tender to the taste; some of it has been cooked a trifle long. But by and large it is a varied and exciting pabulum, very different from the unsophisticated dietry of my youth. Much science has gone to the making of it, from basic geology to atomic research; for today archaeology touches all manner of skills and inquiries which were alien to it in my youth. It has, as I say, been discovered not merely by the public but even by the professors, and its surging expansion alike in the academic and in the less academic world has been the experience of a single generation. In the intervals of war, this double development of the scientific consciousness has been for me an absorbing spectacle or even, as an occasional participant, an absorbing adventure which, on the whole, I would not have exchanged for any other destiny.

The following pages are mostly abstracted from old notebooks and letters, scribbled in many odd places and usually in the immediate shadow of the episodes to which they relate. If they qualify at all for a modest place in the genre of a lively half-century they do so only within the meaning of De Quincey when he wrote that 'the least things and the greatest are bound together as elements equally essential of the mysterious universe.'

Mortimer Wheeler

1. Boyhood in the Provinces

For a quarter of a century I have been an archaeologist, a destroyer of the past, and for nine or ten active years a gunner, helping a little, I suppose, to build the future on good constructive high-explosive. In neither rôle have I been very important, but I have not been a mere supernumerary. The interest of this episodic record, if it have interest, is that it represents an average life in one of the great formative periods of history.

As an archaeologist I have no doubt discovered the tub and overlooked Diogenes. As a gunner I have doubtless aimed at the mountain and hit the hapless mouse. In both capacities I have striven with detachment tempered by an equable enthusiasm. I do not believe in much except hard work, which serves as an antidote to disillusion and a substitute for faith. Spiritual aloofness, in spite of experiment, has been as nearly as possible complete. In my time, the volcano has spouted its ashes and entombed a landscape, but, with the Plinys, I have sate on a hill apart and likened the deadly Vesuvian column to a fir-tree. The ash destroys and then fertilizes; meanwhile it is a picture like any other. At its best, this book will be little more than a scrap-book: probably few lives are otherwise, save those of the very successful or the very humdrum.

*   *   *

When I last looked upon Vesuvius, I was 5,000 feet above it, and its toothless maw was framed in a ruff of snow, superbly sinister. More than six years previously in the dusk I had thrust my military caravan into the Amphitheatre Gate of Pompeii as far as a new bomb-crater would allow me, and all night long that same Vesuvius had leered at me with an enflamed Cyclopean eye. At dawn I had walked into the city, a little gingerly, preceded by a sapper who thrust a bayonet ever and anon into the suspect soil. The reconstructed two-storey houses of the *nuovi scavi* had been bombed with satisfactory nicety by our fellows up above: not their fault—they had been told that a German armoured division was 'in Pompeii,' and the map writes POMPEII in large letters across the blackened mass of the old city, whilst the insignificant modern townlet on the main road is merely *Pompeii*. Poor old bourgeois Pompeii, born to be blasted in one way or another! But on the whole it had assumed a certain unwonted dignity amidst its fresh excoriations, with the faint lingering smell of high-explosive about it. It at least lacked the stark vulgarity of Mussolini's *Via dell' Impero* at Rome, where the shrunken, bony fora, once decently screened, have been rudely exposed like an old lady undressed in public. (What a city Rome would be, were it not for its ruins!)

*   *   *

But the Pliny family has led me astray. I should have begun my chronicle on the Braid Hills of Edinburgh, where on a day of 1893 I trotted along at the level of my father's knees, which smelt delectably of Harris tweed. We sat by the roadside; high above us the telegraph-wires twanged their lonely music, and yet higher above the brown hills a lark was singing, lonelier still:

> 'To-wit to-wee, to-wit to-wee,
> There's naebody on airth can mak a
>   shoe for me, for me.'
> 'Why so why so, why so why so?'
> 'Becas me heel's as lang as me toe.'

They are the first words in my memory, and they abide. I piped them after my father, and so attuned were they to the scene that the landscape in all its details entered with them into my infant mind. Twenty-two years later a young captain of artillery was taking his horses on exercise across those same hills, and halted casually for a ten-minutes' break. As he sat back on the roadside turf, his head came down to the three-year-old level. And there were the same twanging telegraph-wires, above them the same

shoeless lark and the outline of the brown hills, just so. It was by
chance the remembered spot.

*   *   *

Two other inconsequent memories of this time remain, with a
wholly irrational vividness. One is of a camera obscura which still
stands on the fringe of the forecourt of Edinburgh Castle. In it I
gazed enraptured upon the toy-like manœuvres of a white-jacketed
Highland regiment actually engaged upon its morning drill outside
—a picture which linked directly with Waterloo and was an age
apart from the soldiering I was later to know. The other is a
moment of agonizing terror when I was held precariously astride
of Mons Meg, waiting for the explosion which would turn the old
iron into red-hot metal and end the world in searing flames. Below
me, with the acid clearness of a vision seen in terror, stretched
Princes Street along which years afterwards I was to ride in review at
the head of a more modern ordnance. But I have never stood beside
a gun firing without the ghost of a Mons-Meg shiver down my spine.

*   *   *

For the rest, the tribulations of childhood may be assumed.
Really important things—a large frigate with black and white
port-holes, treasured until it was little more than a splinter, a brass
cannon that was let off dangerously with real gunpowder on feast-
days, a steam-engine that never worked but was fraught with
potentiality—hold the fortress of memory against all the onslaught
of routine. When I was four years old, my father migrated to
Bradford as assistant editor of a Yorkshire newspaper, and everything that mattered in my education happened there, between then
and the age of fourteen. But before I come to that pregnant decade
I must say a word or two about my father.

He was a failure by all standards save his own. I doubt whether
until his last years he ever earned more than £350 a year (pre-1914
values), but within him was an inexhaustible spring of happiness.
He was the son of a worthy tea-merchant of Bristol, whom I
remember as a bluff old boy amongst the towering hollyhocks,
poppies, and raspberry-canes of the Gloucestershire farm to which

he retired. My grandmother was a little gentle, good-looking old lady with a streak of cynical piety in her composition. Her piety was at first reflected in her son, whose early endeavour was to enter the Baptist ministry; but her cynicism triumphed, and he broke away to Edinburgh, where he was rather an outstanding student in the great days of Masson and Blackie, and became, incidentally, an advanced freethinker of the militant type of the early 'eighties. Blackie would stride stormily into his classroom of a morning, his plaid flowing behind him, and a turgid stream of Greek of a peculiarly Doric sort pouring from his lips. 'What hae I been haverin' aboot?' he would demand suddenly of some trembling undergraduate—in this instance, my father. And having recognized the words ὁ Γλάδστων in the spate, the victim ventured 'Home Rule, Sir,' and a lasting bond of mutual understanding was forthwith established.

For a time my father, with a young wife, was caught up in a circle which included (Sir) Carlaw Martin, later Director of the Royal Scottish Museum, and J. M. Robertson, later a persistent M.P. and a minor minister, whose elaborately tendentious studies in comparative religion have to be read (if at all) in the limited context of an age when Foote and Bradlaugh were living dangerously as missionary heroes of a liberty only less intolerant than the creeds against which they strove. But his interests lay in music and art, and in lecturing shyly on English literature to audiences which appear to have been attracted as much by his extreme good looks and gentle diffidence as by the matter of his discourses, though these I have no doubt were in themselves very good. A year later his wife died in childbirth, and he began to drift into the weedy backwaters of journalism, from which he never again emerged. Shortly afterwards he married my mother, the niece and ward of Thomas Spencer Baynes, who professed Shakespeare at St. Andrews and left a remarkable relict of rich character, whose ample presence and no less ample largesse punctuated my childhood with awesome happiness. My mother was a courageous but rather nerve-ridden woman, to whom my father's inconsequent interest in everything except £ s. d. remained an irritating mystery. She had much to put up with, poor soul, but survived her troubles with an increasing sweetness to the age of eighty-four.

I have never indeed encountered a mind so universally comprehensive and irrepressibly adventurous as my father's. He lived the most humdrum of lives—he travelled once as far as Nuremberg and once to Bruges—yet his daily existence was packed with adventure. Tartarin had nothing to offer him. He had forded the Kabul River under fire, until he could describe the splash of every bullet; he had shot man-eating tigers whose breath lay hot upon my boyish ears. All men who had striven beyond the frontiers were his heroes. His worshipped familiars ranged in fact from Robertson of Chitral to a porter who had been to Kandahar with Roberts. In one way or another I happen to have done rather more than all the things he dreamed of, but I often doubt whether my facts could even now hold a candle to his fancy. Cycling back the four miles from his newspaper office in the early hours of the morning, he would stop by the way to share the lives of policemen or tramps, or of a particularly reprehensible poacher who became also one of my own boyhood confidants. His simple unspoken admiration for men of action won him friends of every grade, and for years after he eventually left Yorkshire all manner of Yorkshiremen remained in faithful touch with him. For feebleness or effeminacy he had no sort of patience. And his own courage, though never tested, was never in doubt: never tested until, during the last ten years of his life, when he went suddenly blind, it showed itself of a kind that out-tops mere gallantry.

His mind was a map of the by-ways of literature, a scholarly map full of exciting discovery. On wet afternoons I would curl up and he would extract dusty books from the backs of his double-stacked shelves, reading and expounding a multitude of things, some of which I did not understand and others which I understood better than he knew. From my earliest years he treated me as an adult mind, and I mentally hopped and skipped alongside his talk as I hopped and skipped beside his long striding legs on our frequent walks together. As to the latter, he never abated his pace for my little steps, and I learned to walk in an abnormally fast and ungainly fashion. I even learned to mumble my words as he mumbled his round the pipe that was perennially between his teeth, so that I have never really achieved the art of crisp speech. In a way, I am afraid I acquired instead a precocious and partly conscious snobbery which was entirely alien to my mentor. I remember once at the age of six or seven being taken to a rather terrifying Christmas party at the house of the chief proprietor of my father's newspaper, and, becoming increasingly bored with the oafish pleasantries of my fellow urchins, I can still recall vividly the surge of revulsion that finally compelled me, in one of those deadly moments of utter silence, to exclaim shrilly '*Damn* this party, take me away from it.' 'My boy,' said my father to me next day, 'your ancestor Rogers the Martyr was burned at Smithfield for saying what he thought.' He did not develop the moral theme but proceeded to tell me the story of Prebendary Rogers, ending with the burning, which deeply impressed me. 'And then they tied Rogers the Martyr to a stake and piled the firewood round him. And beyond the firewood stood Mrs. Rogers, with a wailing baby in her arms and the tears streaming down her face. And round about the firewood stood the little Rogerses, little boy-Rogerses and little girl-Rogerses, all howling and howling and howling. And old Rogers the Martyr looked upon them and shook his head mournfully and said: "Mr. Executioner, for God's sake light the fire and give me peace." And that was the end of your ancestor Rogers the Martyr.' But not for me—I still find myself thinking guiltily of Rogers the Martyr as the party drags its slow length along and I stifle—or fail to stifle—the midnight yawn.

Save when school was inescapable, the afternoons were devoted to our walks together, my father and I, in unfailingly successful search of adventure and new scraps of knowledge. On one memorable day in the woods beyond Saltaire we might find an unrecorded cup-marked stone (later, I believe, recorded by my father in a British Association handbook). On another we might encounter gypsies gathering strange fungi for the pot, and learn from them to discern the good fungi from the bad. We even (to my mother's horror) put our new knowledge to a practical test and on one occasion, after consuming the dangerous morsels, sat waiting grimly for death. On yet another afternoon, when the mist lay heavily on the hills and concealed our guilt, we hewed most scandalously into the flank of an ancient barrow on Baildon Moor, happily without result. And when the August corn was ripening I was allowed to take my small Belgian double-barrelled gun into the cornfields and disperse the predatory finches: always on one condition, that I ate every bird I shot. My father taught me to shoot, to fish and to trap, but never for the mere sake of killing. Often on a summer's eve I have eaten myself to a standstill after plucking countless corn-fed sparrows and cooking them in a lump of dripping within a stoneware jam-jar. Succulent little mouthfuls they were, and many was the good supper of my own hunting and cooking.

Alternatively, there were the innumerable creatures that we assembled round us (my two sisters and I): two mongrel collie-dogs, mother and son, which we had for years, a semi-Persian cat, a venerable and seemingly immortal wood-owl of unspeakable wisdom that lived outside in an enormous pen of a cage, a dozen fantail pigeons (silly, puffed-up creatures), hedgehogs and tortoises that roamed perilously about the wilderness of a garden, guinea-pigs, green tree-frogs, newts netted in a moorland pond, and, not least, grass-snakes which had a tremendous nuisance-value in my constant guerrilla warfare with my countless maiden aunts. A snake in an aunt's bath was worth any petty punishment that might ensue.

Looking back, I can see how in these impressionable years the insidious poisons of archaeology were already entering into my system. On one day it might be the discovery of a strange medieval kiln in a clay-pit at Baildon; or, further afield on another, the filling of our pockets with Roman potsherds where a stream cuts the flank of the Roman fort at Ilkley. Or again, the sight of the strange crosses in the Ilkley churchyard or of the still stranger cup-and-ring marks on the hill-side above the town, or the picking up of an occasional flint knife or 'scraper' on Rumbold's Moor. But all these things are merely selected moments in a constant succession of incidents, filled out by my father's quick observation and quicker memory—scraps quoted in our stride from Walt Whitman, Keats, Drummond of Hawthornden, Rabelais, Emerson, and broken off suddenly to watch a squatting grouse or an unusual butterfly, or the sloping rain behind the Cow and Calf which marked the rocky limit of the moor. We were a solitary pair, bound by bonds tighter than we knew. And I remember regarding our chance encounters with others as an intrusion upon our privacy.

We might walk a (to me) reluctant mile with Cutcliffe Hyne, really a very fine fellow whose rattling sense of action appealed to my father, or Halliwell Sutcliffe, curiously introspective and inclined to act his novels somewhat embarrassingly before writing them—not that this procedure made his novels more real, it merely made his life more unreal—or Oliver Onions, whose *Compleat Bachelor* had, I believe, just rescued him from a precarious living earned by delineating bedsteads and wardrobes for a furniture-dealer's catalogue, or occasionally Bertram Priestman, for whose gentle drawing-room art my father had an affection that transcended criticism.

For myself, my youthful taste (I may have been twelve) rejected Captain Kettle as mere melodrama, but I took Cutcliffe Hyne's other hero, Thompson, to my inmost heart. *Thompson's Progress* was not the most notorious of Hyne's works but it was far and away his best. It was written from a profound knowledge of the Yorkshire-man, and in particular of the Yorkshire poacher, and matched my personal and precocious knowledge of the tribe. The story, you will remember, is that of a West Riding poacher who becomes a man of property and, from sheer ennui or nostalgia, takes to poaching his own estates. I suppose I already possessed, and have retained, a liking for outcast men, for Hereward the Wake or Gurth the Swineherd or Robin Hood or, above all, for the old marshman in *Dick o' the Fens*. This was to Manville Fenn's writings what *Thompson's Progress* was to Hyne's, a book written with secret pleasure and inward understanding. No one reads it now, but it is a good powerful tale, full of the lurking sinister quality of the reedy waterways; second only to that book of books, Richard Jefferies's *Bevis, the Story of a Boy*, which brought all islands to one's boyish grasp with an intimate actuality that neither Crusoe nor the Swiss Family ever achieved. For the rest, when I wanted to enjoy a pleasant melancholy, Don Quixote perennially supplied the need. There sometimes seemed to be a faint touch of my father in him, although I suppose my wholesome virile parent would have voted rather for Sancho Panza, calling a windmill a windmill even whilst tilting at it.

The school which I entered at the age of nine and left at the age of fourteen (when my schooldays ended), was a procreation of King Charles the Second, the Bradford Grammar School, then

situated at the sooty centre of the city. At that time—I know
nothing of it now—it was a pretty good school under the stern
dictatorship of one Keeling ('Rusty'), a terrifying head master of
the old kind, whose son was to become a distinguished M.P.
Under him were one or two masters of some considerable attainment, above all J. E. Barton, a Newdigate Prizeman, who years
later became head first of Wakefield and then of Bristol Grammar
Schools. Barton, relatively unknown to fame, exercised more
influence upon my generation and that which followed mine than
most public men of his time. He had a pimply, sensitive face, a per-
ceptibly nasal voice, and a prehensile intelligence that grasped very
ordinary schoolboy minds and moulded them into the Barton shape.

The Latin which I learned from Barton was of no great consequence, and indeed in the aggregate I may not have learned much
from him of anything. But he had the faculty of stimulating our
callow minds and of indicating rather than illuminating new
horizons. He would give us some trivial task and then lapse into a
sleep which we would respect with an almost painful reticence
that surprised ourselves if we dimly attempted to analyse it. Then
he would suddenly stir into some semblance of life and begin to
talk. The subject might be Pheidias or Socialism or Modern Artists,
and we knew gratefully that for that day at least Livy was consigned
to limbo. Later, I believe, he turned with increasing persistence to
the more revolutionary modern art, and when I stayed with him
many years afterwards at Bristol his walls were covered with an
astonishingly varied and entertaining collection of -isms and -ists,
to which the senior boys were admitted as to worshipped relics.
His medium was by that time the symposium, and in the evenings
his Bristol study was filled with honest and earnest young tradesmen
striving with one another and with Barton over the bodies of
Picasso and Henry Moore.

That, however, is looking ahead. In my day at Bradford, all this
was just beginning. At that time only a small intelligentsia had
nucleated round Barton, chief amongst them Humbert Wolfe, who
was five or six years older than I and an unquestioned Olympian.
I was immoderately glad, I remember, when Keeling gave us a half-
holiday to celebrate Wolfe's scholarship to Oxford (en route for the
Civil Service and Parnassus). The lid had been taken off something,

and the air once more circulated. In retrospect, it simply meant that an outstanding intellect had been removed from our humdrum paths. But for the moment it meant to me that, in a measure, I filled the vacant place, nature thus waywardly expressing her abhorrence of a vacuum. None of us paid the slightest attention to unobtrusive contemporaries such as Frank Dyson, who was to hitch his wagon to a star as Astronomer Royal, or the amiable Maufe, who was to win a V.C. in one war and to get accidentally blown up in another. The real notables of our school generation, the Men who Counted in our daily life, nearly all of them failed to make good in the world beyond our gates. Of such fragility are schoolboy reputations; I suppose the more gifted of us have our little decade of fruition, sometimes before sixteen and sometimes not till after sixty, rarely both and often neither.

By and large, my school was of no great moment to me, save perhaps that it confirmed me in certain prejudices which I had developed in contact with my father. I had then, as I have still, a deep-seated, barely tolerant contempt for those who have to seek amusement in hitting balls with variously shaped sticks, or in kicking balls of various shapes and sizes through, round or over various absurd obstacles under a variety of inconsequent regulations. I have played one game of cricket in my life, one game of Rugby football, one game of polo, and, as a climactic condescension, one game of croquet. The game of cricket was an Occasion. After a rough beginning, my school-fellows had learned to accept my undisguised scorn of their shibboleths, and a satisfactory *modus vivendi* had been established. I ran various short-lived and mildly scandalous magazines, bred mice, developed a strong line in cata-pults ('Wheeler's,' with double thongs of very sturdy rubber), organized a stamp bureau, and even gathered about me three or four disciples who spent with me one half-holiday a week drawing anything we liked in the Art School. Also, on the slightest provoca-tion I produced large coloured posters which were hung in the school entrance-hall. In return for all these and perhaps other trifling services to the community I was by tacit consent exempted from the impositions of the sports-ground. But on one occasion for some forgotten reason it became essential that, if I was to retain my self-respect, I should play for my form in some idiot cricket tournament. In due course I arrived on the ground with a spotless new pair of flannel bags and the sketchiest understanding of the game. For several hours I stood in a remote part of the field wondering what to do if the dangerous missile should veer in my direction. Happily it didn't. Then we removed ourselves to the pavilion, where we adopted one of three or four critical or slightly blasé stances which I quickly recognized and simulated as a part of the ritual. Finally, the eleventh batsman was ordered out, and I stumbled with an air of nonchalance and a heart of melted wax towards one of the ridiculous little wooden contraptions which appeared to mark the ends of the runway. Again my angel smiled upon me. My colleague the tenth man was the first target for the projectile, and without any more ado the little sticks behind him flew merrily in the air. Whilst I was pondering what A did next, the target came graciously up to me and said (for some reason which remains concealed) 'Sorry, old chap,' to which I wonderingly replied 'Oh, not at all,' and we all crowded back to the pavilion amidst uncomprehended applause. Shortly afterwards I sat in some liquid tar and permanently wrecked my virgin slacks. But on the whole I think that my cricket can be described as faultless.

Since I have strayed into ball-games, I will anticipate. My solitary game of Rugby football is carved upon my bones. It occurred on the plains of Lombardy on a hard winter's day of 1917. As a young major I had to turn out to make up the total, whatever that may have been; and thereafter ensued on the frozen soil a gladiatorial contest which threw the recently experienced delights of Passchendaele into the shade. The game devolved into a series of individual combats which eventually put a whole unit of the 5th Division out of action. Nero at least provided his lions with easy-going Christians, but there were no Christians in this internecine Roman holiday.

No, the palm goes to croquet. The lawn of the hospitable British Legation (now Embassy) at Kabul, was the stage, amidst a galaxy of flowers and with the outliers of the Hindu Kush as a back-cloth. It was an apt setting. Being played largely, I believe, by ladies and clergymen, croquet has no rules and is completely subordinate to scenery and scandal. A sport *sans peur* though scarcely *sans reproche.*

But enough of that. I return for a moment to juvenile caprices, and then on to more manly stuff. There remain two things at which I have little more than hinted. The first was my training as a hunter. In that term I include, not only shooting with shot-gun or rifle and fishing with fly or float or sinker, but an attitude towards all of them that transcends mere slaying and bagging. From the years when I first toddled alongside my father, I was taught to carry a stick as though it were a gun, with all the formality and circumspection and respect that so dangerous a toy demanded. But I was also taught to regard myself as a wild thing amongst other wild things, to tread lightly through the wood without cracking a twig, to share the glade surreptitiously with the wood-pigeon busy upon his beech-nuts, or, most difficult of all, to crawl through the undergrowth without setting the small birds a-chattering. Beside the stream I was taught to peer quietly through the bushes at the basking trout without vibration or tell-tale shadow. From the river-bank, if a disturbed waterhen should plunge below the surface, I was taught to watch amongst the reeds until I could detect the refugee's yellow beak sticking up from the water like a tiny peri-scope, almost imperceptible save to that sixth sense that was gradually emerging in my young mind. In these and a hundred other things my father was my prime tutor, himself always learning as he taught. For the rest I picked up scraps of knowledge from a variety of sources, above all from Will the poacher, who like all true Yorkshiremen had a lurcher of uncanny sensibility. It was Will who taught me how to skin and stuff birds; who took me on a moonlit night silently into Hurst Wood and showed me without a word the round black tufts that were stray pheasants roosting among the bare birches against the bright indigo sky. And I remember, as we emerged from the wood on to the Cottingley road, finding myself looking upwards and upwards, as it seemed indefinitely, past an infinitude of serge trouser, coat and woollen muffler to the broad genial face of Mr. Barraclough, the gigantic police superintendent, looking down upon me over his great moustachios and giving me a magisterial greeting. He was a faithful midnight friend of my father's and knew me well. 'Hullo, Sonny,' he was saying, 'out all alone in the moonlight?' I half turned, then checked, my head. Will and his dog had vanished from my side.

Indeed they lived, those two, almost soundlessly and with a perfect understanding.

In hunting of the normal social sort I have never taken much interest. That pink parade is not hunting in any sense of the term that I understand (yet may the blessed soul of Jorrocks rest in peace). Occasionally on the tufty local moors my father and I would spend a day with the harriers, until my knees could scarcely carry my leaden body home. But we were always on the side of the hare, particularly of Old Charlie, a very wise old hare who frequently gave the field a good run but invariably got away into the inside of a familiar and voluminous dry-built wall. There we sometimes used to wait for him and give him a two-man cheer as he dived to safety well ahead of the pursuit.

All these and other things of their ilk have entered into the fabric of my life. I may not touch a gun or a rod for years on end; then suddenly one or the other comes into my friendly grasp, and I am walking down grouse on a fell in northern Lancashire or chikor in Afghanistan or gazelle (for the pot) in Persia or partridge in Sind, or hooking and likely losing a muscular trout in a snow-fed Kashmiri torrent. These are things that matter, experiences that cannot just be bought. They are bred in the young body and the young mind—bred in the small boy who learns to carry a stick as a gun and to tread the paths of the wild with comprehension.

The other principal thread in the fabric was a consuming ambition to be a painter. I have spoken of half-holidays spent, alone or with a small select company, in the Art Room of the school. Apart from that, every spare moment of my busy boyhood was used up in the production of an endless succession of water-colours, oil-colours, pastels, in a fruitless endeavour to express and evacuate some complex or other that inflamed my mental inside. To me every thought, however abstract, assumed (and assumes) a shape and colour. Friday was privately yellow to me long years before I read, with sharp and jealous surprise, James McNeill Whistler's impatient remark 'Of course Friday's yellow!' Later, when in my university days I dabbled in Greek philosophy, even the *eidos* took upon itself a nebulous form, rather like a Hobbiah. I suppose real artists, like Whistler himself, always have this visual complex, and that musicians for their part, without a second thought to it, hum to themselves the tune of Thursday. Anyway, this pictorial reflex, though I never succeeded in projecting it, has served me on the whole in good stead: it has helped me to objectify most things that have happened to me, even while they were happening, and has so enabled me to spend my life, happily enough, encloistered in a picture-gallery.

There is no need to dwell upon these frustrated efforts; only once did I allow them to escape into the (Bradford) world. When I was twelve years old we spent a holiday at Robin Hood's Bay, and I remember painting there two oil-colours, one a smarmy oleographical thing of cottages impending upon the sea, and the other a slap-dash field of corn thrown on to the board with a palette-knife. The cornfield seemed to me rather free and good, the cottages stilted and awful. But the sudden idea occurred to my juvenile mind to send them both into the Bradford Art Gallery for its autumn exhibition. The oleograph was accepted and exposed to the public gaze ('Exhibit by Boy of Twelve'—some local paper, *not* my father's!), and the cornfield was rejected. 'I knew it,' I remember muttering, darkly and with a secret exultation. Which presents me as a disgusting little prig, and rightly so; *only*, I was well aware at that same moment that I *was* a little prig, and in that awareness may have saved some years of purgatory.

When I was fourteen, my father was asked to take over the London office of his newspaper. I had just attained the glory of the sixth form at school, with scholarships looming ahead, and Barton went to my father with an angry protest. Knowing or guessing something of my father's impecuniosity, he said bluntly: 'You are not taking him away from Bradford, you are taking him away from Oxford.' My father looked at me and I grinned back at him. My mind, far into the night, was already awhirl with anticipatory pictures of London, LONDON. Unregretting, I turned my back simultaneously upon my schooldays and upon Oxford, and shortly afterwards sat excitedly beside my father in the night train to London, with a singing heart and a raging toothache.

2. London and Archaeology

In the early hours of the morning a jingling hansom took us from St. Pancras to Fleet Street, the hooves clop-clopping on the wooden sets through cavernous, silent streets. That hollow, resonant noise, more than any other sound, epitomized pre-1914 London. Across the Green Park of an evening, Piccadilly with its flowing lights dipping sharply into its considerable valley would be atune with harness-bells and the unceasing clop-clop which out-topped all other sounds. But from all the generalized roar of London through the years my memory strikes first the echo of that pioneer journey of the young provincial into an Unknown with which his imagination was yet already familiar; ending with a flash of lamplight across the purple-veined face of the top-hatted cabby as he gleamed amiably down on us from his Olympian throne with the inevitable formula 'Leave it to you, Sir.' Then up a narrow stair to the first-floor office which was to be my father's, and in a sense mine, for many years, and finally to a desk-top on which I rolled up in my coat, my head on a pile of ink-scented newspapers, and sank suddenly into oblivion. . . .

My father's voice was in my ears, and from outside, down in The Street, Fleet Street, rose the intermittent rumble of laden drays dragged by heavy horses against the incline. It was still dark, if possible darker than before, but my father was waiting for me to come down with him and see the dawn. The roadway as we emerged was drenched in a chilly blackness through which cumbrous wagons piled with vegetables were dimly thrusting (as my father told me) towards Covent Garden. And then I looked up and saw a sight which I shall never forget.

Since that day I have witnessed a multitude of dawns, some beautiful, some dramatic, some just ghastly. Indeed, I regard myself as something of a connoisseur of dawns, and by and large am definitely their partisan against those vulgar, blowsy, elderly tarts, the sunsets. But crowned over all my dawns stands that first view of St. Paul's with its topmost pinnacles faintly aglow in a first light which had not yet come to earth. As I looked, the grey stone fabric was warming to life, the flush was slowly, very slowly, creeping down the mountainous flanks, the gigantic Galatea was awakening and had, I remember, actually a strange illusion of breathing. The phrase ῥοδοδάκτυλος ἕως means just 'A.M.' to Homer, but, since that morning, has always relit a living literal picture in my mind.

*   *   *

The next two years were, in the long view, eventless, but at short range were the most adventurous in my life. I was given a map of London and told to educate myself, the proviso being that I should take the London Matriculation as soon as the regulations permitted—in other words, when I reached the age of sixteen. Beyond that point the future was undefined.

I can still recapture the almost tremulous excitement of those years. Unharassed by sex, my eager mind fluttered freely in an objective world, entirely friendless but never lonely. Except for the brief train journey from West Dulwich or Herne Hill to Black-friars, I walked everywhere, map in hand, from the City to Kensington and as far afield as Hampstead Heath, whence I could gaze across the pit of London to the Crystal Palace on the horizon behind my home. Sometimes the train journey was forgone, and I spent my morning with the Watteaus and near-Watteaus in the little gallery in Dulwich Village, or painting exotic birds in the aviary of Dulwich Park, or drawing strange inhuman anthropological things in the Horniman Museum at Forest Hill. Still my passion was to be an artist. My happiest haunt was a room at the Victoria and Albert Museum into which at that time was crowded an incredible number of precious water-colours that invited unending discovery; and next came the long-repeated pilgrimage up the silent stairs to the Diploma Gallery, which Michelangelo and Leonardo shared privately with me and none other. Lastly, there was Turner, still undisturbed in his quarters in Trafalgar Square, doing ever more than Nature can to justify God's ways to man. The British

Museum I abjured as I abjure it today, a place that suffers from a sort of spiritual cataract and out-stares the visitor with unseeing eyes.[1]

There was, too, the constant adventure of my commissariat. I had fourpence a day for my food (I suppose I cost my hard-pressed father less than five shillings a week all told from door to door), and much ingenuity and research went to the composition of my midday meal. On rare occasions, a miscalculation—I was once landed for a whole reckless shilling at a pub in the Brompton Road—entailed drastic retrenchment on succeeding days. Now and then, on the other hand, some windfall enabled me to shake out my sails. I have a particular memory of an evening in a resort called (I think) Wonderland in the Mile End Road where boxing contests were staged with a ceremony worthy of a Spanish bull-fight. In the seat of honour in the gallery reclined His Worship the Mayor of Stepney, dignified president of the jousts. Below, round the ring, sat and tumbled a cross-section of the East End with a plentiful sprinkling of red-coats. Shell-fish and mugs of beer circulated amongst the patrons, and every now and then amidst choking tobacco-smoke two youths would dive under the ropes and proceed with unskilled fists to smear each other sportively with blood. I have taken part in half a dozen of the decisive battles of the modern world, but never have I seen so few shed so much honest gore in so short a time. No doubt it all appealed to the sadistic instincts of the masses and was entirely reprehensible: a hang-over from a lawless age when men still fought with fists and not with physics, and drank when they wanted to, and died without the permission of a Ministry of Health.

In those days I journeyed one morning to Oxford to visit an older contemporary from Bradford who had done the proper thing and was now in his first year at the university. A certain curiosity egged me on, a quite un-morbid desire to explore the magnitude of my loss. As I passed through the narrow portal of the Queen's College I experienced simultaneously a feeling of oppression and relief. The heavy building closed upon me like a county gaol—like one of our *better* county gaols; at the same time,

[1] I regret this remark. It was written before I became a Trustee of the British Museum and, had truth permitted, I should have deleted it.

I knew with acute thankfulness that the door remained unlatched behind me and that no broad arrow or short gown proclaimed *my* servitude. In his cellular room I found Smith, not merely braving the rigours of his three-year sentence but actually laughing uncontrollably to himself. 'It's that ass Warmington,' he explained, 'old fat-headed Warmington upstairs. You see, the poor fellow had his girl to tea in his rooms yesterday and, like the half-wit that he is, consulted us beforehand as to what he should do—you know—to indicate where she could powder her nose afterwards.' (Remember, this all took place before two wars had shaken a lot of social nonsense out of us.) 'Well, we all gave him good advice, and it boiled down to this: that after they had finished tea he should stroll to the window whistling absently and jerking his thumb back in the direction of the bedroom door. We even had a rehearsal so that he shouldn't bungle it. Leave the rest to her, we said, and you're the blue-eyed boy. It all came to pass according to plan. Warmers strolled over to the window whistling the lighter passages from Chopin's Funeral March, and his girl tripped off to the bedroom door. The next thing that Warmers knew, the girl had opened the door and uttered a piercing yelp. He swung round to find that—the bedroom floor from door to window, from bed to washstand, was packed tight with a solid mass of chamberpots, line after line of them rim to rim. You see, not only this stair but four or five others as well had rallied round to help old Warmers in his hour of need, we didn't want his girl to miss the point of his act. She didn't, either,' Smith added a little more soberly, 'but I'm afraid she didn't think it was quite nice and poor old Warmers is back in circulation. Eh ho, these women,' sighed the sapient schoolboy, 'they've no understanding of Life.' A few hours later I left the wide-open spaces of Oxford, where Life was understood, for the virginal seclusion of the metropolis, with no invincible regret and content enough with my experiment.

The routine of my wanderings was varied occasionally in the afternoons by a sortie with my father, now no longer redolent of Harris tweed but cased like a chrysalis in tubular frock-coat and silk hat. In this unsympathetic garb he tore through the streets as he had torn through the heather and the moor-grass, and my lanky frame bumped and ricocheted alongside, occasionally venturing with him into the odorous entrails of the twopenny tube or, rarely, on to a horse-bus—the hesitant prototypes of the motor-bus had scarcely yet begun to litter the streets with their inanimate forms and their groups of errand-boys. Our destination might be a new picture-exhibition at the Leicester Galleries, a concert at the Queen's Hall, or a Salvation Army mass-meeting at the Crystal Palace, with the patriarchal beard of the old General as the battle-standard of a vast host of happy, earnest lads and lassies, formidably beneficent. Thereafter I might be taken back to the Fleet Street office and told to try my prentice hand at a 'paragraph of 300 words,' designed for but rarely printed in the 'London Letter.' 'Cut it down, cut it down,' was my father's chorus. 'If you don't cut 100 words out of the middle, I'll just snip them off the end,' and a large pair of scissors was produced. 'Write as though you were writing a cablegram at a shilling a word.' On rare and exciting occasions I recognized a few of my reluctant sentences in the next day's paper, and was thereby fully rewarded for my pains.

Alongside this welter of experience, early morning and late night saw me at my books. By some special dispensation of the University of London I was authorized to sit my matriculation examination before I was sixteen. On the first day of the examination I was dizzy and uncertain of my footsteps; at the end of the day my father met me outside the examination-hall at South Kensington and almost carried me to the Underground station. There I lay in a fainting condition on a wooden bench, the impress of which I can still feel on my shoulder-blades, and for the first time I smelt and tasted brandy. My temperature, it seems, was 105 degrees, and for a week I was critically ill.

*   *   *

Some months later, at a less irregular age, I matriculated and so officially left boyhood behind me. Indeed, somewhere about that time I slowly and inevitably became aware of changing values from which a curious parental shyness had screened me. . . . Even examinations took upon themselves less the character of an ordeal and increasingly that of an orgiastic ritual. It was some time before I fully realized that to take examinations for the purpose of pro-ducing physical excitement was like burning down pigsties to produce roast pork. Meanwhile I almost sought the examination-room, and in retrospect I ascribe the classical scholarship which I acquired at this period to subliminal sex rather than to superior sense.

Be that as it may, the scholarship settled my immediate future. It took me in 1907 at the age of seventeen to the university, and in particular to University College in Gower Street, which was to become my real home for the next five years. There for the first time I stood squarely on my own feet. In one way and another, mostly by extensive coaching and a little writing, I became there-after to a large extent independent financially of my father, and lived increasingly and promiscuously with alien minds. Chance had guided me well. In the years before the First War, University College was still a college in a truly academic sense, not, as it is today, a hypertrophied monstrosity as little like an academy as a plesiosaurus is like a man. There may then have been a thousand students or less all told, of all faculties and disciplines, within its walls: aspiring chemists, physicists, biologists, artists, lawyers, philosophers, surgeons, psychologists, historians, and just basic humanists like myself. We all knew one another and collaborated in a multitude of capacities. Many—a wholly disproportionate number—perished in the 1914–18 war, to which my generation flocked like sheep to the slaughter. Of those of us who survived, a random memory picks out Paul Nash of the Slade who, until we parted on our diverse paths, was a treasured familiar; Alec Randall, who became an ambassador; William Strang, who ultimately ruled the Foreign Office and retired into a peerage; and others of some-what less picturesque attainment such as C. E. W. Lockyer, who became an Air-Vice-Marshal and Bursar of Peterhouse, or E. N. da C. Andrade, the physicist, or Frank Forsey, who devoted a life of undeviating enthusiasm to the professing of classics at a provincial university. And there was Stafford Cripps.

Cripps, older than most of us, was born on Olympus. More than any other man known to me, he had a quality of presence which is quite inadequately expressed by the cliché *personality*. He filled any room which he entered. In those days he was president of the College Union, and his powerful, sombre countenance is my only memory from the innumerable committee meetings at which (as editor, I think, of the Union Magazine) I used to sit opposite to him. I cannot recall any specific act of outstanding wisdom on his part; on one or two occasions I may even have had the presumption to differ from his judgment; but none could question the ingrowing sincerity of a mind deeply rooted in the fertile phosphates from which the radical humanitarians and reformers of an earlier epoch had sprung. In his subsequent political life the idiom of twentieth-century socialism never quite fitted him. He was more truly of the ilk and age of a Wilberforce, a Robert Owen, or even a Peel. At the early date of which I am speaking, however, his politics had not yet emerged, nor, curiously enough, did he contribute to the actively intellectual life of the college. He remained a remote and brooding genius.

Behind a variegated student-life loomed dim altitudes of another kind. The professors' common-room was in those days a small, crowded, smoke-laden cell where talk was both good and general. A. E. Housman was still there, professing Latin on the 'take-it-or-leave-it' principle; as one with his mind elsewhere, though liable to rally unexpectedly in caustic comment, whether the subject were Martial's text or its luckless exponent. Platt, Professor of Greek, as a conversationalist far outpaced Housman. He could bring a library to bear, with exact quotation, on any subject of today or yesterday from a filled and photographic mind. Beside him, the eloquent silences of W. P. Ker were already a legend. Ker's measured declamations of Milton have made it impossible for me to read *Paradise Lost* save in the remembered organ-music of his slow and resonant voice. Yet his leisurely sampling of literature and of life was the mask of a vivid capacity for unperturbed enjoyment. He was a devoted mountaineer, and in fact died eventually in the Italian Alps. A typical incident—of many—is related of him on one of his ascents. He was leading along a narrow ledge upon the face of a rocky precipice; sheer rock above, sheer rock below. At a turn in the path, some enthusiast had taken advantage of the precarious situation to chalk up on the rock-face in great white letters PREPARE TO MEET THY GOD. Ker paused and looked long upon this timely warning. Then, half-turning to his companion, he remarked in a slow, mildly reproachful voice, 'And in so narrow a place, too,' and passed on.

Others contributed. From the science side Sir William Ramsay and Sir William Bragg brought a distinction which needs no renewal from a mere humanist. The mathematician Micaiah Hill, vice-chancellor himself, father of a vice-chancellor who was also an Air-Marshal, brother of a director of the British Museum, contained as it were in a Parmenidean One the potentiality of an infinite variety. He was the living proof that the Greeks were right in basing our understanding upon mathematics. But he was difficult to know, beyond the ordinary reach of the undergraduate or young graduate, and I was never drawn into his orbit. Much the same is true of the little, cloud-borne philosopher, Dawes Hicks, though his natural sweetness shone through the mists like a rainbow. But my hero was Tonks of the Slade. There was no nonsense about Tonks. He was a late convert to art, and came into the Slade with the clear-mindedness of his scientific training in medicine and surgery. For a time Tonks tried to teach me to draw.

I have spoken before of a lurking ambition to become an artist. In furtherance of this fantastic aim, I made some special arrangement whereby, whilst reading for my classical honours degree, I could spend some time in the Slade School. It was a foolish business; it meant cutting much of my classics, and, in particular, it involved the constant cutting of Housman, for the very good reason that Housman cared least about his individual students. Yet in the long view my glimpses of the Slade were probably a good thing. This was just after the great phase of Augustus John and Orpen and Albert Rothenstein, and the Slade was still in the first flush of the world's art schools. Sickert, McEvoy, W. W. Russell were hovering round it, shortly to be joined by that mild and academic revolutionary, the sculptor Havard Thomas. It was a promised land into which I wanted above all things to enter. But one morning, as I left the studios, I stumbled unexpectedly upon a decision which was to be final: either, as was highly unlikely, I should be admitted to the revolutionaries and starve, or I should become a conventionally accomplished picture-maker and earn a living. Both alternatives on that cold winter's morning were equally repulsive. I continued my journey to a classroom where I was to teach the rudiments of Latin to a scented Egyptian, and never returned to the Slade.

But that was not quite all. My aesthetic inhibitions found some

AGED 3

SEGONTIVM : CELLAR IN SACELLVM. *SECTION AT S.E. END.*

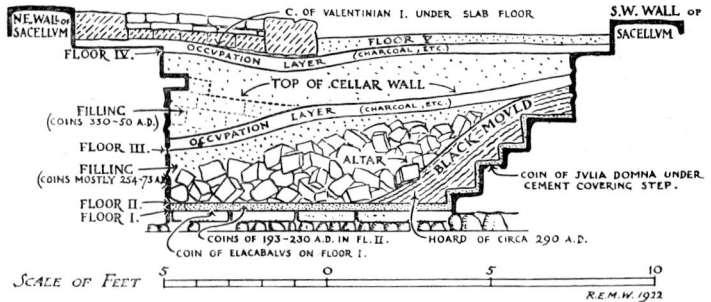

NE.WALL of SACELLVM

FLOOR IV.

C. OF VALENTINIAN I. UNDER SLAB FLOOR

OCCVPATION LAYER

FLOOR V (CHARCOAL, ETC.)

S.W. WALL of SACELLVM

TOP OF CELLAR WALL

OCCVPATION LAYER (CHARCOAL, ETC.)

BLACK MOVLD

FILLING (COINS 330-50 A.D.)

FLOOR III.

FILLING (COINS MOSTLY 254-73 A.D.)

FLOOR II.
FLOOR I.

ALTAR

COIN OF JVLIA DOMNA UNDER CEMENT COVERING STEP.

COINS OF 193-230 A.D. IN FL.II.

HOARD OF CIRCA 290 A.D.

COIN OF ELACABALVS ON FLOOR I.

SCALE OF FEET 5 0 5 10

R.E.M.W. 1922

SECTION ACROSS THE STRONG-ROOM OF THE ROMAN FORT OF
SEGONTIUM, 1922

SEGONTIUM, 1922

*Dame Margaret Lloyd George (centre) visits the excavations. The Author
is on the left, and Wilfrid Hemp and Tessa are in the background*

slight outlet in the study of Greek art under Ernest Gardner, who was at that time the Yates professor of 'archaeology'—a term which, in that context, would nowadays be synonymous with 'art-history.' Gardner was an efficient, unimaginative, not very inspiring teacher, but it was his teaching that drove me ultimately and not unwillingly into professional archaeology of other kinds. Of that I shall speak in a moment.

Meanwhile there is one personality whom I have omitted but of whom a word must be said. Both before and after my time, University College lay under the strong hand of (Sir) Gregory Foster, provost. Foster was an imposing figure of a man, with a sultry countenance and a Socratic forehead that concealed little in the way of academic understanding but a great capacity for administrative push. His ambition was to make University College bigger and wealthier every day and in every way. Alas, he succeeded. He never paused to think that he was nailing down and forcibly feeding a perfectly good goose with the sole object of putting more and more fatted liver on the market. He never reflected that 'It is not growing like a tree in bulk doth make man better be.' There were many things on which he did not reflect, for his was not a reflective nature. And I am well aware that, in saying this, I am less than grateful (if not less than just) to my first benefactor. It was this way.

As a student I had had my share of undergraduate troubles. At seasonable moments in the year strange things sometimes happened —explosions, firework displays, booby-traps and such nonsense— in discreet parts of the rambling college, particularly in the extensive (out-of-bounds) vaults which underlie the building. On more than one occasion mischance had delivered me, not always unaccompanied, into the hands of authority, which meant a climactic interview with the provost and a stiff fine which I could very ill afford. One day in 1910, just after taking my first degree, I was wondering anxiously how to tackle the urgent problems of life, when the provost sent for me. I entered his sacred study with guilt in every fibre of my body and exactly four pennies in my pocket. Foster looked up sternly and paused. 'Do you want a job?' he asked gruffly. 'Well, ye—yes, Sir,' I replied. 'Then you can be my private secretary,' he continued. 'And you can start now. There's your table.' A faint smile flickered across his face, and he turned his back

B

on me. My salary was a very badly needed £100 a year. Two or three months later I was promoted to the office of 'publications secretary' at £120. It was becoming abundantly clear that, unless I made some determined move, I should become a permanent cog in the machine.

My move in fact took three directions. First, in my spare time I worked for an M.A. degree, which in the University of London is a serious undertaking. (I achieved the degree in 1912.) Secondly, I became engaged to Tessa. Thirdly, I applied for a new archaeological studentship which had been established jointly by the University and the Society of Antiquaries of London in memory of Augustus Wollaston Franks.

The candidates for the studentship in 1913 were interviewed by an imposing committee under the chairmanship of Sir Hercules Read. With him were Sir Arthur Evans, the discoverer of Minoan Civilization, Professor Ernest Gardner, I think Reginald Smith, and one or two others whose names now escape me. As a subject for research I submitted the study of Romano-Rhenish pottery, a subject chosen as introductory to the study of the Romano-British pottery which had then, as the result of excavations on Roman sites at Corbridge and Wroxeter, become a manifestly important factor in British archaeology but had received very little scientific attention. I was accepted, and left the room with a sudden sense of responsibility and anxiety. I was giving up an assured if modest income for—£50 a year for two years, with a journey to the Rhineland in immediate prospect. My future was indeed fixed; I was to be an archaeologist; but all else was quicksand.

As I walked away slowly and thoughtfully down the long corridor, I became aware of light footsteps hurrying after me. I turned and found myself looking upon the small, slight form of Arthur Evans, a little breathless with his running. 'That £50,' he said, in his quiet voice, 'it isn't much. I should like to double it for you.' And he was away again, almost before I could thank him. That characteristically generous act of Evans's changed the whole climate of the situation. For the moment I was saved, and I have never ceased to recall with gratitude the kindly impulse that saved me.

Of my journey to the Rhineland, where so much had already

been done in the ordering and analysis of the material wherewith
I was now concerned, nothing need be said here. But, when I
returned, fate had another little crisis ready for me. Three vacancies
for 'junior investigators' on the staff of the Royal Commission on
Historical Monuments (England) had been advertised, and Ernest
Gardner was prepared to back me. Inquiry showed that *six* candidates were to be taken on for three months' trial, after which three
of the six would be selected for permanent appointment. I was
assured that a purely classical degree and no practical training in
architecture were not appropriate qualifications. I promptly undertook, however, to work at night in the Architecture School at
University College, and there in fact, whenever opportunity
offered, I pursued with industry the elements of building construc-
tion and architectural drawing. The training was one which I
should commend to all archaeologists, whatever their chosen path.

On a frosty morning of late autumn in 1913, I cycled across
London to Liverpool Street station for my first day's probationary
fieldwork in Essex. There I was to meet the commission's senior
investigator, Murray Kendall, under whom I was to begin my
tutelage. Kendall was already pacing up and down the platform,
blowing upon his fingers. He greeted me with 'Still a quarter of an
hour to go, my boy. What a morning like this requires is a Little
Reinforcement. Come along.' He strode away to the upstairs
refreshment-room, and briskly ordered: 'Two double whiskies in
new milk.' (There were no 'opening hours' in those days—England
was still a medieval country.) My eyes stood out of my head. I had
never tasted whisky in my life before, and can remember to this day
the fierce, glowing sensation as the 'double whisky in new milk'
found its pioneer way down my unpractised gullet. I remember,
too, how the platform rose courteously to meet me as we hurried
to the train. An hour later Dunmow station received us with a
cold, inhospitable look about it, and Kendall again sniffed the
frosty air. 'My boy,' he said parentally, 'what we need before we
set out down the road is a Little Reinforcement'; and he led the way
to an adjacent inn where the startling ceremony was repeated. The
three or four miles to the village of Stebbing, our goal for the less
serious work of the day, followed in quick succession, and we dismounted at the church. Let me here repeat that my education had

been strangely neglectful of the niceties of English medieval architecture, and, in spite of reinforcement, my heart was by now slipping steadily in the direction of my boots. We looked inside the building, and to my unskilled eye there seemed to be a great deal of involved stonework and quite an array of decorative shields. 'Phew!' whistled Kendall. 'Look at that stone screen. It's a bit of a stunner, isn't it?' I gazed vaguely round and said Yes. 'Well, look here,' Kendall continued, getting out his notebook, 'suppose you start in on the heraldry and I'll have a shot at the screen.' I had been gloomily expecting something of this sort. I hesitated. 'Well, as a matter of fact,' I said, 'I don't actually know any heraldry. Of course, I'm anxious to learn . . .' 'Oh, that's all right,' replied Kendall, accommodatingly, 'I'll do the heraldry, whilst *you* do the screen.' The situation was desperate. 'You know, I'm awfully sorry, but I don't really know screens. Of course, I'm anxious to learn . . .' I added. 'Hum,' said Kendall, and reflected. Then he looked up brightly. 'I know what we want,' he was saying. 'What we want is a . . .' But I was already following him mechanically up the village street towards the Red Lion, which gaped before us like Behemoth.

That night, from the White Hart at Braintree, where we were quartered, I wrote to Tessa a letter of utter despair. 'I shall never in my life make an archaeologist,' I said, 'I just simply can't stand the pace. . . .'

Three months later I was one of the three probationers chosen for permanent appointment. What inference may properly be drawn from that fact, I do not know, but Tessa and I celebrated the occasion by getting married. It was now 1914 and, before we knew where we were, the war was upon us.

3. War Interlude I, 1914–19

WRITING in an era in which war has become a commonplace, I have been wondering whether to devote any part of this chronicle to the miscellaneous war-time notes and diaries which I find amongst my papers. On reflection, I have included a few scraps for the reason that without them my story, such as it be, is excessively syncopated and out of proportion. For a quarter of my working life I have served as a soldier on active service; and the fact that I have enjoyed my soldiering does not reduce the measure of the resultant distortion of my proper work.

For the first of the two war interludes, the plain facts are these. I was commissioned into the Royal Artillery (Territorial Force) in 1914, and for a few months I remained in London as an instructor in the University of London Officers' Training Corps. (My son Michael was born in January 1915.) I was then, as a youthful subaltern, shortly to be captain, posted to command a Lowland field battery at the unfinished Colinton Barracks near Edinburgh. Thereafter, in spite of constant restiveness, I was trapped in various battery commands—field-guns and field-howitzers—in Scotland and England until 1917, when at last I escaped to France. Passchendaele, Italy, the last advance on the Western Front, the march into and occupation of Germany, followed in eventful succession. In July 1919 I returned from the Rhineland to London and to civilian life.

In other words, mine was the common lot of my generation. For the following trifling extracts from my records I can claim nothing exceptional—no V.C.s are won, no battles lost, no high-level stuff redeems the plebeian theme. And that is why I have admitted them. They represent the *genre*, the commonplace, of a phase now passed into history. It was the last war of the horse, and I like sometimes to reflect that I fought one war in a saddle and another in an armoured car. The inherent element of 'explosive evolution' gratifies my archaeological sense.

The great General Pitt Rivers once remarked that 'common things are of more importance than particular things, because they are more prevalent.' With that thought I have, for example, reproduced a day in the life of a battery commander during a major battle. The account was written at the time in my military notebook and has, perhaps, an actuality which justifies its reproduction. It is at any rate a faithful, pedestrian record of the battle-routine of a young field-officer in the year 1918. For the rest, I have dug out two or three bits and pieces which seem faithful to the mood of those times and may therefore be worth a few transient pages.

(I) ATTACK

21st August 1918

The summer night was blotted out by a driving rainstorm. The drivers, bending low in their saddles, had ceased to curse, for the misery of a sodden saddle at midnight, with a long prospect of soaking hours before one, lies beyond the pale of speech. The track was already afloat and would be worse before morning. Fortunately, the Hun was behaving himself like a gentleman.

Crash! A blinding flash, with a halo of flying sparks, lit up for an instant the long column of straining horses and flooded wagons. A team swerved, and the white eyeballs of the startled horses gleamed for a moment in the glare. The night closed its fist once more upon its prey, and the parting shell from the roadside gun added another note to that of the squelching hoofs and jolting wheels.

For the second night in succession, the teams plodded slowly up the last shell-eaten hill-side towards the jagged tooth that had once been a large and prosperous farm. From this landmark the terrain sloped down towards a valley where, a mile away, the British front line wound like a rivulet amongst the foothills. On the opposite side of the valley, some six hundred yards further on, lay the German line with its outpost trenches, machine-gun posts and wire. This line, said rumour, was to be captured in two days' time, and the brigade of field-guns was being put into an open battle-position on this last hill-top for the purpose. The fact that the hill-top was a favourite hunting-ground for the Boche gunner was self-evident and would, under favourable weather conditions, have been of some interest to the miserable mass of humanity which was now grudgingly throwing the rounds of ammunition from the wagons into the old crest-line trench. Under the present conditions, however, nothing was of interest save to get the job done. The last wagon was turning away as a hiss and a bark and a scatter of sparks and steel heralded the nightly German bombardment. The rain was blowing into a grey dawn as the mournful procession splashed homeward.

*   *   *

The Topographical Man was timidly flitting across the skyline, his silhouette bristling with tripod legs like the back of a porcupine. A brigade major and an A.D.C. alternately displayed, doubtless to an admiring foe, the beauties of lemon buckskins. The hedge which fringed the crest ill-concealed a colonel and four battery commanders, each with his attendant minions. 'Thank God,' said the brigade major, 'it isn't much of a flying day, or Fritz would come over and read the whole book. Can't think why R. will reconnoitre at the head of an Army Corps.' 'Damn the Staff,' muttered the battery commanders. 'They aren't going to live here, and don't care how much they give away.' 'Curse the Topography Merchant,' yelled everybody. 'He'll get the whole place shelled brown inside of five minutes.'

Topography came to rest behind the hedge and distributed largesse in the form of map co-ordinates. The landscape was cluttered with maps and instruments. The brigade major gazed skywards apprehensively as two of our flights hummed far overhead towards the enemy. One of our observation balloons chose the moment to desert its moorings. Pursued by anti-aircraft shells it rose and drifted helplessly across the lines, leaving behind it a series of grotesque little tragedies. The grooms, taking the chargers back towards the wagon lines, had been idly watching an artillery aeroplane flying homewards through the line of stationary kite-balloons. There had been a sudden 'crack' like that of a whiplash. The aeroplane had broken into fragments and plunged earthwards;

the balloon had shivered and begun to rise. The cable, broken by the colliding aeroplane, had whirled heavily downwards in vicious circles. The grooms had scattered, but too late to save one, whose head, caught in the lashing coils, was whipped from his body with a blow which nearly cut the horse also in twain. The tragedies of warfare are the 'Accidentally Killed.'

Orders and ammunition had been arriving fast. Here and there small parties of men were cutting wire and clearing platforms amongst the ditches and shell-holes, or repairing some scarcely-discernible track which had been damaged overnight. The communication trenches and observation posts were alive with officers of every Allied army and nationality, from kilts to spurs, from New York to New Zealand. Yet the secret had been well kept. It was vaguely known that They were 'going to do something down south,' that They were 'going to wheel the line north-east,' and that we were the pivot of the wheel; which meant that the Boche would probably not have to move back much of his artillery opposite us. The plan of campaign was condemned at sight by every subaltern who knew how battles should be won. 'The Staff . . .' etc.

Now, at the last moment, the plan developed. The 3rd Division was to go through the 2nd Division after the capture of the first objective. The artillery would be ready to move forward at zero plus 1½ hours, and our 76th Brigade R.F.A. would move first. The same artillery brigade would send forward a section of guns in close support of the advancing infantry. There were indefinite possibilities. After the months of stagnation which had followed the German offensive of the previous spring, a new current of energy and expectation suddenly burst upon the waiting army. The geography of No Man's Land assumed an unforeseen interest, and every track and tree-stump became a focus of urgent importance.

The guns and the final orders arrived with the misty moon. The air was surprisingly thick, and the normality of the hostile shelling showed that the night had well retained its secret. The mist rendered it possible to set the fuses comfortably by torchlight. By midnight all was ready, and the detachments snatched a few hours of uneasy sleep in the neighbouring trench.

'Zero hour will be 4.55 (four fifty-five) a.m. on the 21st.' The moon had been swallowed by a dawn which scarcely filtered through the now dense fog. The control officer, sitting in a shallow pit behind the centre of the battery, could not see the flank guns. The battery commander and the senior sergeant were going from gun to gun for assurance that the routine of battle was in order and that everything was ready for advance. For the first time for many a long day, the officers and sergeants wore their spurs in action, and they glanced at their heels with a schoolboy's exhilaration.

'Five minutes to go!' The man with the dixie of steaming tea hurried on his round. At each gun the ammunition lay in ordered piles, each pile roughly labelled on a sandbag with the number of the barrage-lift for which its fuses had been set. Buckets of water and oil-cans were ready for cooling and feeding each gun as it heated up. The N.C.O. in charge stood by the trail with a tin of tea in one hand and his barrage orders in the other.

'Three minutes to go! All ready, One?—Two?—Three?—Four?—Five?—Six?'

'All ready, Sir!'

'Thirty seconds to go!'

The layers' hands stretched out and grasped the triggers.

'Ten seconds to go!'

'Are you ready!'

'Fire!'

The ridge flared into spouting flame. On every hand, although the flashes could not be seen through the fog, the leaping guns were pouring a hissing mass of steel across the valley. Behind, the 'heavies' were adding their deep-throated chorus to the concert of sound, and somewhere out in front the German line, churned into great columns of dust and debris, threw back the answering chorus of bursting shell and hurtling splinters. The sleepy German who woke to that terrible reveille knew well that it was the dawn of The Day.

'The colonel wants you on the 'phone, Sir.'

I picked up the receiver.

'Can you see anything up there yet?'

'No, Sir. The O.P. is still absolutely fog-bound.'

'Send forward a mounted officer's patrol and try to get some news. No information here yet.'

The patrol disappeared at a canter into the mist. The guns, constantly sponged and oiled, were now hammering the country well behind the enemy's front line. The infantry of the 3rd Division were by this time filing past the batteries on their way forward. Remembering the Hun offensive of a few months earlier, they grinned at the thought that the boot was now on the other foot. 'Give it 'em, boys,' they shouted cheerily to the sweating gunners, who threw their rounds home with an answering grin.

'The colonel on the 'phone again, Sir.'

'The patrol has not returned yet, Sir,' I reported, 'and neither wounded nor prisoners have passed the battery.'

'I have no information here either, and the Division know nothing yet. However, you can send your advance-section forward at once, and follow with the rest of your battery if you like.'

The teams picked their way carefully up the hill-side towards the guns amongst the shell-craters and wire. In a few minutes, the battery was trotting sharply down the narrow road towards the ruined village through which, the day before, our front line had run. The groups of infantry by the wayside raised a scattered cheer and shouted 'Good luck!' as the guns passed by them. The route, picked up with difficulty over the trench-ridden ground in the enveloping fog, led past a dressing-station which was beginning to fill, chiefly with dazed and bleeding Germans. Some of our wounded had walked in, and others were being brought in on stretchers by white and scared prisoners. Our casualties so far had evidently been few. . . .

The battery turned off the road and groped its way amongst the almost continuous mass of shell-holes which had formed No Man's Land. The teams were now in the German S.O.S. barrage, and shells of every calibre were crashing in the mist beside and in front of them. Anything approaching exact location was impossible, but a rough calculation showed that they must be in the region of their destination. As the battery dropped into action, a squadron of cavalry flitted by like shadows in the mist, and a tank waddled up uneasily from the front and finally broke down beside the guns. Leaving the battery to settle into its new home, I rode forward with my staff of signallers in search of news and observation.

No Man's Land in a fog is no place for equestrian exercise, and the tangled masses of wire, the treacherous shell-holes and other obstacles soon brought us to our feet. The horses were sent back to such shelter as could be found, and with my staff I picked a tortuous way forward amongst the debris. In the fog the only sure guide was the broken road, and the Hun was fully awake to the fact. His barrage was now falling noisily on and near it. Dodging from bank to shell-hole, our little party crept forward until at last, with grateful hearts, we stumbled upon the old German main trench where it cut the road. The trench marked the second stage of our journey; in its comparative security we paused for breath.

This trench had, up to that morning, constituted the first German line of resistance. Now, blown to pieces by shell-fire, flattened by tanks, choked with scattered equipment and mangled bodies, only here and there could a stooping man find cover from the flying splinters. In it, the fog-ridden air was heavy with the smell of high-explosive and newly-churned earth, and blood and blood-soaked cloth, and that indescribable pungent, vegetable smell which is the smell of the Hun.

I turned from my map towards the two or three infantry-men who garrisoned the short length of habitable trench. 'Any news from forward?' 'Naw, Sir,' came the stolid reply; 'we've just coom here in support, and we was told to have us breakfast.' He bit another chunk off a well-thumbed crust, and followed it by a slab of bully-beef deftly inserted on the blade of a jack-knife. His eye wandered listlessly to a heap of khaki and webbing which lay crumpled up in a pool of blood amongst the tangled corn-stalks in front of him. If he was thinking at all, he was wondering whether it had any cigarettes left in its pocket and was making up his mind to be first on the scene after breakfast. A fuse-head, ricocheting from a bursting shell, whirred close overhead with an unusual drone. The face of the gloomy breakfaster assumed a shadowy look of interest and amusement at the novelty of the sound. He spoke sideways, without turning his head: ''Ear that, 'Arry? Latest novelty from 'Unland—the shell with the airyoplane propeller on its 'ead!' . . . But 'Arry was busily investigating the pockets of a greatcoat of field-grey, and his ears were deaf to trivialities.

Groping along the zig-zag trench line, as the only available landmark, our party was continually brought to a dead end, where the trench had been entirely flattened and merged into the surrounding landscape. A circular reconnaissance, the scout keeping in touch by shouting, would rediscover the broken line and the party renewed its slow progress. A 13-pounder Horse Artillery battery struggled past us on the heels of a troop of cavalry, the horses gingerly picking their way amongst the shell-craters. Now and then a riderless horse would loom up out of the mist from the direction in which the leading troop had gone a few minutes earlier. Two horses with their mutilated riders under them were lying by the trench, and the team-horses passed with distended nostrils and frightened eyes. Suddenly a horse appeared to sink backwards into the earth. Its rider picked himself up and pulled at the head-collar. The horse struggled and sank further, as into a quicksand, until only its head and neck could be seen. An officer dismounted, glanced at the wretched animal, and put a bullet through its brain. For many days afterwards, that horse's head, odoriferous and shrunken, projecting from the great shaft which led to the layer of some large 'dud' shell, haunted the unholy spot and put the fear of all the horse-devils into the passing steed.

A momentary gap in the fog showed fifty yards ahead a desolate 18-pounder gun and wagon, the teams sheltering in the surrounding craters from the sweeping shell-fire. The horse battery, befogged, was wheeling round and returning. Laden stretchers, borne by Boche and British together, were slowly finding their way back along the track. A batch of German prisoners, many of them laughing weakly and chattering to the two wounded Tommies who escorted them, tumbled into the trench. 'War finish for me' was their theme, and they pulled souvenirs out of their pockets to placate their victors. One of them, seeing my major's badges, saluted with servility. Another rushed forward with a match to light a Tommy's cigarette, and received a Woodbine for his trouble. They were perfect Kamerads.

Everything appeared to be going as well as circumstances permitted. The fog, however, which had assisted the earlier operations, was now a serious hindrance. The infantry and cavalry were losing direction, the guns were blind. The returning wounded knew neither where they had been nor where they were. Until the fog should lift, the battle was in suspense, save for the persistent enemy curtain-fire. . . .

About one o'clock the fog in fact began to lift. By half-past one the sun was shining brightly, and the air was filled with the hum of many 'planes. A little later, one by one, small black specks rising and falling on the horizon showed where German observation balloons were timidly blinking in the sunlight. Where one of these specks had been a moment earlier was now a dense column of blue-black smoke, streaming upwards from a falling furnace of fire. The heavens were pointed with black and white smoke-puffs amongst the plunging 'planes. Some of the smaller enemy guns had slackened fire and were probably being moved back, but the heavier howitzers were raising great columns of dust and debris round and in front of the new battery positions, and high-velocity gunshells were crashing continuously into the village behind. Through this village all roads and tracks leading forward in the sector converged, and our heavy guns were beginning to deploy into action around it.

In the hollow to the right of the battery, a brigade of field artillery was waiting, limbered up, for the fog of war to lift. A troop of cavalry was returning wearily past them. On the left, another artillery brigade was crawling like a swarm of ants up the hill-side into action. In the battery itself, the gunners had spent the morning in digging shelters for themselves in the outpost trench, and were now beginning to dig cover for the guns. They had already done two days' work in half of one, but not every day did they have the honour of coming into action in Bocheland, and they worked with zest. So far they had been lucky, but about this time one of the battery's teams was hit whilst bringing up ammunition through the village. The battery paused a moment, spat on its hands, and turned once more to its spade-work. Curiously out of place amongst this panorama of unconsciously picturesque industry, an official photographer wandered with ready camera.

Word now came in from an officer's patrol that the advance had been checked by intense machine-gun fire in the neighbourhood of the railway ahead of us, and that the cavalry, dismounted, were supporting our tired infantry. With a fellow-major and some signallers, I forthwith set out once more in search of observation and fuller information.

From our temporary observation post on the Courcelles ridge, the telephone-wire was laid forward, the signallers with the unwieldly cable-drum following us across the broken country. The valley in front of the post held the cavalry horses and horseholders, blistering under the heavy afternoon sun. The engineers further back were working feverishly at disused and wrecked well-heads, but in the meantime the country for miles was waterless, and the wretched horses were hollow-flanked and heavy-headed with a ravaging thirst. The enemy shelling, though now more spasmodic, was still unpleasant, and here and there heaps of mutilated men and horses formed islands of death amongst the living. A company of infantry were digging short lengths of trench on the nearer side of the valley, and, close by, near some German trench-mortars, an advanced dressing-station had just been established in the bank of a sunken road. To it was already streaming a long procession of walking wounded, both in khaki and in field-grey. An 8-inch Hun howitzer was sweeping the valley and sprinkling the road with splinters of steel.

To the sound of bursting shell was now added the sharp whispering of machine-gun bullets as they rushed past on their secret course. A shell is tangible and meets one boldly face to face, but the rustling of machine-gun bullets is that of the evil spirits of the night. They are round and about one, almost between the fingers of one's hands and in one's clothes. The skin burns as with a thousand red-hot needles, and life is lived from breath to breath.

From amongst the grass on the top of the ridge could be seen the whole vast panorama of the battle front. A few yards down the forward slope, in the sparse covering offered by shell-holes and improvised infantry shelters, crouched the thin line of khaki outposts. At the foot of the hill the railway embankment, with its mined dug-outs and fortifications, formed the main enemy line of resistance—-a serried line of active machine-guns which, with their broad field of fire up the hill-side, were effectively blocking the way. Advancing towards the railway could be seen the small black columns of the enemy reserves, exempt at present from our artillery fire and but lightly harassed by our few advanced Lewis guns. In the middle distance, amongst the scattered trees and banks, were the pinpoint flashes of the enemy batteries, many of them firing at the ridge over their open sights. One gun was being withdrawn; the team pulled out, and the German officer, sitting on his horse, calmly waved his hand and walked his gun out of action. He was worthy of his regiment.

Targets were more than plentiful. The signallers were beckoned up, and the wire was unreeled to a neighbouring shell-hole. Two of the signallers had been sent back to mend the line, which the test proved to have been broken by shelling or traffic. The telephone was tried again but still brought no response, and we battery commanders could only lie in the grass fuming with impatient helplessness as we saw beneath us the enemy reserves streaming forward unchecked. On the left, our whippet tanks were making a half-hearted attempt to advance over the crest. On the skyline they came under a concentrated fire from the enemy field-guns. One tank came to a standstill—a steel tomb. The remainder turned and crawled back down the slope, pursued by a searching fire. To attempt to advance was suicidal and useless, and it was clear that the battle was finished for the day. Had the fog but lifted four hours earlier. . . .

The telephone was still unresponsive. One of the two remaining signallers was sent back down the wire, and finally the corporal went back to get the line through to the guns at all costs. Half an hour later the 'phone was still useless, and we ourselves turned back down the wire. On the slopes of the hill the corporal lay across the wire, with a small crimson puncture in his forehead. . . .

A fine summer's night closed down on the scene. The air was full of the threatening drone of bombing planes, of the crashing of bombs and shells and guns on both sides of the line. The air round the batteries became heavy with gas. Some of the weary gunners were again at their guns, alternately firing and pausing as the enemy planes passed overhead. The enemy front line was ablaze with anxious Very lights of many colours. The battlefield slept wakefully.

(II) THE BUTTE DE WARLENCOURT

[Years afterwards, in the Ordnance Survey Office at Southampton, O. G. S. Crawford, as the Survey's Archaeology Officer, was laying down the law. In front of him was an air photograph of a region near Bapaume, and he was pointing out with some emphasis to a subordinate that a certain pool of light and shadow on the photograph was *not* a deep pit but a high mound. He looked up and saw me smiling. 'Yes,' I said, 'it is a high mound. It once seemed to me nearly as high as Everest. . . .' And I told him the story.]

* * *

It was two days after the attack. For the moment, things had settled down, and the field-guns had been brought to the rear shoulder of the forward ridge on which, on the first day (as I have told), I had lain in the grass and impotently watched the enemy pulling out below me. He now lined the opposing ridge, and, as the streaky mists of a fine dawn lifted from the valley, I took stock.

Immediately beneath us was the railway. Beyond it, a dusty track or two crossed the low ground, mounted the further slope, where there were a few scattered trees, and disappeared over the ridge, which was lined by a main road. Yet further, amidst more trees, would lie the ruins of Bapaume. Our outpost-line was scattered somewhere along the valley. Beyond it, on the slope lay two German field-guns, limbered up but encumbered by their dead teams. They were presumably the last section of the battery which I had seen pulling out, and a machine-gun had got them. Behind them, on the skyline, rose a great mound. Looking through my glasses, I could see upon its formidable sides the scars of recent digging amongst the scrub which partially covered it.

It was a busy but slightly tedious day. Mostly, we burst shrapnel amongst the trees to dislodge enterprising snipers. Ever and anon we plastered the offending mound, which had definitely been turned into a machine-gun nest and made things uncomfortable for our outposts. And the two German guns lay there, ownerless and tempting.

During the afternoon, I walked along to the colonel (W. L. Y. Rogers, Rugby international, I believe) and we looked over the ridge together. 'No, you certainly can't,' he replied to something that I had said. I accepted his verdict with model discipline. 'It's rather a pity, Sir, isn't it?' I continued, after a respectful interval. 'During the night they could easily slip out and get them.' 'Well then, turn your guns on them and break them up.' 'Yes, Sir, but wouldn't that be rather a pity, too? You see, we've now got masses of German gas-shells, and all we want is a German gun or two to chuck them back with.' 'And what about that mound? Don't be a b. fool. Poppycock!' he added with final emphasis.

In the bright sunlit evening, however, he rang me up. 'I said what about that mound?' 'I'll get my battery to put some smoke-shell over it, Sir,' I replied. 'All right. You can go if you like. Good luck, old chap.'

I called for volunteers, a sergeant and two six-horse teams. There was no difficulty about most of the volunteers. Sergeant Hewson and five drivers were with me on the instant. The sixth driver had hesitated, a known shirker. I sent for him and put him in the middle of one of the teams where he could do no harm. [Nowadays I suppose he would be posted to a clinic and psycho-analysed whilst his mates got on with the job. But this was a war of the past.] Swayles, one of my best subalterns, I left in charge of the battery with instructions to plaster the mound with smoke-shell until we returned. Then at a slow trot we moved over the crest towards the front and No Man's Land, the sergeant behind the two teams and limbers, and myself in front with a slightly strained feeling about the ribs and a growing sense of the silliness of the whole affair.

Past the railway we rode by little groups of outpost-infantry, sitting in shell-holes or short lengths of improvised trench. I recall their startled looks as they saw two artillery teams in so un-conventional a spot, and one or two of them shouted timely advice. I looked up happily towards the mound, on which Swayles's smoke-shell were landing quite prettily. And then, as I looked, our shelling abruptly ceased, and the smoke began to drift away. [I did not note and have forgotten the cause of the interruption.] The mound now looked down upon us at horribly close range, seemingly with a hundred angry eyes. Shortly, however, we found ourselves under the hill, momentarily in dead ground from the summit, and reached the guns without mishap.

There four of us dismounted, and got to work; but, alas, the eyelets of the German gun-trails would not fit our limber-hooks. There was nothing for it but to take the German limbers too, and to lash their poles to our own limbers. With difficulty we extracted the poles from beneath the unimaginably heavy carcasses of the

German teams, fastened them with drag-ropes and, again at a slow trot, began our return journey. The summer dust rose thickly around us from our wheels, with the density of a smoke barrage, and to that fact I ascribe our safe emergence. A shell landed beside us, and as the smoke and dust cleared a little I rode round the teams to check up. The rear gun had jumped its hook and had disappeared in the noise and dust. This was just too bad. I sent the sergeant on with the one gun, stopped the rear team, and circled back with it. The centre driver of it was the scallywag whom I had put in at the last minute, and I observed him as the team turned in the dust. His blue moonlike face had lost all expression, his mouth and eyes were wide open like those of a corpse, his legs were clattering at the sides of his saddle and only the balance of long habit kept him in place. I recall a sudden and unforgivable urge to put a bullet through his head. [Poor fellow.]

A hundred yards back we found the gun amidst the dust. With small available man-power, we had great difficulty in re-hooking it, but another shell landing nearby served as a timely stimulus. Then we turned once more in the falling light and reached the battery without further episode. There I had lined the men up to thank them when I was called to the telephone. 'Send in two names.' Reserving one for the sergeant, who had acquitted himself admirably [and was awarded the D.C.M.], I chose a driver (quite irregularly) by lot, and wondered, as I was doing so, whether the scallywag would draw the winner. In fact, he did not—but he might have done. [The selected driver got the M.M.]

At intervals throughout the night our new German guns fired German gas-shell back to their rightful owners. I last saw those guns, with our battery's name upon them, in St. James's Park in 1919, when a great mass of war-booty was exposed there to the public gaze. But, though an archaeologist, I have never been back to see that awesome castle-mound, the Butte de Warlencourt. I probably never shall; the picture of it is clearly in my mind.

(III) TWELVE HOURS' LEAVE IN 1917

[At this time I was commanding a battery in a Field Artillery Brigade, which would nowadays be called a Field Regiment of

Royal Artillery. With the 5th Division, we had been switched overnight—if a train journey lasting a week can be so described— from Passchendaele to Northern Italy at the critical moment when our allies, the Italians, broke dangerously at Caporetto. We were now parading the plain of Lombardy and the foothills to the north, digging out Italian deserters and awaiting our turn in the new front line along the Piave. With a fellow-officer I took twelve hours' leave in Venice, then officially out of bounds but accessible. That night, on return to my billet in the house of a parish priest some miles from Treviso, I sat up in bed and wrote the story of the day. Here it is.]

It is a hard early winter in 1917 amongst the fields and ditches of the Venetian plains. These few farmhouses and inns are Silvelle— one of the most beautiful names in a land fragrant with such beauties. Otherwise, the only comeliness of the place is that of fields of snow beribboned with frozen dykes.

This is the house of the priest. Like all houses in this country, it is something of a farm. The little wizened priest presides over it furtively, with a shy and smiling courtesy. His courtesy withdraws him generally to the kitchen, where he nods gravely and deferentially to the loud pidgin-English wherewith the British soldiery is apt to appeal to the inferior understanding of the foreigner. Occasionally we succeed in enticing him back into his study which is now our Mess; and tonight, with a little French, a little Italian and much bad Latin, we have for an hour or so taken forty years and a whole Veneto village off his bending shoulders. With much closing of outer doors and jingling of keys, he has unlocked a cupboard in the wall and taken out therefrom a polished gramophone, beautifully kept, with about twenty records neatly docketed and evidently intended to be a representative collection of international masterpieces. With unhesitating tact he hastily conceals the two Wagner records which happen to lie on top, and, after a brief search, produces with evident pride his sample of English music. A moment later the instrument is softly sighing out the overture of the *Geisha Girl*, whilst the old priest, renewed youth in his eyes and a beaming smile upon his cheeks, is vigorously marking the time with two long and bony fingers.

Now the priest has retired to the unexplored hinterland of the house. Swayles [one of my subalterns], pen in hand, is busily consulting Wilcox whether he should propose to the girl in Newcastle or the other one in Cardiff. Cheesman, the captain, is alternately baying with and at a banjo which is obviously master of the situation. A hundred yards down the road, at the next farm, Wandy [my admirable young captain, Prior-Wandesforde] is sitting in the cow-house, holding the plump and somewhat leathery hand of Angela, whilst Angela's father and mother and sisters and brothers sit round in an admiring semicircle. Ever and anon a jug of inky and acid wine is circulated, and Wandy solemnly drinks to Angela's eyes, and Angela, with a little timid giggle, drinks to Wandy. The guttering candles throw a ghostly light upon the gaunt rumps of the great white oxen in the stalls, and the warm air is heavy with the bitter-sweet smell of oxen. Where else than to the byre should the Italian farmer and his family go on a winter's night?—for there is no stove or fireplace in his house. And Wandy goes too because it is warm, and because Angela's hand is plump. Last month, Wandy, aged 19, won his D.S.O. in a flooded gun-pit overlooking Passchendaele Ridge. But this month he is 20, and now a grown man, and he holds Angela's hand and drinks vinegar to the beautiful eyes of Angela.

But there is only one Angela, and the house of the priest is a-cold. Wherefore am I in bed, and by candle-light I write this history of all that happened to some others and myself this day. I will call it

A VENETIAN BLIND

For a moment the scene stirred my companion to reminiscence. He had once seen Athens, when his ship stood off the Piraeus after a snowstorm, and the Parthenon, glistening whiter than marble, thrust into a steel-blue sky. Or, to quote him *in extenso*, 'the rotten hole was like a Christmas card.' And there, the possibilities of the subject having been fully explored by a mind which knew only simple predicates and full-stops, the topic ended. We settled down amongst our coats in the bottom of the gondola, and the Unshaven One propelled us steadily down the Grand Canal amidst a swirl of moist snow-flakes. 'Another damned Christmas card,' added my companion concisely between the teeth, and then, after a suitable lapse, he began to hum a Christmas carol with gloomy humour. The Rialto, strangely new, drifted over us, and palace after palace, strangely old and shabby, floated by. The blue and gold lay threadbare on the mooring posts, and in one place, I remember, a broken shutter hung like a bat from the scarred cliff-face of a deserted mansion. It was once, said the Unshaven One as he came forward on the stroke, it was once the Kaiser's Palace. Venice after three-and-a-half years of war was indeed out at the elbows; her *palazzi* with their teeth out, with tousled hair about their ears, blotched make-up and unseeing eyes.

Things were getting desperate. It was cold, and Venetian snow dissolves as it descends and goes through one like a vanishing ghost, but alas! with more substance. Something had to be done. Worst omen, my companion became eloquent. He was an excellent specimen of the silent British cave-man, and he shall here be known as Taciturnus. Now it is notorious that Britons such as Taciturnus are the most perverse of God's creatures. When the sun shines and all is well, they grumble and blaspheme. But when all is black and the heavens ope their sluices and the clothes cling like seaweed, then do they raise their voices in raucous song and indulge a gawky humour of a type which may best be appraised in terms of horse-power. Something had to be done; for the Christmas carols were now merging into negro ditties in a great crescendo. Something *was* done, more or less in the following terms:

Ego (pleadingly): Taciturnus, you have no soul.

Taciturnus: No, my boy, nor fingers nor toes, and my legs have got the cramp and my nose is blue—I can see it.

Ego: But, Taciturnus, these palace walls which you are now shattering with your accursed Tennessee—think what they have seen, and hidden: the Ten Tyrants—the merchants newly from the Orient with baskets full of precious stones for the shrine of Mark—the loves, the poisonings, the tortures, the triumphs, and, above all, the endless secrets. Why, the whole place is sibilant with secrets, and, with a bit of ordinary luck, we shall find that our gondolier is really a temporarily embarrassed princeling.

Taciturnus (impatiently): Oh, see guide-book.

Ego: You have no spirit of adventure.

Taciturnus: Adventure? Nothing ever happens in this dingy place. Why, they're never even bombed.

Ego: Well, if Venice can't produce an adventure, the world is dead. . . .

Look here, Taciturnus, I *bet* you we can find an adventure.

Taciturnus (entering sullenly into the spirit of the thing): I wouldn't rob you, my boy. But I'll tell you what I will do. I'll toss you for the first adventure!

In the draughty cabin of the gondola we blew upon our icy fingers and tossed for the first adventure. 'Heads,' said Taciturnus, and heads it was.

*　　　*　　　*

Now were this other than a true history we should thenceforward have plunged into the New Arabian Nights or trodden the innocent footsteps of Father Brown. Quivering knives would have pinned mysterious messages to the prow of the gondola, or ghostly shrieks have lured us from our course. Instead of which, two frozen men-at-arms were slowly propelled by an unshorn and evil-smelling marine cabman undeviatingly from one imprisoned water-way to another, until Taciturnus found himself completely outstared by the inscrutability of fate. He had already given the Unshaven One ten lire to sing a Venetian gondola-song; and had then given him ten lire more to shut up. Now, with the monumental patience of despair, he displayed twenty lire before the great Unshaven, and demanded an adventure *instanter—nulla mora interposita* was his nearest approach to the native idiom. With incredible celerity, the pilot comprehended, and the gondola sprang forward with renewed life.

Suddenly, with a noiseless whirl of the sweep, the gondola swung in amongst the bedraggled posts, and from the four-days' growth of the pilot came a strange and penetrating *hiss*. You know how on the Welsh mountains the lithe sentinel sheep hiss as you approach, a quite effortless hiss which can nevertheless be heard three hundred yards away or more. Thus thrice hissed the Unshaven One, and on the third signal there was a rattling of the shutter overhead.

'O thou fool, Taciturnus,' I said, 'dost thou not know yet after thy wanderings that cabmen are the same all the world over? A cab in Paris—a rickshaw, I suspect, in Japan—a gondola in Venice —they are not for adventures but adventurers. Drive on, Antonio!' A fat and yellow arm, brownish-pink at the elbow and lightly clad, was thrusting aside the shutter. Above the arm appeared a well-filled countenance, dark yellow with black and puckered eyes, all framed in thin black hair. Taciturnus was looking upwards through half-closed eyelids as one deep in thought and judgment. 'Yes, Antonio, drive on,' he said, after a pause. 'But, signori . . .' began the pilot in amazement, waving a hand at the same time ingratiatingly and despairingly towards the window. Taciturnus passed him the twenty lire and repeated his order. With more protest and gesticulation we drifted back into the narrow canal. Taciturnus gallantly kissed his hand to the lady, who responded with a high-velocity expectoration.

'You have blundered hopelessly, Taciturnus,' I observed, rather lamely; 'first, you have obviously offended a lady; secondly you have upset all the preconceived ideas of our friend Antonio regarding the British National Character; and, thirdly, we have probably both caught pneumonia. All dirt cheap, of course, at twenty lire.'

'Anyway,' I added, 'the next adventure is still yours.'

As we approached the steps, a naval pinnace full of leave-men approached from the direction of the Lido, where lay an Italian destroyer, for all the world like a broken-down tug-boat. We found ourselves in the midst of a small crowd of chattering mani-kins in tight blue uniforms, and the expressive silences of Taciturnus reacted antagonistically to those hoarse, throaty laughs, which are characteristic of the lower-class Latin. For a moment the arrivals hovered on the steps, much as a released carrier-pigeon circles before picking up its direction. Then, with a few exceptions, they moved off with some common purpose along the cobbled street. An incomprehensible force drew us in their train.

'Who knows, but that this way lies your adventure, Taciturnus,' I suggested. He grunted pessimistically. We strode down the street and turned over a narrow bridge, across which the small crowd had turned in front of us. Down a small alley, across a desolate piazza, and there the gallant sailormen hesitated. Their leaders were gently tapping upon a large, nail-studded door, high up in which was a small grating. The grating was uncovered from within, and invisible eyes peered out. Taciturnus swung upon his heels with a groan.

'Wait a moment, Taciturnus, you are in the presence, not of an adventure, but of a national institution. We have turned and turned and turned again upon our tracks, and lo! there is the same palace of the closed shutters and the aggrieved maiden.'

As I spoke, the great door swung open without visible hand, the gloom within engulfed the sailormen, and the door swung to upon a deserted street.

'To the Latin, meat and drink are but two members of a Trinity,' murmured Taciturnus. Caesar made one joke, and Taciturnus that single epigram. 'Well, Taciturnus,' I said, as we moved away, 'you are a professional soldier and I, thank the Lord, am not. Now, in your profession two failures count as one success, so that I imagine we may regard the two dismal fiascos into which you have led me as one thoroughly satisfactory adventure. It's now *my* turn, and we'll begin right now at St. Mark's.'

We stood in front of the mighty pile of steel plates and sandbags, towering to the great dome which seemed to smile faintly in the winter sun, like a bandaged but convalescent patient. Within was a blackness made luminant by golden mosaic which could be felt rather than seen and was darkened rather than lightened by fifty candles in one of the chapels. You who know bejewelled St. Mark's in time of peace can scarcely picture her in her armour, with her jewels gone, and her columns and her images swathed and swollen with steel casing and sandbags, so that saints looked grotesquely like sausages and the pillars like huge submarine growths. But through all this fantastic panoply shone the unquenchable light of a noble building nobly used. For the chapel was crowded, not with the moneyed tourists of peace-time, but with those poor work-people who, almost alone, remained in war-time Venice—glass-makers, small shop-keepers, a few labourers from the Government yards, a few children.

We passed out silently. 'Now we will see the finest man-statue in the world,' I said. And what else I said about the Colleoni need not be recorded, for I love the Colleoni with a love which began at the age of seven and therefore transcends criticism. As we made our way towards the spot, the air was suddenly a-hum with a sound that our little world knew only too well. We looked at each other with a momentary incredulity, for no one believed that the Austrian or even the Hun would bomb Venice. But there they were overhead, and for an eternity of time there was the quavering, sighing hiss of the falling bomb. As we stepped into a doorway, St. Mark's crashed behind us. An instant later, and the piazza in front roared back at us and the air was filled with dust and gas. The comment of Taciturnus shall remain unwritten. 'The next adventure, Taciturnus,' I observed, 'is yours.' But Taciturnus rose on the crest of a resurgent wave of national vanity—that honest but withal theatrical vanity which everywhere characterizes the professional Briton at a moment of crisis. He suddenly displayed, for the first time in my knowledge of him, a deliberate and meticulous solicitude for Art. 'When we were so rudely interrupted,' he was saying in a cold and even voice, 'we were going to admire the statue of the robber-king. Let us continue.' We went on into the dust-laden piazza, the Camp Santo Giovanni. In the midst, capped by a malodorous cloud, rose the great marble pedestal of the Colleoni; and at the foot of the pedestal lay—well, I need not describe what lay there. Possibly another princeling in disguise, only his disguise was now eternal. We saluted, and hurried on.

*   *   *

The evening train was passing back across the snow-clad Veneto, glimmering under a frost-clear moon. We were three, for on the platform at Venice we had met the Poet, likewise homeward bound. Now the word Poet is a term of contempt amongst soldiers; as when Lord Kitchener called Sir Ian Hamilton 'that damned poet.' But this particular poet of ours was suffered by his more military associates with a tolerance which amounted to affection, even to a reluctant respect. He was an untidy man, but of an inquiring mind which notoriously deprived him of fear in No Man's Land, much as an inspired fanatic is insensitive to pain. Simple military souls like Taciturnus treated him with a clumsy levity but at the same time sought a little shyly sometimes to shine faintly in his presence. On this occasion, Taciturnus, still a trifle self-conscious, as one half-instinctively concealing a somewhat shaken nervous system, was inclined to spread his tail and to strut before the Poet. 'Yes,' he admitted, 'we have been doing Venice. We went into the Cathedral. Topping place. Mosaics and candles and incense and all that. And then we went to see the greatest bronze statue in the world. Freelance soldier-man of the Middle Ages. By Jove, a *topping* statue, Poet. It was great.'

I observed a puzzled expression upon the Poet's countenance. 'Strange,' he murmured, half to himself, 'very strange. I thought they moved the Colleoni to Rome about six months ago! In case Venice should come under fire. Strange.' I kicked the Poet violently on the shin. Taciturnus had not heard, and we could almost see his proud features shining in the moonlight. He had at last met an artist upon his own plane, and Soul had conversed with Soul. . . .

I hastily changed the conversation. 'And you?' I asked the Poet. 'A dull day,' he said. 'I got into a gondola at the station steps, and was pushed about the whole Venetian irrigation system until I froze. Then I turned to the rascally gondolier and said: "Does anything ever happen here?" and he said "Niente." And then I said: "I suppose something happens here sometimes?" and with true Venetian politeness he said "Si, si." And I said "I'd give anything for an adventure." And he said "Give me twenty lire." This seemed a fair offer. So he put the twenty lire into his waistbelt and we went on our way.'

At this moment Taciturnus suddenly showed a mild interest. 'Go on,' he said, as the Poet paused.

'Well,' continued the Poet, 'we found ourselves in amongst the mooring-posts in some small canal near the Palace, and before I knew where I was that thief of a gondolier was hissing staccato between his teeth. Thrice he hissed, and on the third signal a shutter flew outwards from the wall overhead, and with the shutter a rounded arm. Beneath the arm gleamed a pair of laughing brown eyes, and the voice of a dove said "Good-day to you, signor. Come hither to my nest".'

He paused again.

'Yes, yes,' said Taciturnus and I in one breath. 'Continue, Poet.'

'And then,' he began, and again hesitated. 'And then,'

interpolated Taciturnus, 'and then you said to your gondolier "Gondolier, drive on!" Or didn't you?'

'Well, such was my instinct,' said the Poet, 'but precisely at that moment those infernal aeroplanes came over. . . .'

(IV) STANDARDS OF MISERY

> Through many a clime 'tis mine to go,
>   With many a retrospection curst;
> And all my solace is to know,
>   Whate'er betides, I've known the worst.

To have experienced with understanding the worst, both physically and mentally, that is likely to befall one is, I suppose, the soundest assurance of future content. Byron and I and, I have no doubt, the other man have made this cardinal discovery without cross-reference; and I would only add the actuarial truism that, the earlier in life these experiences hit one, the longer the happy sequel. Of the nadir of physical misery I had no doubt in 1917; the mental impact did not come until 1936. Of neither episode need I, nor indeed could I, say much. But I have been acutely conscious of the significance of both from the moment of their happening, and I have explicitly referred subsequent tribulations to the standards thus established, in the comparison never failing to find a sufficiency of elementary solace.

In October 1917 the ridge of Passchendaele, north-east of Ypres in Flanders, was the definition of hell. The cataclysmic rains and such shelling as never was before had churned the whole landscape into bottomless mud, honeycombed continuously with ever-renewed shell-holes, every shell-hole liable to be an actual grave or a pond of slime into which the wounded rolled from time to time and were choked to death. The air was foul with gas, and all night the crash of high-explosive was varied by the sinister pattering of more gas-shells with their scorching effluvium. Upon the ridge, in what had once been Langemarck, a solitary gaunt timber rose defiantly into the air above powdered rubble, the last vestige of *Au bon gîte* (what irony in a name!), blest now by every gunner for a mile round as an aiming-point amidst the uniformity of desolation. Beside it, under the debris, was a small cellar, filled with dead Highlanders; tiny, they seemed, in their little kilts, and green they were, with unforgettable eyes in the dim light. And beyond that I was shown, when I came up to take over command of 'A' Battery, 76th Brigade, R.F.A., a large shell-crater, oozing with a reddish brown, oily stain which was my predecessor's life-blood. Beyond again, on the forward incline towards the enemy, broken duckboards carried at dusk the dejected processions of the hopeless, on their way to the shell-holes in which they would constitute the 'front line.' And yet beyond were distant scraps of greenery where, in the Forest of Houthulst, the Germans and their howitzers occupied a happy land not yet fought over.

Immediately behind the ridge, below *Au bon gîte*, were packed the field batteries, French and British, in an almost continuous jagged line. 'A' Battery occupied six pits below the lip of a stream, the Steenbeek, now a mud-glacier merging into the general chaos. The pits were full to the brim with water; the gun-layers sat in water; the guns recoiled into water, such at least as were in firing order—rarely more than two at any one time. The gunners, thinned by casualties to cadre strength, were voiceless and red-eyed through cold and gas and sleeplessness. Behind the guns was a minute German pill-box, less than five feet high, where the signallers lay and where the battery commander and his officers, crouching over their maps, calculated their incessant barrages and harassing fire; a microscopic cell in which one could just sit up and write by candle-light. Ever and anon a German howitzer-shell would crash upon it, stunning the occupants and extinguishing the candles but happily failing to penetrate, such was the quality of the German concrete and the resilience of the sodden subsoil. I recall how after one of these crashes, in the momentary silence during which consciousness returned to us amidst the choking fumes of high-explosive, the voice of the Irish cook, Doyle, was the first to penetrate—'Och, begorra, and sure the . . . . . .'s entoirely spoilt the parruch!' First things first. But we became fewer and fewer. A shell landed amidst one of my working-parties, killing five men and wounding seven others. A driver bringing up ammunition had both his horses killed and his leg blown off as he reached us. The poor fellow was tied up as best we could and was carried by volunteers to the dressing-station. Of course he died. Every day the hard-driven pack-horses found it more and more difficult to reach us with the much-needed shells and rations. One morning, after a particularly heavy bout of enemy shelling, I walked back four or five hundred yards to the flattened spot known optimistically on the map as Golden Cross, where a battery of 60-pounder guns was deployed. I arrived to find the four great guns knocked to all points of the compass, whilst two teams of heavy-draught horses, a steaming mass of pulped flesh save where a stiffening leg projected with idiotic integrity, bespattered the site. Amidst it all, lone survivor, the battery major was walking up and down aimlessly with tears streaming down his face. Twice within a few hours I had seen men weeping; the sight shocked and embarrassed me, and I turned upon my heel. . . . That night I was summoned by the colonel to a midnight conference about a dawn attack, and I picked my way by compass-bearing across the morass in the noisy, flickering darkness. At one point I flashed my torch to circumvent a shell-hole; the thin light lit up an arm and half-clenched hand, thrust from the mud as though to clasp my ankle, and the macabre memory has not faded. I was suddenly and violently sick. . . .

And now I anticipate. In April 1936 I had been travelling in the Near East without postal address for several weeks. The Trans-continental Express by which I was returning from Aleppo to Boulogne was shunted en route into the Gare du Nord at Paris, and there I bought a *Times* from a passing newsboy. I sat back and opened it. A paragraph-heading at the top of a column read 'Tessa Verney Wheeler,' and below it was an appreciation of Tessa by Sir Frederic Kenyon. She had died three days previously, suddenly, in the fullness of her life. Six weeks ago I had left her well and with her blessing. Twenty-two years ago we had been married, and year by year we had worked as one, as 'the Wheelers.' I pressed the bell-button and ordered a double brandy. My unfocused eyes turned from the unreality of the printed page; at the same time a kindly numbness entered into my mind and threw it also out of focus, a condition in which it was happily to remain during the following days. . . . I was aware of an English family at the door of my carriage meditating entry, and vaguely recognized an acquaintance from the Record Office. He glanced up, spotted me, and with his folk hurried anxiously away down the train without a word. On the cross-Channel boat I saw the little group dodge round a corner as I came aboard; and thereafter a sardonic humour induced me to pursue it from point to point until finally in mid-Channel I cornered it. 'I know,' I said, 'say nothing'; and the heartfelt response 'Thank God' was out before the conventions supervened. At Victoria I was met by Molly Cotton, a treasured friend and colleague of ours. For two days and nights she had met every continental train, not knowing which would be mine . . . in case I didn't know. The numbness slowly passed away, leaving the subtly impaired sensibility of a first 'stroke.'

4. Archaeology in Essex and Wales

In July 1919 I was 'disembodied.' The War Office terminology was cynically exact. For nearly five years I had achieved a little brief authority and a sizeable income—latterly, with field allowances, something over £800 a year, which in those days was not a negligible total. And now once more I was a Junior Investigator under the Royal Commission on Historical Monuments (England) and one of the lowliest of God's creatures. In effect, at the age of twenty-nine I was for the first time (like so many others) confronted with the overdue problems of a career. Also, I had a wife and a small son.

Archaeology. The day on which the Franks Studentship and Sir Arthur Evans had combined to guide my footsteps was irrevocable, nor had I any desire to revoke it. Already I had a clear enough idea as to where such ability as I possessed could most usefully be employed. In the early summer of 1914 I had been surveying for the Commission, under Professor F. J. Haverfield's remote control (I never met him), the Roman remains of Essex. My material might have been the content of a junk-shop, so inconsequent and inconsiderable was it. To continue indefinitely to toy with such *disjecta* was mere foolery; something practical had to be done to bring reason into the chaos, and done quickly, for I was already oppressed with the brevity of life. Amongst the scraps with which I was dealing were vague references, mostly of the eighteenth century, to remains of a Roman building near Pleshey in central Essex, and in what passed for a museum at Chelmsford were fragments of Roman 'Arretine' pottery from the site. Now Arretine pottery, made in Italy, passed out of circulation within two or three years of the Roman invasion of Britain in A.D. 43, and a site which produced such pottery must therefore have been in very early contact with the Roman world. Here was an obvious starting-point for the ordering of Roman Essex. I hurried down to Pleshey.

The village of Pleshey, in the depths of the Essex countryside, is little visited today, but is in fact a notable spot. Above it towers a great Norman castle-mound, with a bailey alongside and, beyond that, the crescentic outline of the old *burgus* in a singular state of preservation. The place was originally held by the De Mandevilles, but passed to the De Bohuns, who, as Earls of Essex, were the great family hereabouts during much of the Middle Ages. It was not, however, in the rôle of medieval historian that I made my way there in 1914, but as an ardent young classic in search of Roman Britain. Alas, I could not find it. The site had long been forgotten, had melted into the landscape. It was just possible that one old, old man might remember it. He was bed- or chair-ridden, that was the trouble, and couldn't move out of his house. I ordered a horse and trap and sought out the ancient.

I found him in his cottage, folded into a chair. He must have been something like ninety years old, but, even in decay, rarely have I seen a finer, more aristocratic face, a mien of greater dignity. I was presented to 'Mr. Boon,' and I started at the name. Of course; here was the last of the Bohuns, whose castle lay in the trees beyond. From which side of the blanket the old cottager's forebears had come was of no matter; here, without shadow of doubt, was a true descendant and simulacrum of an earl who had led at Crécy. It was, I hope, with an added reverence that I helped to lift him into the waiting trap. We trundled off down the road until quietly told to stop. The Fitzboon was pointing over the hedgerows to the exact spot where, in years long past, he had ploughed into the buried walls.

I arranged to return in August to dig the site on behalf of the Morant Club of Essex. On August the 4th the Kaiser Wilhelm II intervened. The site is still untouched by modern hands.

The next archaeological episode occurred in 1917. In that year my field-howitzer battery was stationed for a short time in the barracks at Colchester, preparing Most Secretly to be placed on a barge and landed by night behind the German lines on the Belgian coast. My dreams were haunted by a conglomerate vision of myself in the dual rôle of Julius Caesar and the standard-bearer of the

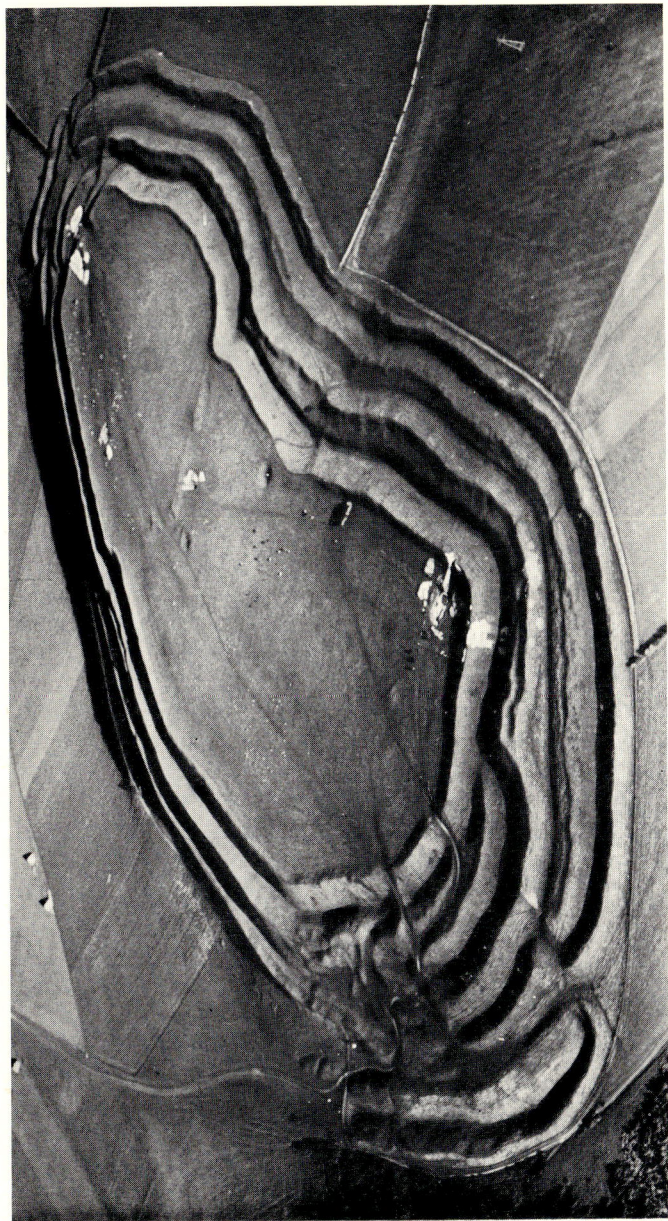

[*Air photograph by Major G. W. G. Allen*

THE PREHISTORIC 'OPPIDUM' OF MAIDEN CASTLE, DORSET, DURING EXCAVATION, 1935

MAIDEN CASTLE, 1937: THE BRITISH WAR-CEMETERY, A.D. 44

Note the Roman arrowhead in the spine of a British defender

10th Legion leaping into the surf between Nieuwport and Ostend whilst the Western Front crumpled up and the Kaiser rushed to proffer me the hilt of his sword. Happily for myself, the Germans got wind of the projected landing and it was abandoned. Meanwhile, during the summer evenings I was quietly conducting an offensive upon the Balkerne Gate of Colchester, without contradicting the rumour that I was in fact building an anti-Zeppelin shelter.

The circumstances were these. The Balkerne Gate is one of the most upstanding relics of Roman Britain, and had been the entry into the Roman city from the London road. A large part of it was, and is, covered by a public-house, but in 1914 a local antiquary had dug into the more accessible portions of the gate and had even begun to probe beneath the superincumbent inn. War and the death of the antiquary in question had left the work unfinished and unpublished. Now, with the concurrence of the Colchester Corporation, I undertook the tasks of clearing up the mess and producing some sort of a report.

My *modus operandi* was to detail, evening by evening, three or four volunteers from my battery and, with their aid, to make what sense I could of the untidy burrows. The nucleus of my gang was my groom, a professional groom of melancholy but co-operative nature, and one of my gunners, Max West, who had been at the Slade School and was not of a noticeably military turn of mind. To these a variety of bodies were added, attracted less by archaeological research than by the homely noises of—and subsequent participation in—the revelry of the tap-room overhead. The excavation, if such it can be called, was conducted largely on our backs by candlelight and was anything but a model of scientific method. But we at least did not do any irreparable damage, and ultimately produced a plan designed to serve until the removal of the public-house should facilitate corrections and additions. The whole operation was one of salvage, and now, thirty-six years later, our sketchy plan is still the only record available. The affair was pleasantly rounded off by the Corporation with a surprising resolution of thanks, which, formidably engrossed and sealed, is amongst my treasured possessions.

This brings me back to 1919; but, before proceeding with my

C

chronicle, I must here recapitulate some of the thoughts which were passing through my mind in that year of decision. First, it was clear to me that the next advance in our knowledge of human achievement outside the historical field was dependent upon fresh and methodical discovery, and that fresh discovery in great measure meant fresh digging. In Romano-British studies, which to me, as a classic, were the starting-point, Haverfield had carried synthesis pretty nearly as far as it could be carried on the existing evidence. In other branches of insular archaeology, much more work of the kind awaited attention: work such as Lord Abercromby, for example, had already carried out on Bronze Age pottery. But those branches lay outside my immediate purview, and, in any case, it was sufficiently evident that there too the stimulus of controlled discovery was an urgent need. And as I looked around me with these thoughts in my head, two other factors stuck out a mile. The first was the utter inadequacy of the pre-war techniques for the recovery and analysis of buried material. At Wroxeter under J. P. Bushe-Fox we had been groping towards something a little more adequate, inspired, as each generation fortunately is, by a filial contempt for our elders. But then the First German War had blotted us out. That was the second factor: we had been blotted out. Those familiar only with the mild casualties of the Second German War can have little appreciation of the carnage which marked its predecessor. It is a typical instance that, of five university students who worked together in the Wroxeter excavations of 1913, one only survived the war. It so happened that the survivor was myself. In other fields were A. W. Clapham and O. G. S. Crawford, both of whom became the closest of my friends. But in my own rather ill-defined province, a sense of isolation was already apparent to me in 1919; in what followed it became a dominant element.

The technical problem was the immediate hurdle. As I pondered more upon it, the more puzzled I became. I can vividly recall the sequence of thought. Between 1880 and 1900 General Pitt Rivers in Cranborne Chase had brought archaeological digging and recording to a remarkable degree of perfection, and had presented his methods and results meticulously in several imposing volumes. Then what? Nothing. Nobody paid the slightest attention to the old man. One of his assistants had even proceeded to dig up a

lake-village much as Schliemann had dug up Troy or St. John Hope
Silchester: like potatoes. Not only had the clock not gone on, but
it had been set back. What had happened?

True, individuals here and there had done creditable work during
the decade following the general's death. James Curle had dug
up Roman camps and forts at Newstead, near Melrose, with no
ordinary skill, and had published his report munificently. Bushe-Fox
at Hengistbury Head in Hampshire had produced a rational sequence
of cultures and a number of penetrating ideas, though his recording
never, then or later, approached the standard of Pitt Rivers. More
typical of the age, at the Roman military depot near Corbridge
in Northumberland there had, about 1907–8, been a nebulous
free-for-all which has recently been illuminated by Sir Leonard
Woolley. Writing in 1953, he tells us[1] that his own first experience
of digging was in this Corbridge enterprise:

'I know only too well [he says] that the work there would
have scandalized, and rightly scandalized, any British archaeologist of today. It was however typical of what was done forty-five
years ago. . . . The committee naturally appealed to Professor
Haverfield as the leading authority on Roman Britain and he, as
he had intended to take a holiday on the Roman Wall, agreed to
supervise the excavations. Somebody, of course, had to be put in
charge of the work and . . . Haverfield arranged with Sir Arthur
Evans, the Keeper of the Ashmolean Museum, that I should go
to Corbridge. In point of fact, I had never so much as seen an
excavation, I had never studied archaeological methods even
from books (there were none at that time dealing with the
subject) . . . I was very anxious to learn, and it was a disappoint-
ment to me that Haverfield only looked in at the excavations one
day in the week and then was concerned only to know what had
been found—I don't think that he ever criticized or corrected
anything. . . .'

Such was my technical inheritance when, in the latter part of
1919, I peered anxiously into the future. Manifestly, my path
thither lay backwards, to the forgotten standards of Cranborne
Chase, before advancing to new methods and skills. But first I must

[1] *Spadework* (London, 1953), pp. 14 ff.

clear up this matter of a career. Listing seventeenth-century cottages for the Commission was great fun, but it led nowhere either professionally or financially. Finance was my immediate worry. I went to (Sir) George Duckworth, the Commission's secretary—a smooth Edwardian placeman with a fair knowledge of wine but none whatever of archaeology—and demanded more pay. His reply was 'Come out to lunch,' and we proceeded to discuss, not pay, but lobster mayonnaise and Sauternes at the Garrick Club. On the way back, as we passed through Trafalgar Square he beamed upon me and said that there was no hope whatever of my advancement. Did I realize that there had been a war? I turned angrily upon him (he had himself spent the war in various comfortable and evasive nests in Whitehall), thanked him abruptly for his lunch, and went my way. An hour afterwards my eye lighted upon an advertisement for candidates for a joint post of Keeper of Archaeology in the National Museum of Wales and Lecturer in Archaeology in the University College at Cardiff. Still fuming with frustration, I sat down and applied for the vacancy, rather as a means of letting off steam than with any expectation or indeed hope of success. I had never heard of the National Museum of Wales, did not know where Cardiff was on the map, and had a growing dislike of museums.

Why I was appointed to the Cardiff posts is still hidden from me. My principal competitor was an established museum-curator of some repute and I had no sort of qualification. I came away from the interview with a heart of lead, not because I had failed but because I had succeeded. Apart from a handsome civic centre, the streets of Cardiff seemed unbearably mean and dingy, the people in them unbelievably foreign and barbaric. For the moment I yearned for London as never before. Having said that, I must hasten to add that my following six years (1920–26) in Cardiff were both busy and happy ones, and that the kindliness with which Wales received a stranger in its midst is unforgettable.

Of the administrative aspects of my work there I will say little although they loomed large at the time. They were mainly twofold: first, to secure some general acceptance in Wales at large of a 'National' Museum situated in the cosmopolitan, un-Welsh and peripheral city of Cardiff; and secondly to bring the museum itself into physical existence. To these two aspects I might add a third: to secure for archaeology a recognized place in the curriculum of the Welsh University, where I was now the first holder of the first lectureship in the subject. A little may be said of each of the two former matters in turn.

First, Wales *versus* Cardiff. The intense local patriotisms of a mountain-divided country with indifferent communications were (and are) natural and proper. Wales, save when united in opposition to England, was an aggregate of parish pumps rather than a nation. The thirteen counties could not for a moment be expected of their own volition to focus on Cardiff; the last thing that the mountains were prepared to do was to come to Mahomet. It was for Mahomet to go to the mountains. And if for Mahomet we substitute a young and rather determined Englishman, that is what happened. My senior colleagues were sometimes disturbed at my frequent absences in the hills, but I knew that my policy was right. By lectures, excavations and other contacts I took the museum into the highways and byways of Wales, and eventually, by offering practical assistance to the poor little local museums up and down the country, built up a Welsh federation of museums with the National Museum in the chair and periodical training-schools at Cardiff. I even produced a book on *Prehistoric and Roman Wales*, to give something of a general picture of the values of Welsh archaeology as a whole. It was not a good book; it was scribbled hastily in railway carriages and country inns during 1923 and 1924; but it was better than anything that had gone before and in some measure served its frankly political purpose, as a primary medium of integration. Looking back on it and on the utter negation from which it emerged as a germ of future achievement, I am less dissatisfied with it than a single-minded and unfettered archaeologist has the right and duty to be.

To the excavations which I have mentioned I shall return. Meanwhile I pass for a moment to the more domestic problems of the new museum. In 1920 the building was a façade backed by concrete and scaffolding. Most of the collections were still housed or stored in a murky suite in the city library. Work on the new structure had ceased and the building-fund was £22,000 in debt. Everything had come to a standstill. After a profitable war, Cardiff was suffering a financial setback which augured ill.

When in 1924 I was elevated at the age of thirty-three to the Directorship of the museum, stagnation had set in with an air of permanency. The situation was a challenge to the new Director; chance and Sir William Reardon Smith, Bart.—but especially Sir William Reardon Smith, Bart.—enabled him to meet it. I have never encountered a character at the same time so rich in experience, so shrewd, and withal so simple, so unspoilt, and so generous as that of Reardon Smith. When I knew him he was the head of the largest and most successful fleet of cargo-ships then running, and he owed his success to his personal inside knowledge of the business from fo'c'sle to counting-house in all parts of the world. He had been born in a cottage at Appledore in Devon and as a youngster had been sent to sea as cabin-boy of a brig. In those days the captain personally provided the victuals for the crew and made what he could out of the deal. Young Smith on his first day was sent to the galley to try his apprentice hand at peeling the potatoes. By and by the captain came down and, observing substantial slices of potato adhering to the peel in the bucket, seized Smith by the scruff of the neck and kicked him savagely into the rigging. 'But if I'd peeled those potatoes properly and economically, I should be in the cookhouse still,' added old Sir William. 'I owe a lot to that captain.' Smith had later commanded a number of cargo-vessels and finally bought the fleet. It was my joy to get him going on the saga of his travels and to hear the seaports of the world roll off his tongue with all the poetry of Homer's 'Catalogue of Ships.' We became great friends.

On my appointment events happened in speedy succession. A private visit to the Treasury in Whitehall resulted in a substantial increase in the Government grant, and a subsequent open battle between myself and the museum treasurer (a useless local alderman) led to the resignation of the latter and the appointment of Reardon Smith, who marked his appointment by coming to my office and writing a cheque for £22,000. With our debt thus cleared, an appeal was launched, and in a few weeks the builders were once more at work. Gradually the great building took shape and some of the rooms were thrown open to the public. Before long the King would be invited to open the museum in state.

This bald summary covers several months of hectic and anxious work. The result had been a victorious answer to the challenge. But what next? I sat back in my office with a sudden feeling of deflation. I was thirty-five, and the rest of my life was already a tramline. But now I had other ideas, other plans in my head, a scheme to which I shall come presently. London was necessary for the development of that scheme. Already in 1921 I had declined an invitation from Burke, Garter King of Arms, to join the College of Arms in Queen Victoria Street as Bluemantle Pursuivant. At that time I had not been ready to return to London; my work in Wales had only just begun, and, moreover, the picturesque but two-dimensional life of a Herald had little permanent appeal for me. But one morning in 1926 a letter from (Sir) Charles Peers in London invited me to the Keepership of the London Museum in St. James's. This time I accepted. I felt that now I could depart with a clear conscience. Behind me I should leave a going concern; I could leave also a successor in whom I had absolute faith, for on my promotion to the Directorship (Sir) Cyril Fox had been persuaded to come from Cambridge to assume the Keepership of Archaeology, and he (I was determined) should now take charge. A whisper in my ear hastened my resolution. It was now or never, and in July of that year Tessa and I left Cardiff with many and genuine personal regrets but with an inward assurance of right judgment.

It is time to return to the archaeology from which these affairs of administration constituted an increasing and not particularly congenial diversion. In 1920 my *venue* had been moved from Essex to Wales but my purpose remained unchanged: namely, to integrate a given portion of Roman Britain by selective excavation, and at the same time to evolve an adequate technique with Cranborne Chase, not Corbridge or even Wroxeter, as my pattern. Opportunity awaited me. Excavations had been begun in the Roman fort of Segontium, overlooking Caernarvon, and in 1921 I was asked to take them over. Apart from some slight exploration in Colchester in 1919, this was the first serious work of the kind that had come my way, and the chance was gladly seized simultaneously to deal with the historical problems of a site which was pivotal in the Roman occupation of Wales and to evolve the necessary techniques for doing so.

The book which, through the benevolent offices of Sir Vincent

Evans and the Honourable Society of Cymmrodorion, ensued with reasonable promptitude as *Segontium and the Roman Occupation of Wales* sufficiently contains our answer to both problems. I reproduce as a sample a key-section drawn in 1922 through the cellar or strong-room in the headquarters building of the fort. The section displays a certain crudity but, with the privilege of advancing age, I can say that it has all the right stuff in it: the clear interleaving of the original structure with dated coins, the cascade of vegetable mould which streamed down the steps when the building was deserted and more or less roofless, the infilling of masonry debris when the garrison returned years afterwards and cleared and rebuilt the structure, and the successive floorings (with their significant contents) with which the cellar was ultimately filled and sealed. The whole bones of the matter are there and at this late date it is fair to boast that, *at the time*, our sections were unapproached anywhere for expressiveness and integrity. Later, of course, such work—and better—was to become a matter of routine.

At Segontium on a small scale we began, too, that association with students which was to enter into our normal practice. I remember (as I have said) being deeply conscious at this time of our loneliness in the field of archaeological excavation and of the responsibility which the hazards of the age had thrust upon our shoulders. It became a mission—one which I have never since forsaken—to gather the younger generation about me in all my fieldwork, to inculcate it with a controlled enthusiasm, and to give it in the formative stage a sense of direction, or at least of the *need* for direction. In return, these young people have served as a recurrent blood-transfusion into my own work. Whether in England or Wales, in France or the East, they have been encouraged to work with me in their tens and hundreds, and my debt to them is beyond acknowledgment. There are lone workers in archaeology, but I pity them. The instinct for transmission is a quality essential to the complete mind as to the complete body; and the pleasure of nurturing the young idea, watching its early flights, and ultimately perhaps almost losing sight of it in the upper air, is an honest vanity not lightly to be contemned or forgone.

Of the few whom we assembled at this early date (1921–22) at Segontium, two names stand out: those of Ian Richmond, then a young undergraduate of Corpus but already alive with the intellectual agility and imagination which were to distinguish his mature scholarship; and Victor Nash-Williams, one of my first pupils at Cardiff and subsequently Cyril Fox's successor in the Keepership of Archaeology at the National Museum and in the lectureship at the Cardiff college. Nowadays, I am at least as much their pupil as they then were mine, and I have never ceased to value their early friendship.

The completion of our work at Segontium and the light which it threw upon North Wales turned our minds inevitably to the South, the archaeological bias conforming nicely with the political need for alternation between what may be loosely called the two halves of the Principality. The map and reconnaissance directed us to the Roman fort near Brecon on the fishful river of Usk. There, in an attractive countryside, was a place which, in spite of its present seclusion, had been a busy nodal point in the Roman road-system; its history could not fail to reflect that of South Wales as a whole. We knew something of its ancient garrison, a cavalry regiment raised originally in Spain. Beside the neighbouring Roman road a tall tombstone, battered and weatherbeaten, gave a ghostly personality to the scene. And incidentally I had observed the temperamental river boiling with fish during that strange ten-minute 'rise' which turns the quiet Brecon water suddenly into a noisy battlefield at sundown. A complacent owner and a co-operative tenant sealed our purpose.

For two summer seasons (1924–25) we worked at the Brecon *Gaer*, and the site produced all that was demanded of it, from Early Roman to Dark Age. In 1926 a monograph on *The Roman Fort near Brecon* presented the southern counterpart of Segontium. It also pointed to the next inevitable step: the examination of the great legionary fortress from which the Gaer and its fellows had depended, as it were the prehensile fingers of a strong hand. The time had come to grasp the hand itself.

But I have not quite finished with the Brecon Gaer. On the whole, it was, I suppose, the happiest and least anxious of all my enterprises. Amongst my students there I have a vivid memory of two young Wykehamists from New College, Christopher Hawkes and Nowell Myres: one vital, ebullient and determined, the other more sedate and reflective, but with a lively twinkle in his eye. The one was a perfect antithesis, or, rather, complement of the other, and I like to think that this happy conjunction of the stars is a continuing phenomenon of a university where one is now the Professor of European Archaeology and the other Bodley's Librarian.

And another memory of those Brecon days is of the Flinders Petries, who came down and stayed with us on one of their rare holidays. The term 'holiday' is a relative one. Petrie's mind never 'let up' for an instant. He had chosen 'stone circles' and cairns for his holiday task, and morning after morning he would go off into the landscape with this set purpose. On the first day I asked him what instruments he proposed to take with him. A look of ineffable cunning came into his eyes as he produced a single slender bamboo pea-stick and—a visiting-card. The pea-stick, he said, planted in the ground gave him the line, whilst the visiting-card, sighted carefully along two of its sides, gave him a right-angle. At night after dinner, by the light of an oil-lamp, he would get out a notebook containing lists of measurements resulting from his day's work in the field, and, with the help of a logarithm-table, would ultimately reduce them to a schematic diagram.

I recall this story as a curious, rather human sidelight on the paradoxical character of a man whose microscopically precise measurements of the pyramids of Gizeh are almost legendary. By his incredible ingenuity complex problems were liable to be rendered excessively simple and surmountable, and simple problems might be tangled into inextricable complexities. But he was a genius in the full sense of that abused term. Younger generations have sometimes blamed him for sinning against their own standards, forgetful that the immense stretch of his working life extended long after his period of intellectual receptiveness had passed. We might as well blame Xerxes for not deploying torpedo-boats at Salamis, or Napoleon for attacking the British squares with cavalry instead of machine-guns. Petrie fought with the weapons that he knew or himself invented, and in his youth fought better than any of his contemporaries in the East.

His unresting mind is my last memory of him. It was years afterwards, early in 1942, when I happened to be engaged upon fieldwork of a non-archaeological kind in Egypt. Petrie had then been living for several years in Palestine, and one day I heard somehow or other that he was dying. I took twenty-four hours' leave, drove across Sinai to Jerusalem, and made my way to the hospital where Petrie in his eighty-ninth year lay placidly upon his death-bed. The picture of him is stamped on my mind. He was swathed in white sheets, and a sort of turban of white linen was about his head. His grey beard and superb profile gave him the aspect of a Biblical patriarch. His mind was running even faster than was its wont, as though it had a great distance still to cover before the approaching end. In the course of ten minutes it ranged without pause over a wide variety of matters, from the copper implements of Mesopotamia to the lethal incidence of the malarial mosquito at Gaza. I left the room quietly, my brain stretched by the immensity and impetus of a mind for which there were no trivialities in life and no place of respite.

But to return to Wales and 1926. In such moments as could be snatched from the busy routine of the museum, I was preparing the way for an attack on the legionary fortress at Caerleon. Immediately outside the fortress lay the great oval hollow which the village folk knew as 'King Arthur's Round Table' but was less romantically the site of the Roman amphitheatre. Here was a suitable starting-point: a familiar site, free from encumbrance, one likely to attract the considerable funds required for a long-term programme of work. I announced the project to the Press.

The following night I was at a public dinner in Cardiff when I was called to the telephone. 'Mr. B. of the *Daily Mail* speaking, about that Amphitheatre of yours, I am coming down by the next train, can I see you at midnight?' By five minutes after midnight the *Daily Mail* had agreed to finance the excavation of 'King Arthur's Round Table' (to the tune ultimately of some thousands of pounds) in return for exclusive news. I am glad to place on record not only the liberality but also the liberal spirit with which the *Daily Mail* shouldered its side of the bargain. But what had happened? Why this unprecedented emergence of the daily Press as patrons of British archaeology?

The answer is not, I think, difficult. Our leading newspaper had already had the enterprise to acquire the exclusive right of publishing Lord Carnarvon's excavation of Tutankhamūn's tomb, and the resultant reports had captured the popular imagination. Archaeology had, almost overnight, acquired a new market-value, and it is fair to say that, since that time, it has maintained its hold upon the public. The Press, films, radio, and now television, have all taken it up, and for my part I wholeheartedly welcome this development. Years before Tutankhamūn came to the rescue, G. M. Trevelyan had been protesting that 'if historians neglect to educate the public, if they fail to interest it intelligently in the past, then all their historical learning is valueless except in so far as it educates themselves.' And apart from everything else, today the public has every right to its archaeology, palatably garnished; for the days of private patronage are over, and most field-archaeology now comes directly out of our rates and taxes, whether we like it or no. It is only fair to add that in the budgets of other countries State-archaeology long loomed more amply than in our own.

In 1926, then, began the excavation of Caerleon, which has continued intermittently ever since with illuminating results. Tessa took charge of the very considerable task of excavating the amphitheatre, and subsequently Aileen Fox, Christopher Hawkes, and, above all, V. E. Nash-Williams, continued within the old fortress itself. Meanwhile, in the latter days of my directorship at Cardiff, my mind had been turning increasingly to the need for systematic training in a discipline which was now emerging from the chrysalis stage and was incidentally now in the public eye. Students were increasing in numbers; archaeological posts were slowly beginning to multiply. Something had to be done about it, and, looking round in my war-depleted generation, I could see no one but myself to do it—such was the poverty of the land. During the early months of 1926 I drew up a detailed scheme for a university Institute of Archaeology such as nowhere existed in this country. The scheme seemed to me at the time a very easy and convincing one: all we needed was the money, and we knew exactly how much. I was an optimist; in fact, it was ten years before the scheme could be partially realized. It had to be insinuated into a massive university system where the new was inevitably (and rightly) regarded as a rival and a challenge to the old and was not therefore lightly admissible. In July 1926 we moved to London and got to work.

*   *   *

Here I must pause for a moment. It would be improper to leave Wales without a friendly and filial postscript. When, twenty years later, I was suddenly called upon to face the immeasurably greater and more complex problems of the Archaeological Survey of India, I was constantly aware of the extent to which my Welsh experience had prepared and trained me. Wales *in parvo* presented just that internal diversity of interests and loyalties which characterizes the Indian sub-continent, and the problems of centralized administration from New Delhi were to offer surprising parallels to the problems of centralized administration from Cardiff. Comparable local suspicion of the intruder had to be overcome, emphasized in both contexts by the fact that the central agent was an Englishman and a foreigner. Emphasized, but not always aggravated by that fact; for in both countries I have found that the sympathetic foreigner, transcending local antagonisms, was not necessarily unwelcome as an unbiased intervener.

Wales, too, brought me closely into touch with that immensely variegated and infinitely fascinating phenomenon which is misleadingly simplified as 'the general public.' To this, war service had necessarily been a rough-and-ready introduction, distorted by special circumstance. Now, in Wales, it was my specific function to bring the arts and sciences to the myriad thresholds of 'the general public.' And this, up to a considerable point, could be done only in the most literal sense, by personal visitation. I recall an extreme instance.

In 1922, when I was working at Caernarvon, I decided to penetrate into the almost unknown recesses of Bardsey Island. With me went my friends Alfred Clapham and Wilfrid Hemp (then Inspector of Ancient Monuments for Wales), and a local acquaintance, Shirley Jones, who in a ramshackle car proceeded to drive us to the little coastal village of Aberdaron, on the end of the Lleyn Peninsula. In the distance, three or four miles away, lay the island in the morning haze.

Now by the shortest line Bardsey lies only some two miles off the Caernarvonshire mainland, and it might seem no great exploit to traverse that modest strait. But in fact it is a matter which requires thought and preparation. The currents in the two miles' stretch are fierce and formidable; add an ill-favoured wind, and the island is inaccessible. On one occasion H.M. school-inspector, having scrambled on to the island, was unable to leave it for three tedious weeks, in spite of the superhuman efforts of the islanders to get rid of him. The story is told of a Lord Newborough of a cynical turn of mind—the Newboroughs have long owned the island—who enjoined in his will, under sundry dire sanctions, that he should be buried on the island on the anniversary of his death, neither a day sooner nor a day later. The anxious heir, his eye on the sanctions, had one course open to him—to build, at extravagant cost, an all-weather landing-stage on the island, not otherwise could trans-shipment be guaranteed. The massive timbers were driven and locked into position; bills for hundreds of pounds were incurred; the bidden day came. There was not a breath of wind, and the lamented peer could have been landed anywhere on the island without any sort of landing-stage! It is said that, as they carried the coffin ashore, the bearers could hear the old man chuckling evilly within. He at least had had his money's worth.

But his tomb is not the only monument which adorns the island. Nearby, he or one of his line set up an imposing 'Celtic' cross to commemorate the 'twenty thousand saints' buried thereabouts. Bardsey must surely have been as saintly as Cornwall. The reference is, however, to the ancient monastery, now marked by a jagged fragment of medieval masonry, which goes back to a happy age when all religious were *ipso facto* saints. Certainly their modern lay successors have been content with a less exacting standard of attainment. Indeed, towards the end of the eighteenth century things had come to such a pass that the Lord Newborough of the day decided to impose a constitution upon the island. On the named day, the gentry of Caernarvonshire, with the noble lord at their head, sailed to the island in a fleet of yachts, and participated in a Coronation. The oldest reprobate on the island was selected for the office and was solemnly crowned by his lordship with a tall crown made of coloured glass and improvised brasswork, which I believe still survives somewhere or other. Thereafter the king, doubtless *suarum legum simul auctor ac perversor*, was responsible for discipline on the island, and succession was ensured by election.

At the time of my visit, 1922, there were still about a dozen families on the island, distributed in the small farms around the foot of the cairn-capped 'mountain' which lends a little distinction to the place. Out on a level spit is the lighthouse, but the lighthouse men had no truck whatsoever with the islanders and in no sense 'belonged.' The kingly succession was still uninterrupted though there had recently been a change of tenant. At the outbreak of the 1914 war the islanders had met under their previous king and had declared themselves a neutral power. I believe, indeed, that they went further and actually proferred their allegiance to the Kaiser Wilhelm II in a document which was intercepted and is still preserved. Consistently, they took no part in the conflict until 1918, when a boatload of seasick policemen landed on the island and forcibly removed those of military age. Meanwhile, the islanders had not been inactive in other directions. Sinkings by U-boats in the Irish Sea had been numerous, and much wreckage, including an appreciable quantity of alcoholic liquor, found its way to the shores of the island. The inhabitants, and not least their king, proceeded (so it is told) to exploit the situation, to such an extent that by 1918 the king had reached an advanced stage of alcoholic poisoning and was no fit leader of his flock. Attempts were made by those who concern themselves with such things to induce him to leave the island and 'enter an institution.' Not unnaturally, the old man refused, and did so with some spirit. Eventually, however, even his insular friends decided that the time had come, and, after much consultation, they hit upon a ruse. On the mainland opposite the island they built a formidable cairn of empty beer-barrels. They then carried the poor old man out of his house and to his dim gaze indicated the promised land. 'Take me to it,' he said faintly, and, for aught that is known, those were his last words. He was taken ashore and hurried in an ambulance to an inglorious death-bed in the Pwllheli workhouse. A successor was promptly elected to the vacant throne. . . .

On the shore at Aberdaron our motor-launch had not arrived. We adjourned to the neighbouring inn. Against the bar was leaning an old salt, with a mahogany face framed in whiskers. To our 'good morning' he vouchsafed a grunt. Unbeaten, we replenished his glass and were rewarded with another grunt. Then, after a long lapse, he spoke slowly in a rather gruff Caernarvonshire singsong— 'Where dit we come from?' I rashly ventured 'Cardiff.' The fog thickened during another long pause, and then from the whiskers came the terse sentiment '*All* sorts comes from Cardiff,' followed by a skilful expectoration towards the door. Shortly afterwards our pirate, without further speech, left the bar and made his way down to the shore where a boy was preparing to hoist the sail in a twenty-foot boat. The potman leaned over the bar: 'That wass the new King of Bardsey,' he said, 'he doess not much like foreigners.' So much we had inferred, but the prospects of our forthcoming visit to the island kingdom were none the happier for our new knowledge.

Eventually our launch arrived. In mid-channel we found the Royal Barge becalmed and adrift. I stopped the launch and offered a tow, which was grudgingly accepted. The gesture was not infructuous. When we landed, we were graciously beckoned by His Majesty to the hospitality of his cottage, and when we left the island that evening three lively lobsters of the most vivid ultra-marine hue were put on board by Royal Command. During a long and difficult journey back to Caernarvon through the rainy dark-ness, the lobsters and I conducted an unceasing battle on the back seat of a lampless car. The lobster is a cunning and unprincipled fighter. . . .

In those days of the early 'twenties it was not merely in North Wales that local worthies and pundits had to be courted and conciliated and reconciled to the new idea of national institutions. In the south, Carmarthenshire was a citadel of home rule, and, in Carmarthenshire, the self-appointed leader in all matters—cultural and social—relating to antiquity was a certain George Eyre Evans, now gathered to his fathers. Eyre Evans was a Character. He had once, I believe, been a Unitarian minister, but had long declined from that estate. His energy was unbeatable, and West Wales was full of stories, true or apocryphal, of his unquenchable zest for acquisition. A little eighteenth-century house in Carmarthen he packed from basement to roof with a medley of heirlooms and curios, obtained mainly from country houses on the most shadowy of pretexts, but including indiscriminately some objects of real worth. The following story was elicited from him as a series of disconnected remarks in conversation—a headlong, mixed conversa-tion, rather like his museum—on one of the last occasions on which

I saw him. I remember that he was attired as a boy scout, and his little white, pointed, Captain-Kettle beard contrasted oddly but characteristically with his boyish dress.

He had long proclaimed that he was the last of his family save for one venerable aunt, his 'only relative in consanguinity.' To this aunt he made an annual pilgrimage in the Devonshire cottage where, in solitude, she impatiently awaited her end. Many years previously she had taken out a policy for the price of £5 to ensure her decent burial, and annually she used to lament to 'young George' that she had not had her money's worth. Ultimately the time came, and George Eyre hastened to Devon to see that at last she had value for her investment. The story that I now place on record was, I would emphasize, told with complete ingenuousness and directness. I have merely filled in a sufficiency of description to complete the picture.

The terms of the assurance policy were, it appeared, that the old lady should be cremated at Woking. George promptly hired a motor-hearse; and as the loved one's father had been an officer in the Royal Navy, he thought it proper or at any rate pardonable to cover the coffin with a Union Jack. At dawn one morning he got in beside the driver and they started off across the South of England.

As they set out, an idea occurred to George. Ideas were always occurring to George; his little brain never lagged on its spiral course, and the axis of the spiral was a devotion to antiquity. It now struck him that here was an opportunity such as had never been offered to him and might never be offered to him again. He had never explored the South of England, and he was deeply conscious of lacunae in his knowledge. By the slightest deviations from the straight road to Woking he could now fill up certain of the more important of these lacunae. He buried his head in his map.

A little later that morning, the incumbent of the benefice of Sherborne was approaching his great abbey church when he became aware of an unexpected phenomenon outside his church door. There stood a motor-hearse, and in it was a coffin partially covered by a rather carelessly donned Union Jack. The vicar hastily produced his diary but found no clue; and, as he looked, a vigorous little white-bearded man emerged at a trot from the interior of the building, followed by a breathless companion. The two men leapt into the hearse and drove off rapidly down the street. It is said that for a long time the vicar did not dare to mention the phenomenon to his friends.

An hour or more later, the ex-serviceman who guards the imprisoned Stonehenge from its admirers, was idly scavenging within the compound when he heard a vehicle approaching at high speed. He paid little attention until a flash of colour passed the corner of his eye. As he turned, the hearse swung noisily to a standstill in the car-park on the opposite side of the road, the Union Jack now rakishly aslant across the foot of the coffin. A little man with a thrusting beard descended, dragging after him the submissive driver, slapped two sixpences down at the window of the hut, and rushed into the sacred enclosure. Almost at the double, the little party dashed from stone to stone, missing none in the circuit; and, before the guardian could resume the processes of rational thought, the hearse was dipping down the hill in headlong flight towards Amesbury.

A large and respectful crowd had lined the approaches to the Woking Crematorium. It had scarcely assembled when it was aware of a mud-splashed hearse approaching at an unconventional pace; but, yes, it must be; there was the Union Jack—though only just— and the crowd, satisfied if a little surprised, gravely doffed as the vehicle dashed by. 'He was always a one for punctuality,' they said to one another as they slowly resumed their headgear, 'but where's the mourners?'

The crowd had filled the road in the process of dispersal, when it saw approaching from the direction of the station a new and stately equipage at a properly reluctant speed, trailing car after car into the distance. The ranks opened and stood uneasily but respectfully as the polished cortège slowly passed on its mournful way. A famous and popular statesman, happily unaware of the rival candidate who had belatedly preceded him a few minutes earlier to the poll, was borne smoothly onward to his last election.

5. London Again: the Institute of Archaeology

I MAY recall that 1926 was for me a year of decision. For two years I had been Director of the National Museum of Wales. The museum's very considerable financial debt had been wiped out, the builders had replaced the duns in its gaunt scaffolded halls, the future was assured: a great deal too firmly assured for the liking of a young man with remoter and more presumptuous horizons. If my boots were not to grow too large in Cardiff to enable me to jump out of them, I must jump now. I leapt therefore into the first pair of shoes which presented themselves to me, back in London. For a time, they pinched. London closed in upon us. The asphalt of Carlisle Place blew cheerlessly into our little basement flat near Victoria. The monstrous bank in Victoria Street was of a size and magnificence in inverse ratio to the minute salary which H.M. Treasury now deposited there as a grudging appreciation of my services to the derelict London Museum; and, at the museum itself, the robust Doric of the Cardiff shipowners was replaced by the pedantries of an ancient courtier. But it was London. All the friendship and co-operation which I had left behind me in Cardiff, and indeed in Wales generally, were inadequate compensation (in the eyes of a young man) for the limiting environment of the Cambrian highlands. By the same token, an invitation which came to me at this moment to be the first occupant of the recently established Abercromby Chair of Prehistoric Archaeology at Edinburgh was unhesitatingly declined. For, as I have related above, my pocket bulged with the blueprint of that Institute of Archaeology which was the next obvious step in the development of our infant but growing science. And London was the only possible milieu for such a project.

Not at once, however, could this new project be exposed to the cold light of a London where archaeology, save in the guise of occasional Egyptology and a little classical art-history, was not yet even on the university curriculum. A suitable climate had to be created, and this was not achieved in a day. The London Museum had to be cleaned, expurgated, and catalogued; in general, turned from a junkshop into a tolerably rational institution. Contacts at the Society of Antiquaries in Burlington House had to be established or confirmed by lecturing and committee work. The Royal Commission on Historical Monuments (England) was on the point of plunging into Roman London and demanded guidance. Not least, the University of London, through University College (of which I was a Fellow), had to be led gently into the garden and up the right path. And in one way or another a carefully considered long-term scheme of fieldwork had to be initiated, if only as a framework for the younger generation of archaeologists which was now coming forward in increasing numbers into a world academically unprepared for it. Into all these various activities I at once hurled myself as lone survivor of the Missing Generation. When she had eventually completed the long and difficult task of fulfilling our commitments at Caerleon—a task to which she devoted skill and diplomacy of a high order—Tessa joined me and trebled the efficacy of the attack.

The London Museum was the basis of our operations. It was a strange institution. A scheme for the establishment of a museum which should fulfil for London what the Carnavalet fulfils for Paris seems to have originated in the fertile mind of the late Lord Esher, who produced it informally as a proposal for a memorial to King Edward VII after his death in 1910. The proposal never received official expression in this shape, but nevertheless went forward with the active support of the Royal Family, who offered Coronation robes and a wide range of Royal personalia. A friend of the Royal Family, (Sir) Guy Laking, was placed in charge, the many gaps were hastily filled up with all manner of improvisation, and six months later, on 21 March 1912, King George V and Queen Mary, with Princess Mary and Prince George, inaugurated the new museum at Kensington Palace. At the time, however, the suffragettes were in full cry, and the expectant public was excluded until 8th April.

I was not sufficiently prescient to join the queue on that morning, but the scene appears to have been a remarkable one. It is on record that for hours, both before and after the actual time of opening, a huge procession of persons of all ages moved slowly and patiently towards the entrance. The wind was blowing half a gale, and the reports speak of 'people falling out of the ranks through fatigue, hunger, and the cold.' The laborious process of collecting sticks, muffs and other potential weapons or means of concealing them, slowed the entry, but the small rooms were quickly packed beyond capacity. By the end of the afternoon over 13,000 persons had passed through the museum. The initial impetus was renewed momentarily when, two years later, the collections were removed to Lancaster (formerly Stafford) House in St. James's, where they remained until they were arbitrarily evicted by government after the Second World War.[1] But in spite of such intermittent popularity, by 1926 the reputation of this young national museum was that of a muddy backwater, with picturesque passages but, on the whole, rank and tangled.

Its original keeper, Guy Laking, I never met, but his reputation still lingers in odd corners of St. James's. He had flair, flamboyance, a pictorial imagination, which stood him in good stead in the first hasty shaping of the new museum. When the remains of a Roman ship were found under the site of the new County Hall at Westminster and laboriously placed upon a dray, he led the catafalque dramatically on horseback through Parliament Square and St. James's Park to his museum, and had the poor broken timbers attractively adorned there with stuffed gulls. He had lively models made of scenes from ancient London, including a lurid 'working' reconstruction of the Great Fire which immediately won the heart of the London child. A prison cell of the seventeenth or eighteenth century from Neptune Street was equipped with a macabre waxwork 'prisoner' who, from a carefully induced half-light, evoked little screams from fascinated visitors. All this was admirable. But the instinct for showmanship triumphed over discrimination; and when on the death of Laking the keepership passed to a dull and pompous commercial traveller whom he had picked up in a railway carriage, the initial sense that it was 'all good fun' shaded into a feeling that the joke was now over.

[1] They are now (1954) crowded back into their original home, Kensington Palace.

In 1926, therefore, I arrived at Lancaster House with an explicit mission. During the following years the stable was swept, piles of irrelevant junk were liquidated, and a series of seven or eight guides and catalogues of a responsible type was published, beginning in 1927 with *London and the Vikings*. These catalogues were written in the evening hours—I rarely went home till midnight; and looking back on them I find them, on the whole, a satisfactory intermingling of *vulgarisation* and scholarship. *London in Roman Times*, published in 1930, is still a handbook not without value, and the last of the series, the *Medieval Catalogue*, prepared by my one-time assistant, J. B. Ward Perkins, and issued in 1940, is a unique study of a neglected subject. Alas, the series has not been resumed since the Second War.

Other work at the museum during these years need not be recalled in detail. It includes enlargement of the staff, extension of lectures to schools (latterly eight classes from London schools received lectures in the museum every week during term), and the institution of an annual inter-school essay competition, for which a silver cup was ceremoniously awarded through the generosity of Ernest Makower and his wife. The Makowers also organized and financed evening concerts at which the public, free or for the expenditure of sixpence, could hear the London Symphony Orchestra conducted by Henry Wood or Malcolm Sargent, or a piano recital by Harriet Cohen or Schnabel. These concerts were a great success. The audience consisted of an astonishing medley of critics, music students, tradesmen, guardsmen with their girls, passers-by and pilgrims of all sorts. They stood or sat about on the stairs or balconies or vacant patches of floor, without any special provision; indeed the slight discomfort contributed to the sense of informality and adventure. No stage separated listener from performer, and the resultant sense of intimacy gave an unusual quality to the scene. 'But what has music got to do with a museum?' asked the caviller. 'A museum, my dear sir, is a home of the muses. Why should we turn Euterpe into the storm?'

And behind the scenes a sort of academic and family life gradually focused on Lancaster House. My constant and outspoken desire to associate students with the museum was officially recognized when, on the death of Reginald, Lord Esher, his son established an Esher

Studentship (subsequently replaced by a Leverhulme Studentship) for research into the history or archaeology of London, and thenceforth the Trustees assumed in this context a specifically academic rôle. But, on a less formal basis, students were in fact beginning to come to the museum in increasing numbers. Lectures were given periodically to university undergraduates there; every evening two or three research students could be found at work to a late hour in a room or workshop partially allotted for that purpose; we became the working-home, too, for the inspector of London excavations appointed about this time by the Society of Antiquaries, with which our relations were always of a cordial kind. Pending the establishment of the Institute of Archaeology of my dreams, the shadow of a research institute was already coming into being at Lancaster House. These small beginnings at least emphasized the need for a full-dress academic institution and encouraged us in our efforts to achieve it.

To that project I now turn. The first task in 1926 was clear enough: to prepare the ground by infiltration. Today, a generation later, it is difficult to visualize the primitive state of archaeological technique and teaching in the early and mid 'twenties. I have spoken of this above, but recall it again because it is the background against which our efforts have to be set if they are to be understood. Those were the days when a vice-president of the Society of Antiquaries could display enlightenment with the remark that he 'agreed with Dr. Wheeler's advice to pay great attention to stratification. Whatever material was being dealt with, stratification formed a very useful principle to follow.' The ingenuous undertone of that observation is sufficiently self-evident. To the great mass of professed antiquarian opinion the art of excavation was a hidden mystery. I went to the British Museum and talked to Reginald Smith in the Department of British and Medieval Antiquities.

Shortly afterwards, in March 1927, I lectured to the Royal Society of Arts on 'History by Excavation,' and the lecture was subsequently printed with illustrations in the Society's *Journal*. It was a slight but pioneer effort to put some of the principles of archaeology before the public. In the discussion after the paper, Reginald Smith rallied generously to the colours. 'The only regret was,' he is recorded to have said, 'that there were not more young men in this country to follow in Dr. Wheeler's footsteps [*sic*], and to take charge of excavations which were calling for attention. He believed that Dr. Wheeler had a scheme in mind for founding in London a sort of school or institute for training young archaeologists, especially in fieldwork. Whether Dr. Wheeler was as capable of raising funds as he was of inculcating the principles of excavation, he could not say; it remained for the future to discover that, but he wished Dr. Wheeler all success in any attempt to make archaeology a national movement.' Following Reginald Smith at the end of the discussion, I added: 'In a nutshell the problem was £70,000, the sum required for the creation and permanent endowment of an efficient school of British Archaeology.'

That was the first public mention of the scheme, but in 1927 the way in front of us was still long and hard. The University of London was not yet prepared for the new enterprise. I proceeded to organize at University College an exhibition of the results of recent archaeological fieldwork in Britain, and the experiment met with some success. This was followed by systematic courses of lectures (unpaid) on British prehistory and protohistory; and a sufficiency of students was forthcoming to induce the college to establish a formal part-time lectureship for me. Most of the lectures were in fact given in the London Museum, but the great thing was that prehistory was now, for the first time, on the books of the university. I took a deep breath and prepared for the final assault.

At that moment a succession of chances intervened on my side. The university was busily planning its new quarters in Bloomsbury, and the Edwards Professor of Egyptology, Sir Flinders Petrie, was not unaware of the fact. It came to my ears that he was drawing up a proposal for the proper housing of archaeology in the new buildings, and I hastened to him with my own scheme. He wholeheartedly suggested that we should pool our efforts, and for some time we interchanged and adapted our various ideas in the course of a series of very friendly conferences. Collaboration was not, however, an easy matter. At this time Petrie lived almost in a dream-world. He thought in terms of thousands of cubic metres of space, three or four floors, top-lighting, extensive storage, oblivious to the basic fact that the university had not even begun to consider the inclusion of archaeology at all and would almost certainly decline to do so! I gradually left him to his dreams and hardened on my own schemes. Nevertheless it was this contact with Petrie that ultimately brought the Institute of Archaeology into being. It happened in this way.

At the time Petrie was greatly exercised as to the future of his unrivalled collections from Palestine. He intended to go shortly to Palestine and to reside there permanently; meanwhile, no existing institution was prepared to house his myriad packing-cases and their contents. He made his dilemma known, and such was the combined 'draw' of Petrie and Palestine that an anonymous donor came forward with an offer of £10,000. Petrie did not hesitate. He generously turned the offer over to me, with the sole condition that the new institute should accept his Palestinian material. At last I could go to the university with a concrete proposal. After much parleying, I was authorized by the university, largely through the friendly backing of its principal, Sir Edwin Deller, to issue a public appeal. The hour had struck.

Not that the way was yet an easy one. The whole burden of raising the necessary funds—very considerably more than the £10,000 already offered—was thrown back to me. But from now onwards there was no looking back. The inevitable appeal committee was formed in 1932 under the lively chairmanship of Sir Charles Peers as President of the Society of Antiquaries. A manifesto was addressed to *The Times*. Likely individuals were approached. A prolonged search began for a suitable building at suitable cost. A staff had to be assembled in anticipation of funds wherewith to pay it. And in all these activities save the last, Tessa shouldered a great part of the burden. Without her tireless loyalty through those days the scheme might easily have fallen short of success. Slowly the fund grew to something approaching workable dimensions.

The search for a building was not the least of our preoccupations. We scoured London for the impossible—a large building at next to no rent. And at last we found it. On the little-known Inner Circle of Regent's Park was a derelict and shabby mansion which, as St. John's Lodge, had long been the town house of the Marquesses of Bute, but had been used or misused as a hospital during the First World War and thereafter forgotten. For the considerable cost of rehabilitation and maintenance, we secured it from the Commissioners of Crown Lands at a nominal rent. Save for a somewhat remote situation—mitigated by the proximity of Bedford College—it was exactly what we wanted. It already possessed two libraries equipped with shelving; a vast ballroom offered lodging to the sprawling but invaluable Petrie Palestinian collection; an annexe would serve conveniently for a time as a laboratory; classrooms and studies were there in plenty for some years to come. Moreover, the building itself, in spite of its present decrepitude, had an air of repose and dignity which matched an academic function. Its nucleus was of the Regency period, and was described in 1827 as 'in the Grecian style of decoration, partaking somewhat of the Etruscan.' It had, however, been extensively altered and enlarged in 1847 by Sir Charles Barry, who screened a new entrance-hall with the present pedimented porch and Doric side-loggias. The great projecting wings, too, are largely of his fashioning, and indeed the whole external aspect of the house is essentially 'Barry Italian.'

The restoration of the building was already under way when, as I have related elsewhere, Tessa suddenly died. She was irreplaceable but, well knowing this, Kathleen Kenyon, Sir Frederic Kenyon's daughter, stepped into the breach with a generous devotion that is beyond gratitude. For more than a decade, which included the Second World War and many incidental trials, the administration of the institute rested upon her shoulders. She would not mind my saying that Tessa would have been proud of her.

Meanwhile, Petrie's collection was rapidly being supplemented by teaching-collections derived mostly from recent excavations in this country and the Near East. Steel cabinets were being made to contain them. Laboratory apparatus (largely at the charge of Sir Robert Mond) was being installed. And a nucleus staff was beginning to lend its services, for modest reward or even for none at all. Frederick Zeuner joined us as lecturer in the novel subject of 'Geochronology' or archaeological environment. Sidney Smith of the British Museum established the teaching of Near Eastern archaeology and was awarded by the university the honorary title of Professor. S. H. Hooke from King's College gave lectures and tuition in Biblical archaeology. Kathleen Kenyon and I (as Honorary

Director) plodded on with Prehistoric and Roman Britain, and Kathleen also undertook to catalogue the Petrie material. Students began to arrive and included, amongst the first, Rachel Clay (now Mrs. Maxwell-Hyslop), who subsequently joined the staff of the institute as Professor M. E. L. Mallowan's assistant; and Barbara Parker, now at Baghdad as secretary and general manager of the British School in Iraq. Alongside this more academic aspect of the institute's work, a photographic studio and teaching in archaeological photography were instituted under M. B. Cookson, and Delia Parker and Ione Gedye established the technical laboratory which was to supply an important feature of our training.

On 29 April 1937, almost exactly a year after Tessa's death and ten years after the first announcement of the scheme, the Earl of Athlone as Chancellor of the University formally launched the enterprise. The occasion was used both by him and by Sir Charles Peers (our chairman) to affirm the principles and intentions that had been in our minds, and it is perhaps of interest to quote a few sentences from their remarks:

'If the essential character of this institute may be expressed in a word, it is this, that it is a laboratory: a laboratory of archaeological science, wherein the archaeologist of the future may learn the essentials of his business. One of the newer sciences is this of ours; not a few of us here today may have known and spoken with the men whom we regard as its founders. It has the vigour of youth; even so we may already look with justifiable pride and confidence—though without insular prejudice—on what has been and is being done by British enterprise here at home and wherever in the world the records of past history offer themselves for investigation.

'In this institute, then, it is necessary that the student shall find three things: namely, materials for study, instruction in the treatment of antiquities, and training in archaeological method in research and in the recording of research. This is the irreducible minimum, and, while the principles of archaeological inquiry are sufficiently defined, there can by the nature of the case be no limit to the elaboration of its technique, and to the recognition of its relations with all phases of the story of nature and of man....'

Thus Peers. The chancellor, who had been at pains to study his brief, replied in like fashion:

'The primary function of the Institute of Archaeology, as Sir Charles Peers has told us, is to provide a laboratory which shall fulfil in the study of civilization something of the function which the laboratory has long fulfilled in the study of chemical or physical science. The institute is designed to provide properly classified collections of material, derived wherever possible from scientifically conducted excavations, for the use of the student and the research-worker under normal laboratory conditions. In this function, the institute has the support of the established museums which by the nature of things can never, with the best will in the world, be expected to cater indefinitely for the individual student. . . .

'In addition to its function as a store-house of material, the new institute is designed to comprise by degrees a home for teaching and research in those spreading provinces of archaeology for which no adequate provision exists at present in London or, in many cases, elsewhere. . . . These new fields include Mesopotamia, Syria, Palestine, Cyprus, and regions of what used to be called "darkest Africa"; nor may I omit to add to this list our own country where, during the last quarter of a century, the body of research has far outstripped our academic provision for it. . . .

'To extending geographical horizons must be added a constantly extending technical elaboration of the methods of archaeological research. At these Sir Charles Peers has already hinted; but I would once more emphasize the need today for close collaboration between the humanities and the sciences in the study of human civilization. The history and prehistory of man is a constant process of adjustment between humanity and environment. It is scarcely to be wondered, therefore, that, as the study of civilization becomes more intensive, more detailed and more accurate, increasing need arises for the collaboration of the geologist, the botanist, the palaeontologist, the climatologist, and other workers in departments devoted to the study of the physical universe. Thus an Institute of Archaeology must,

under modern conditions, be designed not merely as an addition
to existing university activities but as a new means of collaboration between them. . . .'

And so on. All this sounds more than a little platitudinous in 1954,
but in 1937 it still needed saying. To a university to which systematic
archaeology was an innovation, these broad and now obvious
principles were revolutionary concepts. And outside London most
of our universities were in similar case. Liverpool had tried and
failed; only in Cambridge and in Edinburgh were there established
and active chairs, and individual chairs fell short of our ambition.
Let us consider this for a further moment, and then I have done
with it.

In the eighteenth century the Royal Society had comprehended
all knowledge. Separate cells were, it is true, provided outside it for
specific disciplines: from 1707 onwards, for example, there was a
Society of Antiquaries. But the Royal Society was the unquestioned
apex of the pyramid, and a Member or Fellow of the Society of
Antiquaries might be, and not rarely was, a Fellow of the Royal
Society. By the end of the nineteenth century the natural sciences
in their increasing complexity had practically crowded out the
humanities from the senior sodality. The last antiquary to become
an F.R.S. was Sir Arthur Evans, who was elected in 1901. In that
year the cleavage between the humanities and the sciences was
made absolute by the foundation of the British Academy as a
conventus for the former.

For a time there can be little doubt that this formal cleavage was
harmless. It may even have pruned and strengthened both categories
of learning. A generation later its merits were becoming less certain.
Geology was consolidating its position anew and in a multitude of
ways as a basic factor of archaeology. Botany, not least of that
analytical sort which deals with pollenated soils, was increasingly
controlling archaeological chronology and distribution. Climate
straddled a number of phenomena influencing and influenced by
human activity. Solar radiation was recognized as a factor in
archaeological computation; and, later, even a by-product of atomic
research was to prove of vital importance to the study of man.
These are examples; they could be widely extended. But they are

enough to emphasize that re-convergence of interest which in the 'thirties was bringing natural science and the study of man through archaeology back into the same fold.

In a tentative but deliberate fashion this new institute of ours was designed as an explicit recognition of the new rapprochement. It has been criticized on occasion for its emphasis on methods and techniques. Such criticism is praise indeed; for that is its primary and avowed purpose. But that is not to say that either its founders or their successors for a moment envisage archaeology by and large as a mere skill or assemblage of skills. Of course they do not. Archaeology is admittedly the study of human achievement in its more material aspects but its ultimate function is the re-creation of Man—sentient, rational or even irrational Man—in the vicissitudes of his long life-history. To that ultimate achievement a multitude of exact and less exact sciences is now, very properly, expected to contribute, and will increasingly contribute in the future. That is where our institute, as envisaged, enters the picture. It was founded primarily as a workshop in which the relevant sciences could be interrelated and assembled in a humanistic environment and to the better understanding of humanity. It represented the culmination of my efforts, begun almost *in vacuo* after the First World War, to convert archaeology into a discipline worthy of that name in all senses. That it is yet in full running order I should be the last to affirm; but the machine is there, its power is slowly ascendant, and I have no doubt that generation by generation it will be improved, enlarged, reshaped with the gradual aggregation and re-assessment of ideas and opportunities.

6. Lydney, Verulamium, Maiden Castle

DURING all these years, alongside the various activities which I have retailed and others beside them, we had been occupied in the summer months and winter evenings with a systematic series of archaeological excavations on an increasing scale and with growing numbers of attendant students. Starting with a classical bias, I continued for some time to exploit Roman Britain as my most accessible field. When Caerleon had been set aside, chance enabled me to assume the study of a site upon which I had already set my eye.

Between the mouth of the Wye and Newnham, not far from the Welsh border, the Forest of Dean thrusts southwards towards the Severn in a long series of picturesque spurs flanked by glens and streams. One of these, at Lydney, has belonged since the time of George I to the branch of the Bathurst family whose head is now Lord Bledisloe. The spur in question was once known as the Dwarf's Hill, doubtless from the fragments of masonry which projected from the surface, the extensive traces of iron-mining, and the coins and other antiquities which could be—and were—scratched, without more than the most elegant effort, from the intervening surfaces. In 1805 the Bathurst of the day ended the era of polite pilfering in a substantial excavation, during which a large part of the site was laid bare and a considerable mass of entertaining and instructive relics collected for the drawing-rooms of Lydney Park. At the same time a record of the work, notably in advance of the standards of 1805, was prepared in manuscript, though it had to wait for three-quarters of a century before it eventually saw the light of print. A similar neglect had meanwhile reduced the site itself to an assemblage of untidy heaps. In 1928 Lord Bledisloe, reviving his great-grandfather's active interest in the place, invited the Society of Antiquaries to intervene, and I was detailed for the pleasant task. During the summers of 1928 and 1929 we pursued the dwarfs to their nethermost layers and in 1932 published our report on *The Prehistoric, Roman, and Post-Roman Site in Lydney Park, Gloucestershire.*

The title of that report sufficiently indicates that our searches were not fruitless in spite of the very extensive digging of a century-and-a-half ago. The new excavations in fact succeeded in elucidating the main history of the site almost as completely as if it had not previously been cleared; such were the differences between the technical methods of 1805 and those of 1928. In 1805 the diggers worked down to a floor and then stopped. To the modern excavator, the primary value of a floor is that it seals and preserves the evidence beneath it. Our excavation at Lydney was thus, more often than not, a process of considered destruction that must have shocked the shade of our predecessor and was a recurrent anxiety to our patient host. But it is fair to say that the evidence which, with no undue effort, we recovered thereby made the site at once a classic one in the proto-history of our island.

This is not an archaeological survey, but a word or two may be said in amplification of the last assertion. The Lydney ridge had in the first centuries B.C.–A.D. carried an embanked village of no manifest distinction, populated probably by a few families engaged upon farming and iron-mining. Their descendants prolonged this way of life far into the Roman period, with such slight cultural elaboration as the introduction of Roman pots and knicknacks implies. So much was quickly clear to us. At this point, however, a more novel fortune came our way. A squalid hut-floor, dated by coins to about A.D. 300, was found to cover the adit of a mine-shaft, which must therefore have been of earlier date and is probably in fact of the third century. We thrust our way down into the narrow shaft, often less than two feet wide, and found the marks of the miners' picks still fresh upon the surface where the marl-filled joint in the limestone had been followed through the hill-side. The whole scene was as vivid as it was instructive; the Lydney iron-mine can still claim to be the only British example ascribable on conclusive evidence to the Roman period.

But the site owes its major distinction to the fact that about A.D. 370 it became a popular centre of religious pilgrimage. A remarkable basilical temple, a guest-house, a 'long building' of

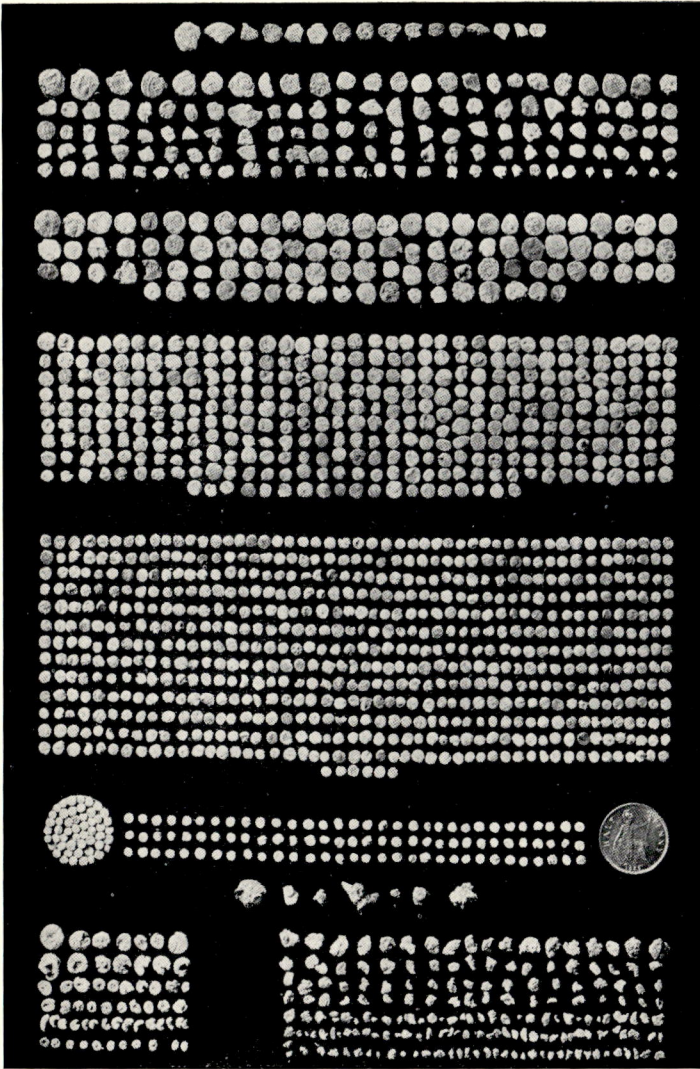

KING ARTHUR'S SMALL CHANGE

Note that 51 of the smallest coins fit exactly upon a halfpenny

THE OPENING OF THE INSTITUTE OF ARCHAEOLOGY, 1937, BY THE EARL OF ATHLONE,
CHANCELLOR OF THE UNIVERSITY

(l. to r.) The Academic Registrar, the Author, the Chancellor, the Vice-Chancellor, Lord Harlech (then
Colonial Secretary)

disputed function, and a sumptuous bath-building attracted worshippers and their humble offerings—several thousands of coins,
and all manner of trinkets and tokens—to the mysterious god
Nodens and the pantheon or pantheistic properties which he had
encompassed. He was amongst other things a healer; those troubled
with their eyes, with unhealed sores, with the ills of child-bearing,
might come to him for relief of their ailments. He had power over
the sun and the sea; fishermen from the Severn must have toiled up
the narrow rocky path to this shrine. No doubt he catered for all
the miscellaneous physical and metaphysical needs of the countryside with the universality of a village store. He flourished in a time
of confused and groping thought, and in a remote countryside to
which the dust of the old temples was more apt and homely than the
specious furnishings of the new church. Anyway, at the end of the
fourth century and in the fifth, when Nodens held court at Lydney,
Ravenna and Byzantium and Jerusalem were an uncommon long
way off if you had the toothache or a broken arm or had lost your
nets in the Severn tide which comes upon you like a moving cliff
at Newnham.

I have just mentioned the fifth century, age of *crépuscule* and
quicksand. That brings to my mind yet another title of Lydney to
archaeological notoriety. One summer's day I was sitting with my
colleagues at lunchtime on one of the walls of the partially excavated
bath-building of which I have made mention. At our feet the floor
showed something of the vicissitudes to which we were becoming
accustomed: the late fourth-century mosaic had been broken
anciently, and roughly made good with a rather uncouth patch of
inferior cement. Beside it lay a pick, and the conjunction of idleness
and opportunity was too much for me. I drove the point of the pick
into the cement patch.

What happened then is graven on my memory. As the lump
of cement came away, the dark soil beneath it was of a sudden
freckled with minute green specks. On my knees I peered at
these specks without touching them further, then called for the
camera and, putting down the only coin in my pocket—a
monstrous half a crown—as a scale, photographed the scene at
short range. Thereafter a quickly measured section was drawn to
illustrate the vertical relationship between the specks, the cement

D

and the mosaic; and finally we proceeded to recover the specks carefully from the earth and to place them in a teacup. The cup was little more than half full when the supply came to an end; nevertheless we found that it contained no fewer than 1,646 of the tiny scraps.

A hasty analysis showed that the collection comprised, with fragmentary Roman bronze coins or their barbaric imitations, an astonishing range of crude smaller coins descending in regulated scale to microscopic stamped discs of which fifty-two could be placed side by side on a single halfpenny! The hoard need not be described further; Tessa published it fully and carefully in our report; but when a newspaper a few days after the discovery hailed it as 'King Arthur's Small Change,' the shot was nearer the mark than it had the right to be. The Lydney Hoard, veritable symbol of the Dark Ages, would alone have justified our two seasons' work on that lovely spot.

Our students at Lydney were restricted in numbers by the fact that the site lay in a private park of which the owner was very properly anxious to conserve the privacy. But students we had about us, and of them two were outstanding. One of these was young Kenneth Oakley, who was later to achieve a high reputation in the twin fields of geology and prehistory. The other was Dermot Casey who, but for the counter-attraction of his natal Australia, would have risen high as a field-archaeologist. He became one of the most skilful and percipient excavators within my knowledge, and was later to rescue me in India. In 1930, when our appointed task was completed, he returned to dig up the adjacent Little Camp Hill, beside Lydney Park house, where he recovered the plan and pottery of a remarkable twelfth-century castle built partly of materials from our Roman site.

In a sense, our work at Lydney was an interruption in the ordered programme of fieldwork which I had mapped out. Already in 1926–27 a study of Roman London for the Royal Commission on Historical Monuments had demonstrated simultaneously the interest and our ignorance of those Roman towns which mark the beginnings of civilization in Britain. Hitherto methodical archaeo-logy had concerned itself mainly with the vestiges of the Roman army, which offered a readier approximation to the historical record. True, for three seasons before the First World War the Society of Antiquaries, in the person of J. P. Bushe-Fox, had dug into the city of Uriconium (Wroxeter), but rather with a view to the classification of small finds than to the recovery of social and economic data on a formative scale. Of all places in Great Britain, the obvious testing-ground for these larger issues was Verulamium, in the valley below St. Albans, where coins indicated a pre-Roman capital, visible remains displayed a large Roman city, and reliable history recorded its continued existence well into the fifth century. The further factors that the site is mostly open to the skies and that it is only twenty miles from Hyde Park Corner were conclusively in its favour. I had long been advocating its exploration when, early in 1930, the city fathers of St. Albans settled the matter by approaching the Society of Antiquaries for advice and help.

The Corporation of St. Albans had recently acquired nearly half the ancient site for use as a park and playing-fields, and had had the enlightened thought that the opportunity might be taken to carry out a tentative exploration there. Alfred Clapham, as secretary of the society, Dermot Casey and I attended upon the Mayor and Corporation at a hospitable luncheon which was served to us in the charming Regency town hall overlooking the busy market-place. It so happens that I have had a long experience of mayors, and am amongst their most fervent admirers. They represent the heart of England, these proud, courteous, friendly, sensible folk, who rise from their railway-ticket offices and their shops to attend in state to the affairs of their fellow-citizens. And the mayor on this occasion was no exception. He was Mr. Ironmonger, the butcher; folk used to come from miles round to buy his honest sausages, and surely an honest sausage is the hallmark of a worthy butcher. We sat at his table, drank an unadventurous Graves, and then rose in turn and made our little speeches. (One of Mr. Mayor's predecessors had in the year 429 entertained at just such a table as this the warrior-saint Germanus when, after paying homage to St. Alban, he had led the local levies to victory against the advancing Picts and Saxons. Just so had Mr. Mayor now invited us to lead the way to new victories, but *these* victories would be won on the playing-fields of Verula-mium. . . .) Thereafter for four summers (1930–33) we industriously sought these victories, toiling at the problems of, and arising from,

Verulamium, and toiling always with the loyal backing of the civic rulers and their officers. It was a happy episode.

I have described elsewhere the carefully studied sequence in which we defined and pursued the manifold problems of Verulamium,[1] and need not repeat the story here at any length. To me the whole episode was of surpassing interest as the first occasion upon which I had had to plan my work in terms, not of a site, but of a landscape. Our work in fact extended over five miles of countryside, and would have been impossible but for the fact that I had an increasing number of assistants and student-assistants, competent to supervise and classify; men like P. K. Baillie-Reynolds or Dermot Casey, women like Kathleen Kenyon or Thalassa Cruso (Hencken) or K. M. Richardson or Leslie Scott (Murray Threipland) —as able a team as could be wished, supplemented by a constant intake of students from a multitude of universities. Above all, on the busy central site of the great Roman town itself Tessa was alike hostess and organizer and director, her scholarly mind firmly on the work in hand but with time and a smile for everyone.

Meanwhile, by car or on horseback it was my task to develop our work *in partibus*. In particular, the search for the pre-Roman city and ultimately for Cassivellaunus himself proved to be a considerably more complicated operation than had been anticipated. The conventional theory from which we started was that the sprawling site of the Roman city which straddled the Watling Street in the valley bottom was also that of its Belgic predecessor. Excavation at a number of points proved the contrary; nothing earlier than the Roman conquest lay beneath it, and its fortifications were of the second century A.D. Our next step was to examine an unexplained earthwork known as 'The Fosse' which projected from one side of it. This was shown to be of earlier but still Roman date, and, since the town is recorded by Tacitus to have been unprotected at the time of Boudicca's revolt in A.D. 61, it was safe to infer that 'The Fosse' was the fruit of that experience. Thence our course led to the plateau above, where O. G. S. Crawford had previously observed a tangle of earthworks in a plantation on Lord Verulam's estate. Here at last success began to attend us. During the next three years we identified three-quarters of a mile of

[1] Wheeler, *Archaeology from the Earth* (Oxford, 1954), pp. 114–18.

the pre-Roman town and a great mass of pottery going back in part to the time of Tasciovanus and Augustus. But Cassivellaunus and Caesar, of 54 B.C., still eluded us, and failure to find the refuge of Cassivellaunus and the footsteps of Julius Caesar was not a prospect lightly to be faced. The search continued.

A mile to the north there was still an unexplained feature which appeared to relate to the pre-Roman site, although ascribed traditionally to the Devil. This was a cross-country dyke or barrier, facing away from Verulamium. Excavation indicated a pre-Roman date for this work also, and enabled us to class it with probability as a territorial boundary of the early city. Its major office in our task of exploration, however, was as a pointer to a seemingly related but mysterious cross-country dyke of far more formidable size, known as Beach Bottom, on the opposite side of the valley.

Precisely at this moment fate smiled upon us. A rumour reached us one evening that workmen digging a sewer through a filled-up section of Beach Bottom had found a shovelful of silver coins. The workmen were 'foreigners' to the district, it was the end of the day, and no time was to be lost. We spread ourselves quickly through the innumerable public-houses of the vicinity and, with an immense expenditure of pints and patience, recovered 'in confidence' forty of the coins 'on loan.' They were photographed and recorded, and were sufficient to show that the dispersed hoard had been deposited early in the second century A.D. But—and this was the significant factor—the men had been working at a carefully measured depth, and a visit to the spot showed that this depth was still a dozen feet above the bottom of the ditch. The great dyke had been filled at least to that extent by the beginning of the second century; and, being indisputably of non-Roman type, its pre-Roman date was assured. I spent the next day in the investigation of its probable function.

The problem was not a difficult one. The dyke was designed to bar an open tract of country between two river valleys and fords: that of the Ver beside Verulamium and that of the Lea near the little country town of Wheathampstead. And on the plateau beside Wheathampstead lay the vestiges of a formidable *oppidum* nearly a hundred acres in extent. This *oppidum* had hitherto been unknown to fame; it now dominated our scene. Excavation quickly showed that, with every probability, it could be attributed to the time of Cassivellaunus. Indeed, in the light of the 'finds' which we unearthed and the formidable character of the defences, there is no known rival to Wheathampstead as the site of Caesar's last, hard-won victory over his redoubtable opponent in 54 B.C.

Those are some of the results of our four years' work at and about Verulamium. Others included a useful new light upon the economic history of a first-class Romano-British city. Where we failed disappointingly was in the elucidation of the 'post-Roman' phase which history had led us to expect. Further search may reveal a little of this shadowy era of civic devolution, but I am not hopeful.

By 1934 a number of variant schemes were afoot for the building of a great new arterial highway through or alongside Verulamium, and the whole future planning and organization of exploratory work there was in the melting-pot. On a smaller scale work continued. Kathleen Kenyon uncovered the theatre with her characteristic efficiency, and the Verulam estate has wisely (and profitably) kept it open for visitors to see. It is today amongst the most vivid relics of Roman Britain. Across the Watling Street from the theatre Kitty Richardson later carried out yet a further season's work. But, pending official decisions, which seemed anything but imminent, we now turned our eyes elsewhere.

For the moment I suffered from a satiety of Roman things. The mechanical, predictable quality of Roman craftsmanship, the advertised *humanitas* of Roman civilization, which lay always so near to brutality and corruption, fatigued and disgusted me so that my Verulamium report fell short in some parts of its record, and J. N. L. Myres very properly rapped me over the knuckles for it. Nevertheless, our work at Verulamium, by a happy mingling of chance and design, had been outstandingly successful, and with the one proviso the report stands. Now, however, in 1934, there was an opportunity to break away from the pretentious Roman machine and to transfer our large and experienced following to other aspects of that pre-Roman Iron Age which had already enlivened Verulamium. Once again the new objective was one on which I had secretly meditated for several years before the moment came for action.

A fair share of voyaging in many parts of the world has failed to blunt the awe and enthusiasm with which I still approach that vast prehistoric fortification, Maiden Castle, near Dorchester in Dorset. Thomas Hardy saw its tumultuous outline daily from his windows, but familiarity only bred fresh wonder at it:

> 'At one's every step forward it rises higher against the south sky, with an obtrusive personality that compels the senses to regard it and consider. The eyes may bend in another direction, but never without the consciousness of its heavy, high-shouldered presence at its point of vantage. . . . The profile of the whole stupendous ruin, as seen at a distance of a mile eastward, is clearly cut as that of a marble inlay. It is varied with protuberances, which from hereabouts have the animal aspect of warts, wens, knuckles, and hips. It may indeed be likened to an enormous many-limbed organism of an antediluvian time . . . lying lifeless, and covered with a thin green cloth, which hides its substance, while revealing its contour. . . .'

In 1934 nothing whatever was known about this monstrous artifact, save that years previously a local antiquary had vaguely found a Roman building within its confines. Sir George Hill said slyly to me one day: 'It's a fine place to dig—and a fine place to leave undug.' I accused him of archaic sentiment, and said something irrelevantly about Tintern Abbey and its ivy; I confessed also to a sneaking sympathy with his point of view; but by August we had resolutely dug ourselves in, and thereafter discovery after discovery issued upon us in unending stream. So we continued with increasing fervour until, by the autumn of 1937, both mind and workshop had reached saturation point and I turned to a less embarrassing sequel.

It is, I think, fair to say that the excavation of Maiden Castle—of such small part of it as came within our compass—touched the imaginations of others than ourselves. T. E. Lawrence stood shyly watching us at our work on the eve of his sudden death. Sir Arthur Evans, small and frail, was blown across our skyline like an autumn leaf before the south-wester which was our normal accompaniment. Sir Frederic Kenyon, as President of the Society of Antiquaries, paid us regular courtesy calls—and, as an unrepentant boy, joined us in a Weymouth fun-fair afterwards. Augustus John and a picturesque entourage might, for a while, temper his science with our art. The poet Drinkwater, solemnly poised on the precarious edge of a pit, might offer his services as our laureate. But it is not of such that I speak when I recall the imaginative appeal of our enterprise. I have in mind the hundreds of little folk from shops and factories and back-kitchens, who streamed on to the hill-top, day after day, and listened to the lecturettes which my students were carefully drilled to offer them, and put their pennies and their shillings into the box or maybe simply spoke their thanks. Years afterwards, in diverse parts of the world, I have come across all manner of people, from privates to peers, who had looked over our shoulders or grubbed upon their hands and knees on that hill-top. When in 1944 I called upon the Viceroy at New Delhi to present my respects, the private secretary who showed me in had worked with us at Maiden Castle. So had an Indian who greeted me at Poona, and another at Calcutta. A Member of Parliament came in the other day and recalled his first essays in oratory as a student-on-duty on a stormy afternoon. When 'turn-overs' still turned over, *The Times* gave us an annual allocation, and the minor Press were with us every week. We politely but cautiously steered the information which went out in these manifold forms, and in one way and another the public for the first time became conscious of the Early Iron Age and the meaning of prehistory. Wireless had not yet, as it has since, become a normal vehicle for archaeological publicity.

All this was, in our view, to the good. Our more conventional archaeological friends sometimes raised their eyebrows and sniffed a little plaintively at 'all this publicity of Wheeler's'! But we were not deterred, and we were right; right not merely because this same public was incidentally contributing in gifts no small part of our considerable funds, but because I was, and am, convinced of the moral and academic necessity of sharing scientific work to the fullest possible extent with the man in the street and in the field. Today, in 1954, he is in fact our employer. Today, ninety per cent of the money spent on field-archaeology in Great Britain comes from our rates and taxes. That was not so in 1934; it might easily not be so now had we, and others like us, not deliberately built up a popular mood to which such expenditure was no longer wholly alien. It was not the least of the results of Maiden Castle that this mood of sympathy and half-understanding was by 1937 in the ascendant. Earlier phases had been manifest at Caerleon and elsewhere, when competitive journalism had whipped up public interest as a rather exotic stunt. Now the public was beginning to come to us of its own volition, the mountain was coming to Mahomet. But it did not come through the unprovoked force of gravity!

Of more scientific results Maiden Castle was singularly productive. Beneath its massive ramparts of the latter centuries B.C. emerged an unexpected neolithic enclosure some fifteen centuries earlier in date. And overriding this were the vestiges of the most amazing and prodigious 'long barrow' yet known, nothing less than a third of a mile in length, with an elaborately mutilated human skeleton under its eastern end. Its date was in the neighbourhood of 1500 B.C. Thereafter, at no great length of time, it was followed by a phase of dereliction that endured for something over a millennium, during which the hill was covered with woodland. Then in the third century B.C. new folk, using iron and crude amorphous pottery, built a stone-faced earthwork, which they subsequently enlarged and elaborated. Two centuries later their descendants were overpowered by masters who may have been refugees from Caesar's bitter vengeance in southern Brittany in 56 B.C. Certainly the new-comers brought the extended use of the sling and its defensive counterpart in the shape of multiple and spreading lines of earth-work, together with alien types of pottery, for all of which southern Brittany is the continental home; and it was under this immigrant control that the great *oppidum* approached its present shape. Ulti-mately, two or three decades before the Roman invasion, Belgic princes, possibly crowded out of the more easterly Belgic zone of Britain by the jealous autocracy of King Cunobelin at Colchester, seem to have taken the place over, restored its fortifications and imposed elements of their own Belgic culture, though again without uprooting the main bulk of the native population.

But of all the episodes recovered by our spades, the most dramatic and spectacular was that of the Roman conquest. The whole process of the Roman attack on the fortress was laid bare to us in vivid detail. Up to a point Suetonius had prepared us for it in his 'life' of the Emperor Vespasian, who, as a divisional commander, led the Second Royal Legion into south-western England in A.D. 43-4. Vespasian, he tells us, reduced 'two very formidable tribes and over twenty fortified native towns (*oppida*), together with the Isle of Wight.' Of the tribes it is a good guess to affirm that one was the Durotriges of Dorset, and it were an unthinkable insult to our most famous earthwork to exclude their Maiden Castle from the 'twenty *oppida*.' In fact no such insult can now be contemplated. The slightest summary of our findings will here suffice.

Maiden Castle has two formidably guarded entrances. That on the west is screened by no fewer than seven ramparts; that on the east is sufficiently elaborate but is of less gigantic proportion. The latter, therefore, we chose for detailed examination, and the gradual recovery of its varied and intricate evolution occupied much of my time during three of our four seasons. As a structural problem it was the most complicated and entertaining within my experience, but this is not the context in which to retrace the laborious processes of ratiocination which led eventually to the reconstruction of its history. I am concerned here with one day only in that history, a day which may be dated within the year 44 of our era, and I will recall it primarily not as a sequence of events but as a sequence of discoveries.

The eastern, like the western, entrance is exceptionally provided with two gateways ('in' and 'out'), which open on to a crescentic forecourt. On both sides of the forecourt approaching roads wind upwards from the flanks of an outer court and outer defences. In the crescentic court we began to find ash and the post-holes of burnt huts. Here and there amongst the ash lay the iron heads of Roman catapult quarrels. As we dug on we came upon rough hollows filled with earth and ash, and in each hollow lay a human skeleton, sometimes two. The skeletons emerged, as our work proceeded, in all manner of contortions and orientations, with all the semblance of having been slung carelessly into their crude graves. Then two or three further features shaped the problem.

First, the dead had met a violent, sometimes savagely violent end. The skulls of many of them had been hacked viciously at the time of death; one of them bore no less than nine deep cuts. The victims had been struck variously on the top, front or back of the head—

in other words, the wounds were battle-wounds, as indeed their repetition suggested, rather than the mark of methodical execution. And in confirmation of this, one skull showed the square piercing of a quadrangular Roman ballista-bolt, whilst another skeleton—most vivid relic of all—had an iron arrow-head embedded deeply in a vertebra. This last unhappy warrior, as he lay grievously wounded, had been finished off by a cut on the head.

Secondly, the skeletons were those both of men and of women; twenty-three men and eleven women were identified. The women had stood shoulder to shoulder with their menfolk in the final mêlée.

But, thirdly, for all the disorderly aspect of the cemetery, the dead had been buried by their friends with a measure of propriety. Most of the burials included bowls or, in one instance, a mug for the traditional food and drink. In two cases the dead held joints of lamb in their hands, joints chosen carefully as young and succulent. Amidst all the evidences of massacre and distraction, this final attention was not the least touching feature of the scene as it lay uncovered before us.

It was now easy enough to reconstruct the succession of events. Before the close fighting began, the regiment of catapults or *ballistae*, which habitually accompanied a legion on campaign, put down a barrage across the gateway, causing casualties at the outset. Following the barrage, the Roman infantry advanced up the slope, cutting its way from rampart to rampart, tower to tower. In the innermost bay of the entrance, a number of huts had recently been built; these were now set alight, and under the rising clouds of smoke the gates were stormed. But resistance had been obstinate and the attack was pushed home with every sort of savagery. The scene became that of a massacre in which the wounded were not spared. Finally, the gates were demolished and the stone walls which flanked them reduced to the lowly and ruinous condition in which we found them, nineteen centuries later.

The sequel was no less apparent. That night, when the fires of the legion shone out (as we may fairly imagine) in orderly lines across the valley, the survivors crept forth from their broken stronghold and, in the darkness, buried their dead as nearly as might be outside their tumbled gates, in that place where the ashes of their burnt huts lay warm and thick upon the ground. The task was carried out anxiously and hastily and without order; many of the dead were still in rigor mortis, contorted as they had fallen in the struggle; in any event, the living were in no condition for the niceties of ritual. Yet from few of the graves were omitted those tributes of food and drink which were the proper perquisites of the dead. The whole war-cemetery as it lay exposed before us was eloquent of mingled piety and distraction, of weariness, dread and darkness but yet not of complete forgetfulness. Surely no poor relic in the soil of Britain was ever more fraught with high tragedy, more worthy of brooding comment from the presiding Spirits of Hardy's own *Dynasts*.

These and other matters went to the making of a substantial monograph which was published by the Society of Antiquaries during the war, in 1943. In that report there are many things which I should write differently today, but I think I may justly say that it has a certain basic and enduring value. The neolithic culture, for the earlier phase of which Stuart Piggott and I had no difficulty in finding Breton affinities, planted that culture fairly and squarely in the Dorset landscape. The egregious 'bank barrow' I have already recalled as an early instance of that megalomania which was to characterize the later Iron Age dwellers on the hill-top. The definitive absence of Middle or Late Bronze Age occupation, with its likely social and climatic implications, was well worth demonstrating in a countryside so densely littered with vestiges of Bronze Age mortality. The succession of Early Iron Age cultures, ranging from the third century B.C. to the first century A.D., yielded a mass of documented material which will for some time to come provide a yardstick for the local archaeology of this period. The significance of the great slingstone hoards in relation to the development of multiple defences was first recognized here. The episode of the Roman invasion has not elsewhere been so vividly illustrated. The evidence for continued habitation for a generation after the Roman impact threw a new, or at least a newly emphatic, light upon the cultural transition from Iron Age to Roman Britain, culminating in the abandonment of the site after the foundation of Roman Dorchester (it seems) about A.D. 75. The partial reoccupation by a Romano-British temple-precinct in the latter part of the fourth century, long after the formal Peace of the Church, underlines the equivalent evidence from Lydney and other late sites. Finally, the lonely Saxon warrior who was laid to rest upon the summit of the hill about A.D. 600 at least reminds us of the scarcity of pagan Saxon relics hereabouts. These are not negligible additions to knowledge, and, in saying so, I am lauding, not myself, but the magnificent team—Mrs. Aylwin Cotton, Miss Kitty Richardson and more than a hundred others—who, before and after Tessa's death in 1936, identified themselves with the work. And for two years of our work, there was Tessa herself.

It was at Maiden Castle, too, that we brought the multitudinous task of recording as nearly to my satisfaction as I shall myself be able to carry it. In particular, the development of an area-excavation by accumulative squares was an elaboration first systematically worked out here on the basis of trial and error, and the drawing of the Maiden Castle sections was an advance, technically and pictorially, on my earlier efforts. These and other matters of technique I have discussed in another place,[1] and I need not now tarry over them.

[1] *Archaeology from the Earth* (Oxford, 1954).

7. Near Eastern Episode

BEFORE passing on to the aftermath of Maiden Castle, I pause to recollect an episode which had perhaps some direct, certainly much indirect, effect upon my future. In the spring of 1936 I went East for the first time. In those intercalary years of the 'twenties and 'thirties, under the easy conditions offered by French and British mandate, the Near East was alive with excavators of many nations. The quality of much of this work was highly suspect, but in the mass it was an insistent reminder of the prime importance of the East to the student of human achievement. Our efforts in England, although on an increasing scale, seemed increasingly provincial and irrelevant. It was at least abundantly evident that, as director of the new Institute of Archaeology which would shortly be opened in London, I must needs have something more than paper-knowledge of the Near Eastern field. With not a little searching, funds were just sufficiently forthcoming for a solitary pilgrimage, and I said good-bye to Tessa. I remember turning back as I went down the stairs of our little Park Street flat, and can still hear the words which followed me in her quiet voice: 'Good-bye—and remember, you are very precious.' That was the last time I saw her.

On the Messageries Maritimes liner which carried me from Marseilles to Port Said I foolishly travelled first class. In the evening I sat in a boiled shirt at a table with two formidable she-dragons from Oxford and a highly scented and obviously very affluent cigarette-merchant from Cairo. I gulped my coffee and fled to the lower classes.

Leaning against the rail in the second class was a little Englishman of communicative disposition. Without excessive encouragement, he proceeded to outline his political views and his private affairs. He was an employee of the ——— Oil Company, on his way back from leave to report for duty at Kirkuk. He expected to be

sent again to one of those little lonely stations which dot the pipe-
line at intervals of something like a hundred miles for general care
and maintenance. At each station are (or were) perhaps four or five
British technicians, maybe an odd wife or two, and there they are
in the desert for a two-year term, hating one another with an
increasing and ingrowing hatred as the months drag by. . . . This he
told me, and more, of these remote, rather pathetic human oases;
then he turned brightly to me and said: 'But I'm doing all the
talking. Now, sir, tell me what *you* do.' 'Oh,' I replied, with a hint
of apology in my voice, 'I'm—er—an archaeologist.' The little
fellow was silent for an appreciable space; then he looked up with
wonder in his eyes. 'Coo,' he said, '*that's* an OUT-OF-THE-WAY
JOB!' . . .

From the poop, where the fourth class were impounded, came
bursts of song and merriment. Looking down towards it from the
promenade, I could dimly discern, under a swinging lamp, a
sergeant of the Foreign Legion, a creole and one or two other
assortments, dancing to a hand-drum and a banjo. There alone in
the whole vast ship, it seemed, were real, living people, uninhibited
by Oxford Greats and unemasculated by Cairene lubricity. And
then amongst them I spotted Peter Murray Threipland.

Peter I had vaguely met in England. His father had commanded
the Welsh Guards, but the son had, for reasons hidden from me,
side-slipped into archaeology. He was now on his way out to join
Sir Leonard Woolley at Antioch, and preferred to travel steerage,
sharing a dog-kennel with a bug-ridden Levantine. In my ridiculous
boiled shirt I suddenly felt heartily ashamed of myself. Of course,
that was the way to travel, sitting at night in the swinging shadows
above the churning propellers amongst these happy polychrome
outcasts. . . . I eventually clambered back to my exalted stateroom
and had a bath.

In Cairo I found the Emerys living upon a dahabiya (small
sailing-ship) on the Nile, and went with them to Sakkara, where
they were digging up very early tombs equipped with desiccated
table d'hôtes laid round the corpses on little dishes. W. B. Emery is
now Edwards Professor of Egyptology at University College,
London, and was then in the earlier stages of successful discovery.
His wholesome work, as I was shortly to find, bore little resemblance

to the sort of thing which awaited me across the frontiers in Palestine.

Of my tour in that country and subsequently in the Lebanon and Syria I will say little. The intricacies of the law of libel are beyond my ken, but I believe that the plea of truth is no sure shield to the offender. It will suffice to say this: that from the Sinai border to Megiddo and on to Byblos and northern Syria, I encountered such technical standards as had not been tolerated in Great Britain for a quarter of a century. With rare and partial exceptions, the methods of discovery and record were of a kind which, at home, the Office of Works would have stopped by telegram. The scientific analysis of *stratification*, upon which modern excavation is largely based, was almost non-existent. And the work was being carried out upon a lavish and proportionately destructive scale.

Method indeed there was of a bizarre sort, and the most elaborate machinery. Excavation-headquarters were equipped to the point of luxury. At sundown the tables burgeoned with hospitality. Nothing could have been more courteous than the welcome extended everywhere to the visitor, whether by Briton, American or Frenchman. Card-indexes, log-books, ingenious instruments for surveying, drafting and photography, were displayed with confidence and pride. Only, the fundamental canons of the craft were simply not comprehended. I left the Near East sick at heart, ferociously determined to make my new institute in London first and foremost an effective medium for the enlargement of technical understanding. Without that, archaeology of the sort which I had witnessed was in large measure destruction.

But here and there amongst my memories of this episode are brighter moments. When I last passed by El Audja Hafia, on the southern edge of the Negeb, the three or four buildings which had constituted the settlement were charred ruins. In 1936 they housed a tiny penal colony, clustered round the well which was the only water-supply for many miles, and consisting of a police-sergeant, three or four constables, and about twenty sentenced murderers or olive-tree uprooters. (To uproot another man's olive-tree, the product of many generations of growth, was a crime second only to murder.) They were, it seemed, a tolerably happy or at any rate philosophical community, prepared to make the best of the fact that escape into the waterless desert meant death. And now a little variety had been brought into their lives by the Colt expedition, which was busily exploring the neighbouring city-mound. With the arrival of yet another stranger, myself, they felt that something had to be done about it. They threw a party.

The night was lit by a full moon when we assembled on a small square platform raised some two or three feet above the desert. Poles at the corners supported a roof of thatch over the open sides, and chairs were placed in the middle of one of the sides for Colt and myself. Flanking us were the policemen, and round the other three sides squatted the convicts, all amiable with anticipation. Above, a lamp hung from the roof in competition with the moon. The inevitable accompaniment—thick coffee—was brought in a huge dixie by the colony's attendant, a full-blooded negro who lived in a hole in the hill-side with a camel, a donkey, a wife, and unlimited piccaninnies. From foot to shoulder he was swathed in a white blanket, and I remember vividly how his face and arms shone purple in the moonlight as he busied himself with his task. From the folds of his blanket he produced a solitary cup. Then the function really began.

The cup was filled from the dixie and passed first to me. Under the appraising eyes of the murderers and olive-tree uprooters, I slowly gulped the coffee, making feeble show of the explosive belches which are the polite accompaniment of Arab coffee-drinking. The cup was returned for a refill, handed to Colt, and then successively to the sergeant, the constables and the convicts. In a black and sticky condition it returned to me, and thereafter throughout the evening it circulated, unwashed, round and around the assembly. Belches pierced the night like pistol-shots.

At last the stage was prepared for Act II. A rug was placed in the centre of the floor, and up the steps was led a little old grey-bearded man bearing a square, single-stringed fiddle and an arched bow. He was placed upon the rug, and, with his sightless eyes turned upwards to the moon, began an endless nasal chant, backed by three or four notes scraped from the solitary string. His theme (I was told) was the endless epic of Abu Zeid, whose adventures are almost congenital knowledge to the Arab and permit of infinite elaboration. Police and criminals were alike enraptured, and the moon had fallen far down the sky before their guests ventured to disturb them. The scene in the moonlight, with its easy picturesqueness, will remain in the memory long after the sins of Palestinian archaeology have entered limbo. . . .

North of Latakia, on the Syrian coast opposite Cyprus, Claude Schaeffer was digging the ancient city of Ugarit, an uninhabited spot known today as Ras Shamra. I left the car on the main Antioch road and turned on foot up the long by-way, rendered impassable to wheels by recent rain. I had dragged my feet through the heavy mud for half a mile or so, when I heard hoofs behind me and a police-officer on an Arab charger cantered up alongside. He sprang from his horse and listened to no protestation: I must take his mount and he would follow on foot. There was nothing for it but to leave Sir Galahad and his impeccable riding-boots imbedded in the morass, and in ten minutes the spirited steed had discharged me, a trifle impetuously, into the midst of as surprising an excavation as it has ever been my fortune to witness.

The approach had in some sense prepared me. Against the sky, the mound of Ugarit had bristled like a fretful porpentine with what I now discovered to be the rifles of a company of soldiers. In the midst of them—yes, more criminals, toiling with pick and shovel, whilst Schaeffer leapt amongst them sternly ordering, correcting, exhorting, with Alsatian verve. By courtesy of the local commandant, the labour problem had been solved, and Ugarit was fast emerging from the dust of ages. . . . We walked down to Schaeffer's little house by the sea, and his charming wife ordered in the lunch. The *pièce de résistance* was a chicken. In itself, that was no unexpected phenomenon; but this chicken was no ordinary Oriental bird. It is well known that Oriental chickens lead a hard life which conduces neither to size nor to succulence; or, as Odile Schaeffer put it more gracefully, they are *trop sportifs*, and in consequence rarely reach a balanced maturity. But this chicken, as I say, was an exception to the rule, a handsome, well-conditioned bird of Occidental proportion. Odile thought rightly that an explanation was demanded. 'Yes,' she said, 'it *is* a very special chicken. You see, it was given to me by a murderer,' and she told the story. Amongst the criminals employed by her husband had been one who nursed a grievance. True, he had murdered a man—that he did not dispute. But the French court had sentenced him to no less than *eight years' imprisonment*, and that was a gross miscarriage of justice. What had he done? He had killed a man who had insulted his wife. What else could a gentleman do? Would any of his friends ever have spoken to him again if he had *not* killed the man who had insulted his wife? He had laid his logical case with emphatic protestation before Claude Schaeffer, and Claude, understanding the East, had represented the case sympathetically to the French High Commissioner. The sentence had thereupon been halved, and the previous day had terminated. What did the newly released murderer do? He went straight off to the hen-roosts of Latakia, stole the fattest chicken he could find, and brought it back to his benefactor's wife as a token of gratitude. 'You see,' added Odile, 'he was always exactly what you English call the *perfect gentleman*. Now let us carve this admirable chicken in the honour of a very charming murderer.'

But from the criminology of the East it is time to return to the archaeology of the West.

8. Northern France

THE inevitable sequel to Maiden Castle began to emerge at an early stage in our work there. By the end of our first season (1934) it had become increasingly clear to us that, whatever the insular contribution to the cultures (neolithic and Early Iron Age) with which we were dealing, we could not place our results in a sizeable context without a first-hand investigation of the equivalent material across the Channel. Geologically and geographically, the granite outcrop of Cornwall and the chalk downs of the southern counties are an extension of the identical formations of northern France, and it was fair to suppose that cultural links might be proportionately significant. Historical relations between Brittany and Britain in the first century B.C. made our supposition something more than guesswork.

Accordingly, in the spring of 1935 one of my young colleagues, Leslie Scott (Mrs. P. Murray Threipland), volunteered to carry out a reconnaissance. Her admirable report was sufficiently encouraging to induce Ralegh Radford and myself to join her in a further survey in 1936, when we made a rapid tour from the Manche to the Atlantic coast, visiting earthworks and museums in rapid succession. By the end of it our further course was clear.

I had in mind three main problems. First there was the question of the earlier neolithic culture of Maiden Castle; secondly, there was the problem of the sudden arrival, at Maiden Castle, of multiple defences and developed slingstone warfare; thirdly, there was the question of the origin of certain new types of pottery (bead-rim bowls, jars with countersunk handles) which were associated with these specialized military developments. The first of these problems was in principle straightforward: the link between our earlier neolithic and Brittany was established, at least in part, by the material in the Breton museums, particularly that at Carnac. Secondly, a cursory examination of selected earthworks in western

Normandy and Brittany pointed to southern Brittany as the main focus of the multiple system; and since southern Brittany was the historic home of the Veneti, who had regular trading-relations with Britain before Caesar's time, the problem began to take a reasonable shape. So far as could be seen, too, from the scanty material available in the undeveloped French museums, the pottery which had troubled us had Breton cousins. The third problem therefore fitted into the picture; but clearly, in addition to more detailed ground survey, we should have to fill some of the many gaps by fresh digging. We prospected.

Near Huelgoat, in the middle of Finistère, we found an *oppidum* after our own heart. The so-called Camp d'Artus, one of the very few of its kind thought worthy of mention in the *Guide Bleu*, was for its great size (some seventy-five acres) without rival in the former territory of the Osismi of north-western Brittany. Moreover it had a faint outer fortification which, at a stretch, might enable us to include it amongst our 'multiple' earthworks. We had no hesitation on the spot in selecting it as our starting-point. We proceeded to tackle the Ministère des Beaux Arts, under which the ancient monuments of France were administered.

Here we encountered a formidable setback. Most certainly we could dig the Camp d'Artus—*but* of course we should have to insure against fire the whole State forest in which the camp was situated! We tried to laugh this off; but no, we must quite definitely insure the forest. I accepted the challenge.

For weeks I tried to persuade French insurance agents to look at the matter in a sensible light. Replies came in the form of shrugs and 'millions of francs.' I was nearly beaten, when one day I came across a Lloyd's underwriter with a sense of humour. The situation was saved; I forget what his premium was, but it was of the order of 7s. 6d.!

That is not quite the whole of the story. Properly impressed with the vulnerability of the forest in which we were working, I issued strict injunctions against smoking, and myself suffered the tortures of the damned by the scrupulous personal observation of my veto. But one morning as I entered the forest I saw flames amongst the trees and a column of smoke rising high above the fire. I broke into a frantic gallop and burst upon the scene. Against a handsome larch, and eagerly licking its trunk, was a fire, sure enough; upon it was a tin can containing a mess of bubbling bilberries, gathered from an abundance round about; and gleefully surveying the brew was a posse of the village children. I leapt with a roar upon the fire and trampled it out, whilst the startled children fled to a respectful distance and stood wondering at the scene. It took hours of explanation to persuade the brats and their parents that this perfectly normal, and hitherto unquestioned, procedure must, with the best will in the world, cease during our sojourn. Vividly in my mind was a Lloyd's underwriter far away in blessed ignorance, happily fingering his 7s. 6d. whilst flames swept the forests of Brittany to the tune of untold millions.

Amidst such vicissitudes our work at Huelgoat developed, until a Gallic Wall of the Caesarian period stood revealed before us, with its timbering and its masonry. At dawn one morning we met our vigorous friend Claude Schaeffer, who came to inspect us on behalf of the French government, and I think we were able to display to him an orderly British excavation in full blast, the first of its kind, I suppose, in the annals of Breton archaeology. We had an admirable team, with my Maiden Castle foreman, William Wedlake, in charge of a gang of puzzled but amiably co-operative Breton peasants, and my photographer, M. B. Cookson, who endeared himself to the villagers and taught them more than he learned from them.

Alongside excavation, our ground-survey proceeded upon a carefully considered plan. With suitable rotation, our large party was divided into two sections. One section assisted in the work of excavation; the other section was again subdivided, and in small groups, each under a leader, combed the countryside within allotted areas. Uncritical lists of earthworks had been compiled from miscellaneous literary sources, and with these in hand and an unblushing use of sixth-form French a great deal of material was collected. At short intervals the groups would report back to head-quarters, and where necessary their work was followed by further investigation. In that way, Brittany and most of Normandy were covered systematically in a pioneer fashion. I have no doubt that sites, and even important sites, were missed, but the resultant maps may be regarded as reasonably representative. Such work on modern standards had not previously been attempted.

Meanwhile, excavation was extended from Huelgoat to a small multiple earthwork of a characteristic south Breton type, near Quimper; and we then moved eastwards to the neighbourhood of Avranches, where a better-known *oppidum* at Le Petit Celland produced another Gallic Wall and abundant native coinage of the Caesarian epoch. In the following year, 1939, we moved into eastern Normandy, and tackled other types of fortification at Fécamp and at Duclair, where our armies were later to cross the Seine, doubtless in the steps of earlier folk. By now our assembled material began to make sense, to fall into rational categories. A number of conclusions began to emerge.

First, in northern France, west of the Seine, we were confronted with a series of widely separated 'camps' or *oppida* of great size and of a date, where tested, approximating to that of Caesar's campaigns in the fifties of the first century B.C. These large *oppida* stood out from their smaller neighbours as centres on a tribal rather than a local scale and could in fact, in some instances, be ascribed to specific tribes. Thus the Camp d'Artus, at Huelgoat, was the obvious rallying-point of the Osismi of Finistère; Le Petit Celland might be associated with the Venelli or Unelli of the Manche; further south the seemingly unfinished *oppidum* in the Forêt de Fougères might similarly have served the Redones; further west, the Curiosolites probably included within their territory the immense *oppidum* at Guégon, near Josselin; and further east, in Calvados, the vast *castellier* of St. Désir near Lisieux, with its Gallic Wall, can only have been the focus of the Lexovii. The story was not yet complete, but its outlines were taking shape. The Veneti of southern Brittany had many small fortifications, significantly comparable with those of Cornwall, though seemingly no large *oppidum*; their ultimate citadel was their famous fleet. But they were exceptional. For the most part each tribe or confederacy, under the momentary cohesion imposed by the Roman invasion, now built itself a great fortification capable of containing the tribal levy and of focusing defence. These new *oppida* were few and far apart; in some instances at least they must greatly have exceeded purely local needs. They represent strategy rather than tactics, and strategy on an unwonted scale. They are a comment on Caesar's *Commentaries*.

But, as we approached the Seine valley from the west, we began to recognize a somewhat different emphasis. Beside and beyond the Seine lay Belgic Gaul, which had already, before Caesar's time, distinguished itself by its lonely and successful resistance to German invaders. The Belgic tribesmen were tough fighters who sought safety less in massed concentration than in a network of stout fortifications of an individual type which we, in 1939, were the first to recognize and investigate. Both Fécamp and Duclair were of this 'new' kind, and we found eight or ten others in Seine Inférieure and the adjacent fringe of Eure. They have huge ramparts of earth, broad, flat, canal-like ditches and large in-turned entrances, and are commonly situated upon commanding promontories. Nothing like them occurs further west, but one example has been identified, appropriately enough, in Kent. It is sufficiently clear that they represent *par excellence* a distinctive Belgic fashion. We were hot upon their trail when the end came.

The latter stages of our work in 1938 had been uncomfortable enough. Day after day in that September the cathedral bell of Avranches had tolled its mournful tocsin; in response, day after day successive classes of the military reserve had left their fields and workshops and had stumbled into the market-place with their bundles and their womenfolk about them. In the unreal respite of the following summer we resumed with half-minds. By mid-August the suspense became unbearable, and, as I shall tell, I suddenly handed over to Kitty Richardson and fled the scene.

9. War Interlude II, 1939–43

THE day after Mr. Neville Chamberlain had stung his fingers upon that nettle danger at Munich in 1938 I stood in the foyer of the Café Royal in Regent Street, awaiting my luncheon guest. Beside me, similarly unoccupied, was a minor Secretary of State, and I can still hear his words. 'Today,' he said, 'I am ashamed to be an Englishman.' That evening, and on many evenings afterwards, I got into my car and until after nightfall toured the Territorial depots of London. It was not merely that war seemed likely; I now savagely hoped for war, for a national opportunity to obliterate the disgrace of Munich, and was determined to be in at the kill. But for weeks my quest was frustrate. I was forty-eight years old and had not donned a uniform since 1919. My nearest approach to achievement was at Fulham, where I was put second on a list for the command of a field battery. (I believe that the battery fell subsequently into Japanese hands.)

And then suddenly things began to happen. I ran into Colonel King, who was high in the counsels of the Middlesex Territorial Association; and Colonel King knew of me as an active antiquary. Why that qualification should have fitted me for military responsibility I know not, but I shall be forever grateful to King and to his colleague Colonel Passingham for thinking that it did. They passed on to me an order from the War Office to raise a new light anti-aircraft battery at Enfield, 'at a time to be notified.' With a glad heart I departed meanwhile for my projected archaeological season in Normandy, expecting from day to day a stern summons to duty and Enfield.

None came. By the middle of August 1939 the international situation had tightened beyond bearing, and one Friday afternoon

I suddenly handed the archaeological destinies of Normandy over to my partners, Miss K. M. Richardson and Miss Theodora Newbould, and took the night-boat from Dieppe. After breakfast I went straight from Victoria Station to the Association's headquarters nearby. The moment was exact; the War Office had just issued executive orders and my arrival was acclaimed. By lunchtime I was in Enfield for the first time in my life, searching for a vacant house from which to recruit 'Enfield's Own.' I found one in the London Road.

Alas, it was a Saturday, and the house-agent had vanished with the keys. I ran him eventually to earth on a golf-links a few miles away. In the King's name I dragged him from the second green, and by the middle of the afternoon I was installed. On a window-sill I drafted a forthright appeal to the patriotic citizens of Enfield, bidding them rally to the colours at No. —, London Road, on the Monday morning. A visit to the local newspaper office—the only printing establishment open at the week-end—speedily produced a liberal edition of the appeal, tricked out prettily in red, white and blue, and ending with a resounding 'God Save the King.' By Sunday morning it adorned the windows of nearly every shop in Enfield. Nor were the local cinemas behindhand; their films were thenceforth punctuated by the new battle-cry hastily scribbled on lantern-slides. Urgent telephone conversations with a variety of military depots produced the necessary recruitment forms and a medical officer. By Monday morning at eight o'clock we sat on borrowed chairs behind an improvised counter, and with combined curiosity and anxiety awaited custom.

'We' had now swollen to five. To the medical officer and myself had been added J. B. Ward Perkins (now Director of the British School at Rome), long a friend and colleague of mine, and my son Michael (a youthful barrister), together with a young sergeant of the regular army from headquarters. Michael and Ward Perkins were awaiting their commissions but were meanwhile a tower of strength. With the exception of the sergeant, we were all still in civilian clothes; we were learning our job and improvising as we went along. On that morning we sat awhile and waited.

The start was a slow one, and it must have been after nine o'clock when the doorway was filled by an immense figure. For a moment the newcomer surveyed with mild surprise the threadbare scene in front of him, and then a quiet, pleasant voice mounted up within him, and he announced his name with a suspicion of hesitation, almost apology. 'A. Goodman, solicitor' went down on the form, and thus a Cambridge graduate headed our list of gunners. Unambitious but out to do his bit, Gunner Goodman had become a quartermaster-sergeant when I parted from him two years later, and I wish him well. He was followed by a thickening stream of schoolmasters, tradesmen, mechanics, labourers—a mixed lot typical of those fine early days of the war, when the spirit of service was universal and unabated. By the end of the week our number was full to overflowing. In the absence of uniforms, the new unit was arrayed in brown overalls and was thus reviewed, at my request, by the brigadier in a carefully chosen cul-de-sac where the most inquisitorial of inspecting officers could not expect manœuvre. For the finer nuances of the parade-ground we were not yet ripe, but we came to attention and stood at ease like guardsmen.

During that week my new officers, carefully handpicked from a long waiting-list, began to arrive. Amongst the first was Bill O'Bryen, with three M.C.'s from his first war, a Rolls Royce and a chauffeur. We promptly enlisted the chauffeur and gave him a pass to take the car home. Then there was Clive Brook, who did his best to surmount the medical examination, but was held up by a lameness which preserved him for his art and his public. And there was Henry Wynn-Parry. He was at that time a K.C., and is now an eminent judge of the High Court. How he passed the sight test is known to himself and his Maker; nor was it ever discovered whether his monocle was an aid or a mask. But he entered our office with a snuffbox and the air of a *School for Scandal,* and was thenceforth, until he went to the Staff and then on to the Bench, the *provocateur* of every sort of satisfactory devilry. We made him a captain on the spot—those were days of wise if astonishing freedom in such trivial matters as rank and promotion.

Yet, looking back, I can see that it was the women, not less than the men, who enlisted 'Enfield's Own.' Mrs. O'Bryen, known to fame as Elizabeth Allan, Mrs. Clive Brook, Kay Hammond, and Mrs. (now Lady) Wynn-Parry, promptly established an exceedingly efficient and attractive canteen in which, amongst all else, they cooked indefatigably and served cheap midday dinners for our hungry soldiery, and certainly attracted by their charm and cookery far more recruits than all my red-white-and-blue posters and public parades together. For everyone, they were great days, those of August and September 1939, days of selfless effort and single-minded purpose. Our initial armament was limited to a few rifles and half a dozen archaic Lewis guns. Our official war-time destiny was to guard the Enfield Powder and Small Arms Factories. But that was no sort of destiny for men of good and adventurous heart. From the 48th Light Ack-Ack Battery we grew rapidly into the 42nd Mobile Light Ack-Ack Regiment of four batteries, of which three went with me in 1941 to the Eighth Army in North Africa. The fourth battery, alas, steamed straight into the hands of the Japanese on Java, and its fate shall be unspoken. . . .

As in my First War interlude, I propose not to linger over the tedious details of regimental history. Instead, I will print a few abstracts from surviving letters to my most constant correspondent, Sir Cyril Fox, and will supplement them with stray notes from my war-time files and diaries. If these *miscellanea* have any merit, it is once again that of actuality, for they include nothing that was not written down within a few hours of its happening.

(II) EXTRACTS FROM LETTERS TO SIR CYRIL FOX

28 Oct. 1941

[On board a crowded troopship in the South Atlantic]

> In the wild October night-time, when the wind raved round
>   the land,
> And the Back-sea met the Front-sea, and our doors were
>   blocked with sand. . . .

Well, more or less. One sits in shorts and many overcoats—those a tribute to the latitude, these to the October gale. Even the flying fishes, that sprayed like soapsuds at our bows, have given up, and the gloomy, humourless shark that nosed our sides has slipped back into the Atlantic. The spectacle of the heaving ships is a fine and solemn one, the warships like thoroughbreds amongst a pack of mongrels. Day after day, week after week, one eats prodigiously and drinks carelessly and gambles trivially, and devours anything in the shape of poetry with a cerebral hunger that might be hard to believe. Only occasionally Things happen, in a reiterant fashion that lacks adventure, and anyway may not be told. And one lectures to the troops on Cecil Rhodes or Ibn Saud or the Delta, or cries 'Hard luck, Sir' at a monotonous variety of organized sports. One also studies the Art of Killing, in a detached academic way. And at night one treads gingerly between countless bodies prostrate on the decks. . . . In short, one lives another existence, and I should be hard put to it to say now whether I've always been a Commanding Officer or whether I'm still a Slippered Antiquary at heart. . . . P.S. Albatross on the port bow. I've just run out to call in all bows and arrows.

4 Feb. 1942
[Egypt, beside the Great Bitter Lake]

If I remember, old Dr. Donne described letter-writing as 'a kind of ecstacy.' I dare say he wrote, as I am writing, with the shadow-bars of a lantern across his script. But he scarcely had the compensatory stimulus of all the stars of the Orient overhead, and lake-water lapping on the shore within a few yards of him, and the long dim line of Sinai beyond. The Wilderness of Sin has its points, and I have spent much time of late upon its chilly sands, learning to live rather like an embattled Bedouin. One trains incredibly much for incredibly little fighting, but we are very ready and very eager for what may, and will, befall. Waiting and waiting is inclined sometimes to weary the flesh. A commanding officer is not allowed of course to have a Hump, but the influence of all these camels is accumulative and insidious. . . . There are many many camels, I'm afraid. However, I've no doubt we shall win this war in the fullness of time, and every camel will have the O.B.E.

Burlington House [the Society of Antiquaries] is both remote and present. The other night I lay under the sky on the beach of El Arish and woke up suddenly before the dawn. The sea had the tail-end of a gale in it, and at high tide (as tides go in these parts) was crunching the sandy pebbles noisily in my ears. It was irrelevant and comforting to think then of the domesticity of Burlington House and the gentle life it stood for. One lay with a quietening sense of complaisance and permanence; until suddenly the palms stood out against parallel red and yellow strips along the eastern horizon, a flight of duck passed overhead, and my men were making a fire of sand and petrol and twigs behind me.

All this is rather solemn stuff, but it jumps with the night. War in one's old age is different from war in one's first youth. So much that mattered once matters so little now. The knight-errant must have yawned after his second dragon.

Tonight, by moonlight, I pulled out in a boat after duck with my gun. No duck but a perilous fusillade from the rifles of the zealous (Sudanese) Camel Corps, who 'thought' we were hashish-runners. The error, when discovered, was received with shouts of happy laughter by the Camel Corps, who were not even ashamed of their own bad shooting. What matters? . . .

2 May 1942

[Egypt]

. . . Stonehenge and the Prescellys have a sense of durability about them which is lacking in all this fretful ironmongery—although even this has its moments of quietude. The night before last I was out in the desert on a training expedition with an armoured brigade, and at nightfall we drew into close leaguer, head to tail in thick-set files of vehicles. The day had been unbelievably hot and dusty, and I happened to have a bit of a fever on me which didn't help a lot. But with the night a little breeze sprang up and passed lightly over one as one fell asleep on the sand beside the car. The looming horizon of tanks a few yards distant, with their porcupine of guns, was black and solid and comforting against a moon-filled sky, and the only noise was the intermittent padding of the sentries. It was a moment of complete and satisfying peace; and I lay convinced that daffodils and meandering streams have no monopoly of Elysium.

We have looked upon our dead, but for the most part life is busily slow. . . . Always occupied—even hectically occupied—but mentally never stretched. Much fibre is wasted upon the suffering of fools—and I've no doubt that the other fellow thinks the same. One pines more and more for the idiom of one's own folk, and for enterprise that is devoid of self-interest. . . .

I'm just back from three weeks with the Higher Tactics. Across the valley were more pyramids than seemed necessary for one landscape, and in the middle distance a triangular sail would wander slowly through the long ribbon of cultivation. Blistering days were spent amidst a plague of ladybirds, and bugs fell upon one at night from the rafters. Nevertheless, an interesting and intelligent interlude. Such are the trivialities of existence. We are still fighting for tasks which, if no more honourable than those we are doing, might at least prove more exciting. Meanwhile, one is occasionally a little richer for experience. I probably told you of my voyage to Rhodes? Or didn't I? It is not secret—it was, as a matter of fact, extensively referred to some days later in the Egyptian Press, which got it from the Air Force. Briefly, it was this way.

As an anti-aircraft gunner I felt that I could never really get round my job without some first-hand knowledge of the receiving end of the business. From my familiarity with military compart-mentalism, it was equally clear that, as a commanding officer, I should never receive official sanction to carry out the necessary investigation. The answer to the little problem was not difficult; a whisper in the ear of the group-captain commanding a bomber landing-ground near Suez brought a laugh and a promise. Two days later, with twenty-four hours' leave in my pocket, I was locked into the front gun-turret of a laden Wellington bomber, and in the evening, en route for Rhodes, we came down for refuelling at a landing-ground on the North African coast. There, as ill-luck had it, an enemy squadron dropped a load of bombs on us by last light; they knocked out only one of our nine planes, but blasted the runway and so shortened it to an uncomfortable minimum. Later, in the prison of a moonless night, we—the five of the crew—were a little tense, I think, as the bomber, with its heavy cargo, sluggishly gathered momentum down the runway towards the little red lamp which now marked the nearer lip of the intrusive crater. At the last moment we just lifted over the lamp; I climbed forward thankfully into the circular gun-turret, and was again locked in.

These things, and those that followed, are routine to our Air Force, but to a mere landsman they were new enough. There were, as I say, five of us: the pilot, a grand boy (Canadian) of twenty, the sergeant-navigator, the bomber, the tail-gunner, and your cowering colonel as front-gunner, cold and chewing peppermint to keep back nausea. Out over the sea we went [at 130 m.p.h.] in a wall of blackness broken only by an occasional dim cotton-wool cloud. At one point far below a lamp waved up to us—'Some poor fellow down in the drink' was the comment over the 'phones. Three hours, and, in spite of the periodical 'Do you see anything?' from the alert pilot, I was lapsing into semi-conscious-ness when the sharp voice of the rear-gunner pierced the ear-phones with 'Fighter on our tail!' Simultaneously, things happened: the pilot, reacting instantly, threw the heavy Wimpey on its side and we dropped like a knife into a cloud. This unexpected operation I accompanied with my mind rather than my body; the latter seemed to remain aloft, poised in the empyrean, and I remember observing the hands which grasped the two machine-guns in front of me as curious and alien objects. . . . We emerged once more into the lonely night, and shortly made out the shadowy eastern end of Crete. It had a friendly look to it—at least it was land! Thence we veered north-eastwards, and presently the slightly intenser darkness below us was the island of Rhodes, with the vague mass of the Turkish coast beyond.

It was now 1.30 a.m., and in ten minutes we were due to drop our bombs. But getting to Rhodes was easier than finding the target when we got there! Our mission was to bomb and machine-gun the larger of two aerodromes, but for several minutes we patrolled the island from end to end without discovering any shape in the blackness. The enemy (Italians) were either asleep or unusually cunning. If only they would open fire and give the show away! The stillness was a little eerie.

At length we spotted what seemed to be a runway; and as we circled over it the night was suddenly pierced by a searchlight. The blade of it cut straight through us and for a moment the sensation was that of a blow on the face. Then the pilot repeated his escape-manœuvre and we dropped out of the glare. Imme-diately there were two, three other searchlights, and some leisurely

HUELGOAT, BRITTANY, 1938

Dr. Claude Schaeffer (on left) visiting the Author's excavations on behalf of the French Government

ON THE BATTLEFIELD OF EL ALAMEIN DURING THE LAST DAY OF
THE BATTLE

tracer-shell bent beneath and behind us; the target was no longer in doubt. We made five runs up the course at 3,000 feet, discharging our load piecemeal; whereafter we swung out to sea, came down nearly to sea-level, and groped our way back inland between two hills vaguely visible above us on our flanks. At the expected order from the pilot 'Let them have it,' the front- and rear-gunners lowered their twin Brownings, firing several hundred rounds blindly at what we trust may have been the target. I say 'blindly' because the dazzling flash of the machine-guns and the smoke which quickly filled the turret blotted out the scene. As the fog cleared we were already rising fast and turning towards home.

But not yet! We were perhaps ten miles from the island when the agonized voice of the bomber came over the 'phones—'Oh DAMN. We forgot to post our letters!' (Our 'letters' being several packets of crude leaflets printed in Greek and designed to stiffen the antipathy of the island peasants to their dastardly Italian masters.) A speedy five-way debate over the telephone followed. Should we push the infernal leaflets into the sea and say nothing, or should we go back and do our stuff? Cowardice prevailed: we turned back to the island, which was now well alight, and dropped our subversive literature on it through the bomb-chute. I remember hoping that the packets would hit someone—friend or foe, I cared not—on the head, in bulk. . . .

My excellent adjutant, Percy Stebbing, the only member of my unit who was in the secret, met me at the Suez landing-ground; and as I left the mess-table an hour later after a short and silent breakfast, I heard one of my subalterns whisper to another behind me—'I say, the Colonel must have had the hell of a good party in Cairo last night! . . .'

10 May 1942
[Still Egypt]

. . . How long they will permit me to stay out here I don't know. You see, I'm seven years over the age-limit and they've been applying it very strictly of late. *In sha' allah.* I sometimes find myself reflecting a little bitterly on those younger members of our craft [archaeology] who so reluctantly, if at all, gave up their

E

peaceful calling and, at the best, took upon themselves gentle jobs at no great discomfort. How can . . . and . . . face themselves at the shaving mirror or go quietly to their beds at night? Or am I stupidly bitter? I think not. This war will be won by blows and by bleeding, and there are enough intelligent women in the world to do all the jobs of . . . and his tribe at least as competently as they. I suppose I'm old, but I grudge youth nothing except security, which is not the privilege of youth in these days. Oh hell! I'm sorry, but I feel strongly. . . .

11 June 1942
[The Western Desert, at last]

War is a natural condition of man. Whether war be good or bad is not in question: nor is the canon of rectitude whereby such niceties may be judged. But, for good or ill, to regard war as a temporary lapse from a normal condition of peace is to invert nature and to falsify history. What major moment in the course of human culture has not had war for its background or its stimulus, is not rooted in contention? Is not the Parthenon a war-memorial? And was not the whole movement of the Renaissance a marching and counter-marching of armies? That turbulence of the spirit which gives rise to masterpieces and major discovery is but a parcel of an unrest which finds equal expression in the call of the trumpet. Peace and plenty, perhaps; but peace and poetry—where can you find them joined, save amongst the polite and little men? . . .

Sorry, my dear Cyril, but this is the first night for some time that I have been able to have a candle after dark, and my pen has run away with itself and got bogged in platitude. I won't do it again. The war is still, for some of us, spectacular rather than really dangerous, but there is a slight improvement, and I have had a brief sight of a modern battle. It is a Thing. A cloud of twenty or thirty Junkers 88 wheeling and diving in the air, their little black bombs dropping from them like strings of beads. Stukas, fifteen of them, tumbling about the sky and filling the air with the swish of their falling salvoes. And, most moving of all, a modern armoured brigade moving grandly into action. It is Miltonic; at the same time unreal and acutely real. . . .

Today I lunched with a company of the French Foreign Legion, a lunch partaken in a 30 cwt. truck but lasting in all *three hours*! A vast deal of chemical was absorbed, and the rations were tricked out into the semblance of a four-course *déjeuner*. The captain was *not* a Frenchman, no, he was a Breton, subject to much ribald good humour from his Norman juniors. We talked of everything save the war, and parted with alcoholic poisoning and a restored sense of proportion. They're a grand lot, these Free French, at heart—and stomach. But they're a pain in the neck to the British military mind.

6 July 1942

[Written at Burg el-Arab on a hot summer's day at the end of the retreat of the Eighth Army to El Alamein, where the first battle of that name was still in doubt a few miles away under Auchinleck. We occupied a reserve position in 'box' formation. Everyone was pretty tired]

The El Alamein Line

The air is vibrant with the clubbed sound of guns,
Beating on forty miles of desert dust.
Unwilling men fight on because they must,
Because some are called Free and some called Huns.
Yet all are choked with the same quenchless thirst,
All seared with the same fiery blinding sand,
All loathe alike this dead and evil land,
All fear at heart the harsh pulsating burst
Of bomb and shell and sudden earthy blast;
All are consumed in hate and lurking dread,
All are impatient both of dread and hate.

As thus I wrote an Arab goatherd passed;
Across the sand his whimpering flock he led,
Secure and happy in the hand of Fate.

A sonneteria, my dear Cyril, bears the same relationship to a sonnet that a cafeteria does to a café. I found it easier to write a sonneteria than a letter. We live, these days, from dune to dune. We are unbeaten. . . .

27 July 1942

[In the desert somewhere behind the El Alamein Line]

This afternoon the air is so full of sand that a London pea-soup is daylight in comparison, and I have just been to the necessarium on a compass-bearing. As for my pen, it is so clogged as almost to justify my handwriting. Somewhere out in the dust is my little command, and for the rest there are a good many miles of desert between us and higher authority, so we are pleasantly isolated. Your letters, with their news of marrying and giving in marriage, are good to read and are a link with another life which will come very pleasantly to me again, if so it be. Yet, this life gets its claws into a fellow. My batman, an old Cockney soldier, remarked to me today—'Leave to Alexandria? Not for me, Sir. The Desert's in me blood; and when I goes 'ome after the war I'll take a sackful of sand with me!' He almost meant it.

I've been turning over the pages of my field-notebook, and amongst map-references and orders I've come across some highly remarkable *vers libre* (save the mark!) dating from the first day of the retreat: *libre* if not *vers*. (What a devastating habit this is of bursting into verse in moments of crisis—and on the spot, too!) It is a terrifying effort but does represent an actual picture, however pedestrian. Take a deep breath—here it is:

Bel Hamid, 12 June 1942[1]

The steel-black road to the West stabs the white sand
And plunges into the quivering horizon.
The car jolts and sways from rut to cratered scar,
And those within are hot and unpeaceful.

[1] The final retreat of the Eighth Army to El Alamein began (very unexpectedly) on this day. The writer was driving forward to visit some guns south of Tobruk when the first wave of the retreating army engulfed him.

A lorry, and another, looms and takes shape out of
   the haze,
One with men clinging about it, another with a portéed
   gun;
Then more appear, tanks, guns and yet more lorries.
Now they spread beyond the road, on both sides,
And the dust rises in an angry turbulence from their tracks.
At last the whole landscape is moving eastward in a
   great flood
Against which the westering car weaves falteringly.

A few miles further and the car is fenced by a solid wall
Of pressing transport; an officer stands in the road,
His face plastered white with sand, like a clown's;
The question, 'Tell me, where is the Hun?'
Brings back the casual answer, 'Just behind that ridge,
And coming along quite nicely.' The mass
Surges eastward again, in unanxious but unordered haste. . . .

Yesterday was heralded by achieved success;
Today a great army
Has snatched Defeat from the very jaws of Victory.

Since then, the great army has turned and is fighting back, so I
can send this balderdash without being accused of defeatism.
Eventually we shall win. Meanwhile we need a little heaven-sent
impatience. My love to you both. . . .

16 Sept. 1942

[At the control-headquarters of the anti-aircraft artillery protecting
the landing-grounds behind the El Alamein Line]

Beyond a radius of 10 yds., my dear Cyril, the desert landscape
is blocked out by a wall of moving sand—the usual afternoon
sandstorm. It clogs my pen and trickles through my hair. It's
probably got into my brain. But I'm just back from four days in
Cairo, my first leave since arrival in the Middle East. The full Nile
flood, chocolate with the snows of Abyssinia and vast leagues of

rich alluvium, tumbled refreshingly under the bridges. I slept excessively and had many baths, bought a book or two, and explored that astonishing monument, the walls of Cairo, with the veteran Creswell. In an embowered house beneath the pyramids I lunched with the R. G. Caseys, an assortment of admirals, and two American ambassadors, who surveyed the world with the good humour and the detached curiosity of schoolboys. There was a high-spot during luncheon when, under the guidance of a demonstrative admiral, a convoy-mat, escorted by heavily armed pepperpots, was safely brought into port beside the *corbeille de fruits*. Otherwise there was comfortingly little 'shop.' The German push had been counter-pushed with success; for the moment relative peace reigned and war was no longer intruding upon the preparations for war.

The previous fortnight I had spent mainly in a lorry, ringed by telephones, at rare intervals reading Gordon Childe's *Man Makes Himself* (which I had bought in Alexandria), sometimes ordering guns to fire, always with half an eye on the plotting-board spread under a light-proof tarpaulin on the ground below me. On the board half-a-dozen enemy bombers would suddenly be marked, advancing in line abreast across the Cretan sea. By successive plottings we would trace their landfall and see them hiving off to their targets. Two or three would come our way, and I would order the guns to stand to. . . . On one occasion, I remember, only a single enemy bomber was marked on the board and, tired of waiting for more exciting stuff, the telephonists (their receivers strapped to their heads) began playing whist on the board all round the solitary foe. Now and then a fresh plot would come in, and a hurried search would be made amongst the assembled cards for the plot-mark, which would be moved to its new position, and the game without ceasing would appropriately readjust itself. Eventually the bomber arrived overhead, shells bursting about it, and malevolently dropped its bombs just outside. Following the almighty crash, there was a great scatter of bits and pieces over the tarpaulin, and then a piping voice from one of the players—'Now, boys, we can move the f . . . . . . b . . . . . . off the f . . . . . . board and get on with the f . . . . . . game.' Which they f . . . . . . well did, without further interruption. Almost immediately afterwards the aforesaid f . . . . . . b . . . . . . was brought down by one of our nightfighters, and *Man Makes Himself* proceeded evenly to the end of another chapter. I'd like Gordon Childe to know that his *chef d'œuvre* is meeting with a proper appreciation in the midst of Man's next 'Revolution.'

But these things are *nugae*. I hope and think we are on the verge of a more exciting destiny. What the hell of a time to live in! I wouldn't have missed it, would you? . . .

8 Oct. 1942

[Still Egypt]

. . . The extremes of this life are remarkable and significant. This morning—machine-guns; tonight a hundred miles away and only a vagrant bomber overhead. Time is bridged by all this animated ironmongery, with the result that barbarism and civilization are now a geographical, not a chronological, problem. You may live like a desert-rat one day, and the next you may sit in comfort and listen to the very excellent symphony orchestra that Malcolm Sargent has pushed off in Palestine. Of course there is an alternative: live in the Balham High Street and read the *Daily Mirror* version of what it thinks you (not *you*!) think life to be. I have only one complaint about soldiering—so much of it is so unutterably boring. I suppose that on the balance the Balham High Street is far the more exciting of the two.

Anyway, Cyril, congratulate me. I'm now in the *crack Division* of the British Army! This means a seat plumb in the front row of the stalls for anything that is going, and that'll probably make the Balham H.S. look silly. It's a grand and gratifying thought. My work now *is* nearly done. I boast that I've been able to lead this gang from the suburbs of northern London right into the very middle of the picture. The rest doesn't matter now. Almost for the first time a little sense of achievement has trickled into my consciousness. Forgive! It was better than staying at home with a red hat round my head. . . .

Please know, my dear Cyril, what a godsend your letters are. They are the needed antidote to the mental inhibitions of war.

20 Nov. 1942

[The second Battle of El Alamein—'the sixteenth decisive battle of history' as Montgomery had foretold it—had come and gone. In my letters to Cyril Fox during the battle it was the subject of security-ridden *disjecta* and unprintable verse. The series is resumed nearly a month later, on the fighting march to Tripoli. Winter was closing in]

There's three parts of a moon away up outside, and a howling icy wind around and about. If I stuck my head out I'd see something of a rolling stony desert country in front of me and a stony little hill at my back. But I won't stick my head out. Instead, I'll stay in this blacked-out armoured car of mine with the lamp in the roof and a thin draught sticking like a needle through a vacant rivet-hole. I've been turning over the pages of honest William Cobbett's *Rural Rides*, and have just lighted on the following: 'From the top of this land you have a view of a circle which is upon an average about 70 miles in diameter. . . . You see the Isle of Wight in one direction, and in the opposite direction you see the high lands of Berkshire. It is not a pleasant view, however. The fertile spots are all too far from you.' Good old Farmer Cobbett! What a revealing passage. And he might with considerably greater ease have written thuswise of this devilish landscape. Here one is not in a place, one is in a six-figure map-reference. There is no house, no tree; but to emphasize the vacuum there is, 100 yds. from me, sitting proud and alone and irrelevant on the desert, an enamelled bath in first-class condition! . . .

Well, here we are for the moment, on our west-faring. I remember how I watched the birth and waxing of the last moon, knowing in some secret detail what it portended. On the first night of the attack at El Alamein, about 3 o'clock in the morning, I lay down in my coat amongst the din and went easily to sleep. At 6 I woke, turned on my back and opened my eyes. The sky was a dark indigo but illumined by a sort of premonition of dawn, and across it lay two wan searchlight beams, in a St. Andrew's cross. It was the pre-ordained signal of success. As things turned out, the signal was premature, and twelve days of rather sticky fighting followed. My regiment behaved properly and there were a good many gaps in our ranks [we actually lost 5 officers and 52 men] but they did not exceed expectation. Personally, my batteries being all deployed to a variety of formations, I had an easy time of it, with the free run of the battlefield; a close-up view of a modern battle, including a German tank-attack. There's something curiously obscene about a tank waddling towards you—ten, fifteen tanks crawling loathsomely. Just before this counter-attack, Field-Marshal Smuts was brought up along the shore by a cloud of attentive staff officers who busily expounded to him the principles of war and their local application. Now hereabouts the shore-line is of dazzling white sand (powdered gypsum) and the sea an incredible blue; and after listening patiently but with manifest inattention for some considerable time, Smuts turned blandly upon his entourage with the remark: 'Thank you, gentlemen, but now at last I really do know what the colour *ultramarine* actually looks like.' . . .

Christmas Day, 1942

[A little west of Mussolini's 'Marble Arch,' on the borders of Cyrenaica and Tripolitania]

Are you good at flowers? I'm bad at them. Birds, fishes, butterflies, yes; but not flowers. Through the open doorway of this steel curricle I look upon the sandy desert of Tripolitania, with its hummocky lumps of dingy camel-grass under a rushing wintry wind and a pale sun. There is no general sign of *colour*, and yet, probing among the camel-grass this morning, I have found an astonishing number of secret flowers: some I can only call daisy-lions, some small white poppies, sprays of yellow and purple that are just *flowers*. Such is my learned contribution to the *Herbarium Tripolitanicum*, the choice fruit of a few hours of invigorating solitude. For today, the first time I think for 3 years, I'm alone, almost. I'm at my Advanced Headquarters, with only two wireless operators, and they are in their wireless truck 150 yds. away. The rest of my folk I have sent back for 24 hours of glut and goodwill. If you think of the unrelenting publicity of the desert, where every detail of one's life is performed in the market-place and scarcely a thought partakes of privacy, the restfulness of these few hours will be a little understood. It's a good Christmas Day.

And, like a proper pagan festival, it's founded on good feeding. We sat down, my two signallers and I, to a monstrous great midday dinner prepared by themselves, with a full-dress MENU beside each plate:

CHRISTMAS DAY 1942

DINNER

MENU

Chicken soup.

Braised (query) pork chops *à la* Western Desert.

Baked beans.

Boiled potatoes.

Bartlett pears and Cling peaches with cream.

Coffee.

Cigarettes—State Express 555.

How's that for a blow-out? And if the winter's wind did blow a little on our soup and cool our coffee, what of it? Buy that luncheon for your 3s. 6d. plus 10s. for holding your hat and another 5s. for looking at the waiter! How's that for the Forward Area? I'll tell you: bloody good. And for the cool of the night in front of us I've got a bottle of rum in the box behind me, and the Old Buccaneer had none better. . . .

7 Jan. 1943

[In Tripolitania, on the desert near the coast. The writer had evidently been reading *Moby Dick*]

What ho, Cyril! It's a cold day of winter and I've issued a tot of rum to all hands. ' "Drink and pass!" he cried, handing the heavy charged flagon. . . . "Round with it, round! Short draughts—long swallows, men; 'tis hot as Satan's hoof. So, so; it goes round excellently. It spiralizes in ye; forks out at the serpent-snapping eye. Well done; almost drained. That way it went, this way it comes. . . ." '

And on the strength of it I've given the troops a lecture on the Post-war World. 'For the making of it, each individual man of you is personally responsible,' I shouted, glaring from one spade-like face to another. 'Now go and wash yourselves in the sea, and take a rope with ye!'[1] At that moment three Hun ground-straffers came charging and rolling by through our encampment at 50 ft. and we shot one down; I've just sent a man to the smoking ruin of it. Are you alive, *really* alive, my dear Cyril, this brisk winter's day? Do you hear the Middle Sea spewing and sucking along the foreshore behind those blanched sandhills? Are ye alive, Cyril, spinning the world around ye like a top? For sure you are, most vital of men. And what is your news? The postman happens by in these remote parts now and then, and I hope he may empty your brave penmanship from his sack at his next happening—a letter from the real to the unreal, for this life of mine has no tangibility, and already one of my correspondents has referred to me as a 'myth'! On the whole I'd rather be that five-shillingsworth of chemicals which is a man. My love for you both is at least not mythical. . . .

[At this point there is a ten-weeks' gap in the correspondence, coinciding with the entry into Tripoli—see p. 143 and the advance into Tunisia. The letters are resumed at the time of the Battle of Medenine and the capture of the Mareth Line, though the busy military life is scarcely referred to in them.]

19 March 1943

[At Medenine. About this time the writer assumed command of the 8th Army's strange and wonderful anti-aircraft brigade which had been brilliantly led by Brigadier Calvert-Jones. It was anything but a conventional brigade of its class and included as special problem-children a mixed battalion of Free French, survivors of Bir Hakim]

. . . Here, on the edge of the mountains, the spring flowers are a riot. They have been and will be obscured by the smoke of battle and related irrelevancies, but it isn't a bad scene. If you find me

---

[1] Owing to bathing casualties from the under-tow along this coast, it was an Army order that a rescue-rope should always be available.

writing henceforth a little patronizingly, there is reason: in spite of my regimental address I am in fact in command of a brigade, a pretty large body of men of more than one nationality. My age (I'm now very near the uttermost limit) bars my formal promotion, but that doesn't matter—I'm doing the job. After Tunis I imagine that I shall go home. Probably it's time. It's been a long journey. On the other hand, there's some suggestion, apparently, that I should go to Turkey and Iraq in a civilian capacity. . . .

7 May 1943

[The active advance towards Tunis continues: actually outside Monastir, near Sousse]

Since your letter of 29th March the military life has been pretty strenuous in these parts. I've left my regiment, bless it, and have been wielding a full-size brigade—I was, in fact, formally made a brigadier this afternoon. Don't laugh! Instead of sending me home, they've made me a full-blooded bouncing brigadier, all dripping with red tabs and platitudes, and well on the way to Cheltenham. In the future I suppose I shall be regarded as a 'retired brigadier who dabbled a little in archaeology.' It's a funny world, excessively unreal. But if in years to come you ever hear me begin a sentence with 'When I was a brigadier in the Eighth Army,' you have my full and free permission to kill. . . .

Outside, the rain is tapping on the roof of my caravan, and somewhere up above is the drone of a night-fighter, with a bomber or two in the distance. About me in the blackness are the olive-trees, amongst which I took my shot-gun this evening for half-an-hour—result, one pigeon for the pot. Nearby is the small town where yesterday I visited the gaol with the local native potentate, the *kadi*. To my mild embarrassment, at the conclusion of the visit he insisted on releasing two of the prisoners 'in my honour'—a pretty gesture, I thought, and anyway the scallywags inside looked no worse than the scallywags outside. It's a pleasant prolific country where all is sloth and fleas and potential evil—proper breeding-ground for the Barbary pirates. . . .

13 July 1943

[After Tunis my headquarters were withdrawn to the vicinity of Tripoli, whence I flew from time to time to Algiers in connection with the planning of the invasion of the Italian mainland]

I'm sitting back in my canvas chair, my dear Cyril, during the lull between episodes. It's hot, damnably hot, and the old brain is numb and secluded. In fact, it's only just ticking over. If it is reflective, that is because it's so much easier to reflect than to shine forth. It is at this moment dripping ink only as my body is dripping sweat. It is just about as sentient as my foot. Not a well-chosen moment in which to write a letter. This isn't a letter.

Looking back, I can only confess, Cyril, that I have profited by my wars. I should have been a fretful and restless man without them. Caught up in them, I have at least enjoyed something of the anxious stability of the whirling top. . . . Always timely, the cook is now beating upon his suspended tin. I must telegraph to my body that lunch awaits its tolerance. . . . Body apart, there's nothing like a slab of luke-warm bully beef as plaster to the soul. . . . Send me a book please, Cyril, a book tasting of flora and the country green, and costing not more than two bob. . . . And I'll let you into a plot, but not now. . . .

7 Aug. 1943

[Still Tripoli, but referring to a session at Algiers with the planning committee for the invasion of Italy]

Your letter has gladdened my eye after a bumpy aeroplane and 1000 + 1 miles of sea and mountain. . . . I hope to be with you all in December. . . . It's this way. The other day I was [at Algiers] returning to my tent in the evening sun, when my Corps Commander [General (Sir Brian) Horrocks] dashed along with a signal in his hand and the remark—'I say, have you seen this—they want you as (reading) "Director General of Archaeology in India." Why, you must be rather a king-pin at this sort of thing! You know, I thought you were a regular soldier!' If the General ever paid an extravagant compliment, he did so then, although there was, I thought, a hint of pain and disillusionment in his voice. Apart from that, the proposition was a complete bombshell to me. Without any sort of pre-warning, the India Office was asking for my release to take up a key-post in a country I'd never been to in my life! However, I gathered my wits and said I'd accept the offer after the next battle but *not* before. It would obviously have been regrettable to miss all the carefully planned fun at this rather exciting juncture of the war. So I'll join you for a couple of months later on, with the snowflakes and the robins, before going East. Meanwhile I have some very active, tricky and interesting work to hand. And by the way, it is only fair to the Honourable Mysterie of Brigadiers to say that your very kindly reference to my now having 'less personal risk' does them less than justice!! They're no heroes, but a red hat on a hostile beach isn't really much safer than a khaki one!!! However, I'll see you at Christmas. . . .

30 Sept. 1943

[The Salerno landing, of which a little will be said on another page, is now of the past, and Naples lies a few miles in front of us. The scene is night at the Amphitheatre Gate of Pompeii]

I have just turned up the light in my caravan and have shut the door. Before that I had been sitting here and smoking in the darkness. High up in front of me the inflamed eye of the volcano blinked at me beneath the Plough. Now and then was added the flash of a gun, and the leisurely whine of a mortar shell. At the foot of my steps is a bomb-crater, and a hundred yards away in the darkness is the amphitheatre, ruined now as in A.D. 79. It's all astoundingly unreal, but it's many months since I had any close contact with reality, with accepted things. . . .

It's been a stiffish battle, but full of new interest. For the first time for some considerable period I've been really *busy*, as distinct from being merely occupied. It's a good ending to the chapter.

Your letter of the 12th has lifted me buoyantly through the day. First, let me say how overjoyed I am to know that you are to be the next president [of the Society of Antiquaries]. No other choice indeed was thinkable. No other man has the constructive imagination essential to carry our science (and art) over the critical transition from war to peace. For that transition will assuredly occur during your presidency, and it will demand all your finest qualities. And you'll be happy, as one whose faculties are fully stretched. . . .

Secondly, thank you for all you say about my new adventure in the East [as future Director General of Archaeology in India]. . . . In cold blood I'm sometimes a little terrified when I think of the immensity of the task. Then my blood warms up and the giant shrinks. I think that what I'm most terrified of, in prospect, is the element of loneliness. . . .

(III) JOURNEY TO TRIPOLI

[In action, the troops and batteries of a light ack-ack regiment were normally attached to other formations and units, with the result that its commander was liable to be under-employed. Hence this care-free journey, undertaken (be it emphasized) before the author had attained to the responsibilities of brigade-command]

Bir Dufan does not loom large on any map and is absent from most: an obscure carfax of desert tracks, normally derelict but now, on the 18th of January, 1943, a scene of some slight and various activity. A rough German landing-ground, mined and sketchily cancelled by ploughing, was being cleared by our sappers. On the fringe, an armoured-car of the 12th Lancers had just blown itself up on a mine. Up a side track an advance post of some kind was being established. A brigadier sat gazing, a trifle desperately, at a vague map in his car; and a peaceful evening sun lit and softened the inhospitable landscape.

Here was the designated rendezvous of the tactical headquarters of the Eighth Army and one of its armoured brigades with which I was to join forces. Behind me, as a regimental commander, followed my wireless truck and the 'C.O.'s troop' of three Bofors guns, with their lorries. A code message was brought to me by my signaller: the plan had been changed, and both the brigade and Tac. Army had swung northwards, away from us, towards the coast at Zliten.

Similar examples of mutability had prepared us for this, but it was now abundantly clear that, with our growing mastery of the air, my appointed task—the long-range reconnaissance of defiles ahead of the advance—was become a fool's game, fraught with inevitable frustration. I spread the map a trifle impatiently upon the ground and called my two subalterns, Ashton and Plunkett, to me. On the map we drew a straight red line from Bir Dufan to Tripoli, and, after a word by wireless to my distant adjutant and a final 'brew up' in the waning light, we set off into the unknown, leaving the two wings of the Eighth Army to perish without us on our distant flanks.

Our compass-bearing was 309 degrees and the crow-distance 100 miles. Beyond that the map told us little of significance, save for an Italian place-name or two far ahead of us. In the falling darkness and the rising moon we set our course across a desert plateau that might have been designed to speed the night-traveller on his way. For twenty miles or more our nine vehicles and our guns surged forward steadily abreast in desert-formation, until a slight mechanical casualty and a sudden breaking of the ground brought us to rest for the night. We slept well in a fold of the ground, with the guns around us on protective summits.

Next day, after repairs at first light, we set off again on our 309 degrees. The declivity in which we had bivouacked led us downwards to a wide and tumultuous *wadi*, broken by steep hills and bounded by a landscape that can fairly be called mountainous. The horizon was a rigid tableland bitten sharply into segments and all of it flushed with rose and purple. Our course flowed in and out amongst the foothills, deviously and laboriously reconnoitred up the major slopes and down hill-sides that gave anxious thought to the drivers and their commanders. The ground was now hesitant, rock-strewn and treacherous upon vehicle springs, now soft and sandy or newly ploughed, where speed and determined driving alone forced the wheels through. Sometimes the guns and tractors were heeling over like ships in a storm, and the gunners perched upon them clung precariously, sustained (I am prepared to believe) as much by the majesty of the scene and by the sense of adventure and uncertainty that attended the whole episode, as by the odd bits of ironmongery within their grasp. The guns and tractors crossed country that day which I at least, without this stimulus, would have regarded as untraversable by them.

After descending a particularly broken and difficult ravine, we debouched upon a small grassy plain dominated by the ochre-coloured wreck of a Roman pele-tower upon which the Moors had left their later mark. There we lit our fires and fed. As always, the halt was the signal for the sudden and magical appearance of Arabs from the empty landscape—the hidden cultivators of the little patches of soft ground in the *wadis*, the obscure keepers of the flocks of goats that thenceforth appeared here and there amongst the hills. Our empty petrol tins and spare cigarettes found new owners, and we resumed our journey. The country became if possible rougher, and the bottoms of the *wadis* were now steep-sided fosses which often demanded wide detours and anxious crossings. More ruined towers stood out upon the hills, rising naturally from the rocky summits, and to them were now added buildings of other sorts: the remains of little Roman temples or tombs, each some forty feet square, sometimes with broken columns standing amongst the debris, and the vestiges of Roman farms, with the gaunt side-stones of their vanished olive-presses. These little buildings crowned the dome-like hills of the wild landscape in impressive numbers: on one occasion there were no fewer than six of them simultaneously within view.

At length the vestige of a path—a tenuous track amongst the tiny tented villages of which we now caught fleeting glimpses here and there—guided or sometimes misguided our advance; and at length in a V-shaped gap between two hills flashed for a moment the white buildings and dark trees of another land. Our compass-course had served us truly, and at the due instant the Italian colony of Breviglieri shone upon the scene. We were all of us, I think, suddenly sensible of a new interest, almost a new hope, as the disciplined handiwork of man was shown to us momentarily in that rugged framework.

We approached the long and straggling colony along a re-entrant slope which defiladed us, by a few yards of rising ground on our right flank, from all but the most distant buildings. In front of us the foreground, beyond which the hills fell sharply to the houses and the trees, was bounded by the ruins of yet another Roman tomb. The ground about was a carpet of flowers, through which a half-finished military trench cut its way. I halted the convoy. Below us, a few hundred yards distant, lorries were clattering noisily, but with a noise which was not quite of our own kind. On our left two Arabs were approaching us, and I sent for them. 'Inglesi?' we asked them, pointing towards the village. No, no, by no means Inglesi; only Italiani—many Italian troops. With one of my subalterns I crawled up the slope on our right and looked into the valley. Some five hundred yards below us, amidst tillage, were three of the small white cottages which the Italian Imperial Government had built for its lesser farming; Italian soldiers were wandering in and out of them, and a machine-gun stood upon a roof. Beyond them were larger farms, more soldiers. Between ran the highroad; motor-cycles and lorries, some Italian, some apparently German, were hurrying intermittently along it, whilst further up the opposite slope four empty lorries stood upon a farm track. There was no doubt as to the correctness of our Arab informants. To prevent evil communications, we forthwith impounded them.

The situation demanded an immediate plan. We had come for the fun of it, and here was material in abundance. It would have been easy to man-handle the three guns to a hull-down position on the crest and to have blown some of the lorries to pieces; on the other hand the soldiery could readily have found refuge from our two-pounder shells, the occupied houses up and down the valley could have brought us under immediate cross-fire, and with our un-wieldy lorries we could not have escaped attack from tracked or even wheeled vehicles at speed. Without escort, direct attack was suicide, and the only justification of this somewhat irregular expedition would lie in the avoidance of avoidable disaster.

Accordingly I decided instead to withdraw the guns a short distance to some defensible position, and to organize a commando-raid upon the village later that night.

Slowly the convoy turned upon its tracks. The noise of its coming and going had merged in the traffic of the road below, and it was furthermore clear that no hostile approach was suspected by the enemy from the direction of the almost impassable hinterland over which we had travelled. We rumbled away unnoticed, or at least unrecognized. If, instead of three Bofors guns, we had had two companies of lorried infantry, we could, then or after dark, have taken the whole garrison with ease. As it was, we withdrew some two miles and formed a close leaguer or 'box' in the ruins of one of the hill-top shrines. On another hill-top four hundred yards to a flank I placed a Bren-gun with three men; and the whole of our little force commanded a small but difficult *wadi* which we had placed between ourselves and the enemy to impede a rushed attack. The position was a strong one, and every man was confident of our strength.

I then called for volunteers, three from each sub-section, to form a commando for the raid after dark, and nominated the junior subaltern and the senior sergeant of the party. It was now about 18.00 hours. We had a cold supper, and I named 20.00 hours as the time of starting. At 19.30 hours I reviewed my force, gave it words of advice and a tot of rum, issued sign and countersign, and, punctually at 20.00 hours we set forth in two small columns, thirty yards apart and each man ten yards behind the man in front. Our objective was a house where we had observed soldiers on the nearer side of the colony.

A difficulty which I had in fact anticipated now made itself manifest. There were a number of small tented villages hereabouts, each armed with countless dogs of uncanny susceptibility. My untrained commando was shod in ammunition boots which were not designed for stealth, and the night air soon re-echoed to the barkings, wheezings, whinings, rumblings of countless mongrels. We pursued a circuitous course to avoid approaching the tents too nearly, navigating by the stars and an approximate compass-bearing, and led on by the noise of traffic in and about our destination. Finally, we turned northwards at right-angles to our previous course, at a point from which it was estimated we should reach the fringe of the settlement. As the event proved, in the absence of opportunity for reconnaissance we had turned four hundred yards too soon and, when we reached the road, were several hundred yards from the settlement. The latter was, moreover, hidden from us at this point by the sharp and broken hill-side; only here and there in the distance could a white building be discerned in the moonlight in gaps of the hills. We made our way down to the road, intending to follow its course in a deep *wadi* that ran alongside it.

As we emerged upon the road, a car bore down upon us from the direction of Marconi. We deployed with commendable speed, two men beside the road, others on the slope of the *wadi*. My subaltern Plunkett and I with a gunner stood on the road and, as the car approached at speed, vigorously called upon it to stop. Instead of obeying, the car accelerated and one of the occupants fired through the glass. The car was in turn immediately riddled with our bullets and brought to a standstill about forty yards up the road. The officer, an Italian air-force major, was dead on the back seat and the driver mortally wounded. We pulled the driver out of the car, tied a shell-dressing round him, and left him visibly beside the road.

By this time, overladen amateurs that we were, we were beginning to feel the effects of our unaccustomed tramping across the hills. We made our way southwards up the steep hill-side and rested awhile. But the alarm had been given. Lights were flashing here and there in Breviglieri, and shortly afterwards vehicles began to stream down the road towards the scene. Exhaustion and inadequate numbers prevented further action on our part, and we laboriously climbed back across the hills to our guns. Eventually at 23.40 hours the blessed challenge 'TRIPOLI' was wafted to our ears, and with the countersign 'MONTY' we entered our leaguer. The shooting had been heard by the guns, and the results anxiously awaited. . . . And so to bed.

Shortly afterwards, and for some considerable time, an enemy plane flew round about us at a low level in the moonlight, but we were not otherwise molested.

* * *

The following morning at first light and before sunrise, when the valleys were rivers of white mist, Plunkett and I went down to the fringe of the colony to observe. Already as we moved forward we heard the noise of departing lorries and motor-cycles, and when we reached our observation post a more peaceful scene met our eye. Most of the soldiery had departed, though a few still moved about amongst the adjacent cottages. Farm carts at several of the farms were being piled high with household goods. A cart led by a soldier and followed by a man with a bicycle, a woman and three children, was coming down the road. For an hour or more we watched such scenes as these.

Later I got into wireless communication with my main H.Q.,

forty miles away at Zliten. Breviglieri and Marconi, I was informed, were still held in force by the enemy. Our eyes, however, had told us a somewhat different story, and late in the afternoon our Arab friends—-we were now on excellent terms with the local villagers— told us in broken Italian that the Italians had 'gone away in their machines.' Further reconnaissance confirmed the report; accordingly, at eight o'clock next morning, again in swathes of sharply-defined white mist, we set out for the village, my scout-car plus a Bren-gunner at the head, and the three guns very ready for action. Our ghostly arrival, thirty miles or more ahead of the Eighth Army, took the inhabitants by surprise. They flocked to their doors as we passed, one or two of the women in tears, but most of the folk gravely saluting. Here and there a uniformed policeman stood amongst them, and a young fellow with a rifle over his shoulder cycled out of the mist upon us and collapsed with astonishment. Peace reigned, and in due course we turned from the road and resumed our 309 degrees along a track marked (without excessive confidence) upon the map. Penetrating through farms and farm-lands, we eventually re-emerged in the wilder Arab country and approached the great escarpment below which lay the plain of Tripoli. Here our troubles began.

Reconnaissance failed to reveal any egress down the escarpment. *Wadis* were broken or inaccessible, the mountain-sides precipitous. We breakfasted in the warming sun—breakfasted royally, for the Arab villagers brought us an abundance of eggs. Meanwhile, on the map I chose a parallel path some six miles further west, and decided to go back to Breviglieri for this second venture.

We had returned to within a mile of the colony when the hill-top in front of us was suddenly lined with excitedly bobbing heads and waving arms. The Arab population—some fifty persons of all ages and sizes—had turned out from the fringes of the town to warn us. 'Germani, Italiani' were back again in Breviglieri. They had just come in, many of them. Our experience of the local Arab had given us a high opinion of his veracity and accuracy, and we accepted the information. In other words, we were between the enemy and an impassable escarpment.

Accordingly, I refrained from proceeding further to the settle-ment (from which a single machine-gun could have picked us off) and, instead, turned westwards across country, parallel with the main road. In this fashion we in fact struck the alternative track more quickly than we should otherwise have done, so the enemy at least saved us a little mileage.

On the new track we again turned northwards towards the escarpment. For some miles, our path served us well. Then, however, my scout came back with different news. The path had become a mere goat-track, clinging precariously to the precipitous sides of the cliff.

I placed the guns in a defensive 'box,' and, as in all such crises, ordered a 'brew-up,' and went forward. On the summit of the last rise I looked down for the first time upon distant Tripoli, feeling much as the crusaders must have felt on sighting Jerusalem the Golden. Smoke was rising above the town and, further east, a black sooty column stood above the landing-ground of Castel Verde. Beneath my feet lay ample confirmation of my path-finder's gloomy report. The sheer sides of the involuted mountain barrier were rendered further untraversable by intermittent ledges of vertical rock-face.

Over four hours' hard scouting produced no answer to this problem. About 16.00 hours we gave up the search, footsore and a little tired, and set our course again westwards towards the hills above Tarhuna with the intention of following on the morrow the road Tarhuna–Tripoli to the foot of the escarpment and then taking once more to the desert for the last lap.

Our path that evening led us towards an unbelievably beautiful sunset, through fields and orange-groves, past the high upstanding Roman mausoleum at Gasr Doga and past a solemnly-gay Arab wedding in full blast. That night we slept amongst olive-trees above Tarhuna, to the noise of the barrage which heralded the taking of the pass.

Next day, to give time for the tolerable clearance of the pass after the night-attack, we put in a morning's vehicle maintenance, and then set off at 12.30 hours for the road. There we inserted ourselves into the incipient traffic-stream and, with it, flowed down the escarpment, by-passing mine-craters and minefields on which the sappers were hard at work. Towards evening we turned eastwards off the road at the foot of the hills and, in the moonlight, bore again northwards towards Tripoli along a rough and sandy track.

We had been informed that the 11th Hussars were already in Tripoli, but six or seven miles along our route our scout contacted an armoured-car patrol of that regiment which had been watching two German armoured-cars and four enemy guns in a *wadi* some three miles further on. We accordingly reversed for a mile to prevent rush-tactics on the part of the enemy and went into a box-leaguer, once more with double sentries and a Bren-gun post on a commanding flank. During the night the armoured-car patrol retired past us with a view to rejoining its squadron on the main road and advancing upon the objective. There was now no one directly between ourselves and the enemy, but the night was peaceful, save for the glare of fires in the direction of Tripoli.

Shortly before dawn on the following day, 23rd January, I sent Plunkett to the main road for tidings. He returned with the information that Castel Benito appeared to be in our hands and that, in the absence of news, it was assumed that the way was reasonably clear to Tripoli. Accordingly with our scout well in advance, we set off once more northwards across the sand. For ten miles all went well; then suddenly we found ourselves embedded in a hopeless sand-sea, and, having struggled on inch by inch for a time, I went forward to prospect.

There was only one course open to us if we were to be in the van of the Rush to Tripoli: to join the main road without more ado and to follow it northwards to our destination. Just before midday we struck the road, our goal the harbour of Tripoli. At 12.45 hours we entered the city, and at 13.00 hours the guns were in action on the quays—the first A.A. guns in Tripoli. We surveyed the wreck-filled harbour and ate a contented meal.

(IV) ANCIENT MONUMENTS IN NORTH AFRICA, 1943

'When the British Forces advanced into Libya in the autumn of 1942 immediate steps were taken for the preservation of any archaeological monuments which might come into our possession during the course of occupation.' Such were the opening words of a circumstantial written answer given in the autumn of 1943 by the

Secretary of State for War to an inquiry in the House of Commons as to measures taken for the preservation of ancient monuments in Cyrenaica and Tripolitania. In those righteous words, and others which accompanied them, the Secretary of State had unhappily been misinformed: not to put too fine a point on it, his office had been guilty of communicating an impudent lie. At a distance of a dozen years, the truth of the matter can be told with detachment, and is perhaps worth recording if only as a characteristic exemplification of British improvidence and improvisation. The contemporary documents from which the story is recounted lie before me as I write.

The facts are these. Greek, Punic and Roman enterprise had strung the congenial Libyan coastline with a series of flourishing commercial cities, whilst in the hinterland farms, tombs and churches of Roman Imperial and Byzantine date almost humanized a present wilderness of rock and steppe. At certain of these sites, particularly at Cyrene, Lepcis Magna and Sabratha, the Italians had cleared and partially restored considerable and imposing groups of buildings. The motives behind this work were mixed, as was its technical proficiency. In part they sprang from the established Italian tradition of spectacular if superficial research; in no small measure they were political, whether the intent were to advertise the splendour that had been Rome's and was now reincarnated in Fascist Italy, or whether to lure tourist traffic and advertise Fascist colonization. Whatever the motive at any given site and moment, the work had been elaborately organized and lavishly financed. And now all these resurrected splendours were the playthings of roving armies little less alien and indifferent than the Asturians and Vandals in whose footsteps they trod.

To do it justice, the Afrika Korps had behaved itself commendably well amidst the recurrent temptation to destroy. I can recall no instance in Libya of major damage attributable to German wantonness. (Later, in Italy, a different verdict could be given.) The British Army, with the breath of freedom in its nostrils, was less inhibited. Not for nothing was the admirably flamboyant Highland Division ('HD') known to its envious friends as the Highway Decorators. Not for nothing had the battle-worn apostles of a common weal come from the antipodes to undo Italian imperialism, its past, its present and its future. The colonnades of Lepcis and its underclad statuary were fair game.

Now let me make it clear that, in spite of the subsequent assertion in the House of Commons quoted above, at the time of our advance into Cyrenaica and Tripolitania in 1942–43 no steps of any kind had been taken by our military authorities to safeguard museums, records, works of art, 'monuments,' whether during the active process of occupation or during the subsequent military administration. The idea had presumably not been put to them, and in their busy preoccupation with other things there was little likelihood of its spontaneous emergence. Certainly no blame for the omission can be attached to the Eighth Army. Although a professing archaeologist, I had not myself envisaged the problem in any clear fashion.

It was on the night of 19 January 1943, on the summit of a stony monticule behind Breviglieri, that the need first thrust itself starkly on my consciousness. As I have narrated elsewhere, we had that evening boxed our guns in the ruins of a tiny Roman building, from which many other similar vestiges had been visible on adjacent hill-tops in the dusk; and I reflected that down on the coastal plain lay the great Roman cities which must now or shortly be battlefields in the main advance and thereafter easy meat for any dog that came along. . . .

In Tripoli I went straight to the Brigadier Royal Artillery at Eighth Army headquarters. He listened with a ready understanding which I am glad here and now to record. During the lull in the battle whilst Tripoli was being stocked for the next phase, I might take a few days off and see what action, if any, could be taken. With Major J. B. Ward Perkins, who had recently rejoined me from hospital in Alexandria, I set off on a lightning reconnaissance.

There were three primary objectives: the Three Cities which gave Tripolitania its name. Of these, the modern Tripoli (ancient Oea) is dominated by its medieval and later *castello*, in which were an archaeological museum and a central depot of archaeological records. It was already swarming with navy and army, of whom it is painful to record that the latter were the grosser and more persistent offenders. Inevitably, the archaeological workshop had been forced and, almost as inevitably, cameras had been abstracted and the records dispersed. With highly exaggerated authority we harassed the senior officers on the spot, and a somewhat precarious security was established. Further along the sea-front, the Fascist Library, which I had in fact glanced into on the morning of our entry into Tripoli and had found to be of considerable value, was cleared and stacked under an intelligent welfare officer with Italian aid. And then we hurried eastwards to the spectacular remains of the second of the Three Cities, Lepcis Magna, sixty miles along the coast. Through and by this city the right wing of the Eighth Army had fought its way to Tripoli.

Since the war the British School at Rome, under Mr. J. B. Ward Perkins who happily became its director in 1946, has carried out brilliant research work at Lepcis, and the great Romano-Punic city, birthplace of a Roman emperor who was fated to die at York, is now familiar in many of its details to all who are concerned with classical antiquity or indeed with the general history of civilization. On that day in January 1943, only partially aware of the potentiality of the site, we nevertheless approached it with a combined sense of anticipation and anxiety. The scene, as we found it, more than justified both emotions. Between the roadside grove and the sea with its Roman harbour, great stretches of the city had been cleared and re-erected by the Italians, and the most casual glance indicated the astonishing value alike of its architecture and its sculpture. Of more immediate concern to us was the fact that the small roadside museum had been ransacked and the epigraphy on the monuments which fringed it brought lightheartedly up to date. Through the ruins swarmed the momentarily idle troops of a famous division, with Satan in active attendance. The Royal Air Force was hunting for a spot amongst the debris for the insertion of a formidable radar-station. To complete the picture, a divisional commander, sought out by Ward Perkins, turned upon his heel with the remark: 'What would it matter if the whole of these blank ruins were pushed into the sea?'

Our brief initial visit to Lepcis was, in short, not without incident; but, always wielding an authority which it would have been very difficult locally either to substantiate or to dispute, we bluffed our way through a number of fairly effective measures. Large OUT OF BOUNDS notices were placed at strategic spots and the vague attention of the military police directed to them. A few groups of the soldiery were summarily assembled, and potted lectures of a propaganda character given to them amongst the ruins. The Royal Air Force, as a body of men of notorious culture and education, was invited to take a high-brow interest in the place and (incidentally) to move its radar to a less crucial locale. And we discovered shortly that the gallant Eighth Army, though destructive enough in all conscience, was not our only foe, for the local Arabs made an organized raid upon a wall-up store in the reconstructed Roman theatre and visibly recorded their displeasure at finding nothing more negotiable than books and archaeological photographs. On a subsequent visit the helpful town-major of the neighbouring townlet of Homs, Major Wisdom, supplied an enthusiastic Sudanese sentry who was placed outside the museum, thus rendering approach a chancy matter to all concerned.

The third of the Three Cities, Sabratha, forty miles west of Tripoli, was not yet in our hands. We employed the brief interim in associating ourselves more or less officially with the chief political officer in his headquarters at Tripoli, and there we found in Lieutenant-Colonel Blackley a staunch friend and colleague. Henceforth we were armed with something more substantial than the supposititious status under which, a few days previously, we had started our crusade. How far if at all the remote and ultimate head of the Civil Affairs Branch, Major-General R. R. Hone, was a party to our activities at this time I cannot say, but my slight contact with him at a later stage in Cairo made it clear that he would readily have taken our part and may in fact have done so.

Meanwhile, within the week the Army was once more on the move and I had to return to my regiment. Before returning I drew up and presented a sharp and detailed report on the archaeological situation, as a result of which, by some special arrangement which I marvel to look back upon, Ward Perkins was attached for a month to the political officer to continue our salvage-work, with my long-range collaboration. The range shortened for a moment as Sabratha fell. On a bright sunlit morning, in the wake of the forward troops Ward Perkins and I drove our jeep gingerly through the modern entrance into the excavated Roman town, avoiding the mine-craters which bestrewed the approach. In front of us a white flag drooped from a long pole projecting from the window of a building which we subsequently found to be the museum. Other low buildings were grouped under the palms, but not a living thing was to be seen. We dismounted and advanced cautiously with a weather eye upon the suspect ground. Suddenly, at first with hesitation and then almost tumultuously, Italian civilians with their womenfolk were about us with ingratiating smiles and a crescendo of talk. Their leader, a little man whom we afterwards knew as Dr. Gennaro Pesce, Chief Inspector of Antiquities, was gradually isolated, and negotiation began.

My Italian is negligible and Ward Perkins was then less proficient in the language than he is today. But with the aid of borrowed phraseology the situation was quickly clarified. Here, at the western end of Libya, had accumulated the whole of the Italian archaeological personnel of the two provinces. From as far afield as Cyrene and Ptolemaide, from Lepcis and Tripoli, they had been swept westwards with the retreating Axis forces, and now here they were, forty-six men and a number of women, ponded back on the borders of Tunisia. Their relief on being liberated from their German allies was manifest and genuine. With an immediate Latin sense of the appropriate, the womenfolk withdrew and, with such poor scraps of food as they could muster, began to prepare a luncheon of welcome on long trestle-tables under the trees.

Ward Perkins and I summoned Pesce gravely into an office and closed the door. How far was the place mined? Pesce would immediately show us exactly where the mines were. Who were all those folk outside? Pesce would immediately provide a complete list of them, showing where each was normally employed. Were the contents of the museum intact? Pesce would immediately show us the olive-grove in which all the principal sculpture had been buried—without the knowledge, he was careful to add, of the Tedeschi (Germans). While the lists were forthcoming, we drew up a series of regulations which Ward Perkins put into approximate Italian. The pencilled pages of my notebook read as follows:

LEPCIS MAGNA, SABRATHA, TRIPOLI
Regulations for the safeguarding of antiquities.

1. The senior Italian official at each place will be responsible to the Superintendent of Monuments and Excavations, and

through him to the British authorities, for safeguarding excavations, workshops and stores.

2. At LEPCIS MAGNA every day, throughout the hours of daylight, 3 Arab custodians shall be on duty in various parts of the excavations under the direction of an Italian supervisor. At no time during daylight shall the number of custodians be less than 3, and at no time shall the Italian supervisor absent himself from the excavations, unless properly relieved.

3. At Sabratha similar arrangements will be made so far as personnel is available.

4. At each of the 3 places the senior official will prepare in a notebook a weekly report of work done and of matters requiring action. This report will always be available for inspection by the Superintendent of Monuments and Excavations or by the British authorities.

5. Pending the appointment of British police to assist in safeguarding the sites and collections, all difficulties will be reported immediately by the senior Italian official to the nearest British official.

(Signed)   R. E. M. Wheeler,
Lt.-Col.

2 Feb. 43   for D.C.P.O. TRIPOLITANIA.

With the Italian version of these *ad hoc* regulations in hand, we sallied forth. Pesce summoned the forty-six Italians and they stood before us in an uneasy but attentive line whilst Pesce, flanked by Ward Perkins and myself, informed them that, as soon as facilities could be made available, they would be carted back to their normal stations, and that the following regulations would be observed. He read the document down to the concluding date; and then he put it behind him and leaned forward, the whole five feet of him, raised and shook a minatory finger, and added a sentence of his own with a look of extreme ferocity. I promptly called him to me and asked him what the blazes he had added to my instructions. Ah, he said, he had wanted to make quite certain that the colonel's orders would be strictly obeyed, so he had added 'And the colonel says that if any one of you disobeys these orders in the slightest particular, you will be sent IMMEDIATELY to an Internment Camp—

and you all know what a British Internment Camp is like!' Such was the force of careful indoctrination! However, it worked; thenceforward we had no trouble whatsoever with the Italian staff, and the luncheon that followed was the preface to a friendly relationship which has lasted to the present day.

Thereafter, I passed on into Tunisia and to the command of a brigade, leaving Ward Perkins to the strenuous task of rehabilitating the Italian archaeological department and, through it, of ensuring some measure of archaeological maintenance and protection both in Tripolitania and in Cyrenaica. With limited time and means he wrought wonders. The rare combination of a practical scholar and a combatant soldier qualified him alike to appreciate the technical problem and to deal with uniform in its own idiom. When, a few weeks later, he returned to command our old regiment in the closing phase of the Tunisian campaign, he left behind him along the coast an Italian staff once more busy upon its proper vocation and a British administration sympathetically disposed.

I would emphasize again that all this happened in the opening months of 1943. The 'Monuments, Fine Arts and Archives Branch,' which, fortified by the powerful blessing of the Allied Commander-in-Chief, subsequently accompanied the Allied invasion of western Europe, was not yet in being. From Tunis, indeed, Ward Perkins returned again to his work of salvage, but the absence of any clear direction in the matter from higher authority was still ominous and discouraging. Soon after the end of the African campaign my brigade was withdrawn to Tripoli for special training, and there, meditating upon the forthcoming invasion of Sicily (a top secret to which I happened to be a party), the archaeologist within me was filled with anxiety. In June I took up my pen and wrote to the titular head of all archaeology, the President of the Society of Antiquaries of London. After outlining our makeshift efforts in North Africa, I pleaded urgently for action.

'There are many difficulties,' I wrote, 'but it is fair to say that a great deal has been done by this initial work of salvage and protection. The Civil Affairs Branch under Major-General R. R. Hone has been very sympathetic to our efforts, and we have arranged that for a period of three months Ward Perkins shall be seconded from combatant duties to look after the archaeological remains, etc., of

Tripolitania and Cyrenaica. With no staff, without even a policeman, the task is wellnigh impossible, but I have no doubt that the impossible will be done. . . .

'All this business has brought out a vital need for a small but properly-thought-out organization for the preservation of works of art and antiquity in newly occupied European territories. This organization should be a part of the Occupied Enemy Territory Administration. It should, I suggest, be based upon geographical areas, to each of which, irrespective of the priority of military operations, a qualified archaeological official should be earmarked forthwith under OETA. This official should enter the new territory with the foremost troops, and, working with the provost authorities, should, on a prepared scheme, institute *immediately* the necessary preservative measures. Subsequently, he should be responsible for reorganizing and tightening up the appropriate local administrations under the jurisdiction of OETA.

'I cannot of course indicate the military order of priority in respect of Europe. Nevertheless, a glance at the map is sufficient to indicate certain zones as particularly urgent. It is immediately necessary, therefore,

    (i) to divide potentially occupied Europe into its appropriate cultural zones;

   (ii) to earmark an appropriate and experienced archaeologist for each zone;

  (iii) to get him incorporated in the fabric of OETA; and, above all,

  (iv) to get this laid on *from the highest level* through the War Office.

'There you have it. What about it? I flew up to Cairo and talked to Harlech about it (he was on his way through from South Africa to London) and I also pulled other strings. But Grigg, or even the P.M., should be got hold of. The matter is URGENT.'

That visit to Cairo at the beginning of June had been a desperate effort to secure by direct action some provision for the safeguarding of the 'monuments' of Sicily in the impending invasion. I flew the 1100 miles from Tripoli and went straight to General Hone at the Civil Affairs Branch. He was all sympathy and understanding but was himself on the point of transfer and unable therefore to act. 'Go and see George about it,' he said.

Now 'George' was the name of the secret headquarters where General Montgomery and his staff were planning the Sicilian operation. The building lay, if I remember rightly, somewhere off the Sharia Imad ed-Din, on the way to Old Cairo, and preserved its anonymity with the aid of two barbed-wire fences and a posse of white-spatted military policemen. My red hat carried me through the door and, after much inquiry, I was directed to a basement-cell occupied by a lieutenant-colonel and a wing-commander. In the former it was not difficult to recognize Lord Gerald Wellesley, and my spirits rose. Here at last one could talk without preamble, and it did not take us long to reach the question, 'What, if anything, is being done?' No one knew, but a wireless inquiry would be put through forthwith to Allied Headquarters at Algiers. Whilst this was being attended to, we discussed forthcoming events. Lord Gerald was himself commander-designate of an area in Sicily and would of course do everything within his power, though he regretted that his memories of Sicily were not more recent and more detailed. 'Even a Baedeker would help'; but it was scarcely the moment for a British officer to buy a Baedeker's *Sicily* in a Cairene bookshop!

Nevertheless, 'Baedeker' suggested a train of thought. The Cairo papers had that morning announced the arrival of Lord Harlech, then High Commissioner for South Africa, en route for a conference in London. I hurried from 'George,' found Lord Harlech on the telephone, and met him shortly afterwards on the terrace of Shepheard's. There we discussed the situation, and he undertook incidentally to let Lord Gerald Wellesley have the missing Baedeker from London.

From Shepheard's, since it was still too early to expect a reply from Algiers, I made my way for tea and talk to the rambling tenement-building on the top of which Archie Creswell lived, somewhere near the Abdin Palace. Professor K. A. C. Creswell, then Professor of Muslim Art and Architecture in the Fouad University, was and is amongst the most treasured of my friends. Not the least of his titles to fame is his monumental work on Muslim architecture, but to his familiars an abundant and tireless scholarship

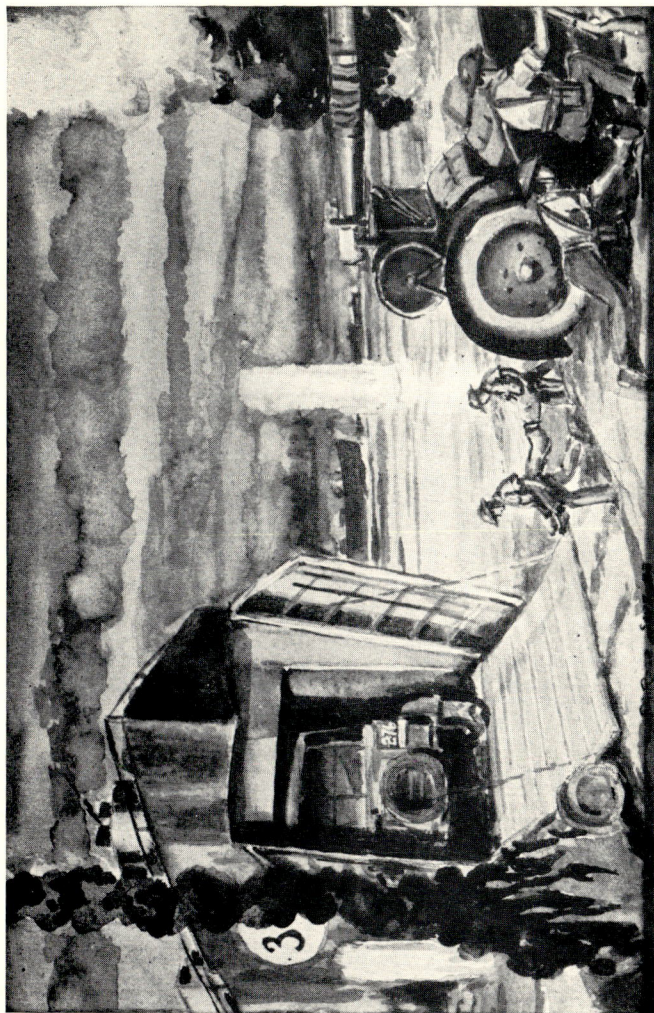

[From a sketch by P. G. Rose

THE LANDING OF THE 12TH A.A. BRIGADE ON THE BEACHES OF SALERNO, SEPTEMBER 9TH, 1943

THE MUD-BRICK FORTIFICATIONS OF PREHISTORIC HARAPPA, PUNJAB, BEFORE AND DURING EXCAVATION, 1946

is merely one of his virtues. For something like thirty-five years his small, neat frame, with a collar always immaculately starched whatever the temperature, has stalked through the streets of Cairo with a benevolence that is on occasion a source of embarrassment and even peril to an innocent companion. Evangelical humanitarianism is, be it remarked, subject to misunderstanding in the East; it is a manifest shock to the Cairene carter to find that the insistent and savage belabouring of his quadruped can be regarded as other than a routine mode of progression entirely acceptable to Allah. The following is a typical convergence of events: (i) Arab carter thrashes hopelessly overloaded donkey; (ii) Creswell leans over the side of his open car and thrashes Arab carter; (iii) crowd assembles and blocks the narrow street; (iv) Creswell spots a distant and reluctant policeman, leaps from his car, thrashes his way through the crowd, and collars the reluctant policeman when on the point of escaping; (v) Creswell compels reluctant policeman to march the offending carter in front of him to the nearest police-station; (vi) crowd makes away with cart and donkey. To his friends it has long been apparent that Creswell bears a charmed life. For his prowess is not limited to the reform of donkeymen. Whether by similar or parallel methods, he has so impressed the Cairo municipality that quite impossible things have been done to the civic architecture. When I first knew the imposing medieval walls and gates of Cairo, they were encumbered and largely concealed by a welter of slums and shacks, at one point by a Muslim cemetery. Today, great stretches of these walls stand revealed in the north-eastern quarter of the city and are one of the most dramatic sights of Egypt. The work of clearance is a tribute to the enlightenment of the municipality, but the prime source of light is Creswell and none other. No greater testimony to his powers of radiation could be found than in the removal of that most inviolable of obstructions, a Muslim cemetery.

Even Creswell, however, has had his moments of adversity. On one occasion we were traversing the fortifications of Saladin in the quarter which I have mentioned, and were persecuted by a small imp who whined and begged at our heels with a more-than-usually maddening persistency. Rebuke failed, and at length Creswell turned upon the juvenile delinquent and gave him a sharp crack

F

with his stick. The little wretch ran off yelping and peace descended upon the scene. But only for a brief span. We were perched precariously, I remember, upon a sort of Mappin Terrace when suddenly out of the blue a whirlwind barrage of brickbats descended upon us. The young monster had sent round the fiery crescent, and there he stood above us with a host of evil allies, heaps of ammunition piled in their cupped *gallabiyehs* and murder in their fly-bitten eyes. The situation was one of instant and deadly peril. Passchendaele and Salerno were picnics in comparison, and Mons was an advance compared with our retreat. The highly trained missile-throwing street-Arab of Cairo is no proper opponent for two defenceless pedestrians, and as we moved away I found it politic to grasp Creswell's right arm firmly, happy enough to leave our dignity with Saladin's successors. . . .

But before this digression I was climbing the long stairs of Creswell's tenement, stepping over recumbent forms until I at length reached his hospitable eyrie. He opened the door with his usual welcome ('Take off your jacket if you're not wearing braces'), and disappeared into his kitchen to boil the kettle. On a sudden inspiration I darted round his bookshelves. There in a corner was Baedeker's *South Italy and Sicily*. Lord Harlech's mission was null and void. In an instant the little red volume was in my pocket, and I turned to greet my host with his tea-tray. . . .

Back in 'George,' a reply had just come through from Algiers. It appeared that two Americans, whose names meant nothing to us, were, somewhat vaguely as it seemed, going to keep an eye upon the churches, temples and collections of Sicily. We glanced sceptically at one another, admitting however that the Americans were at any rate half a move ahead of us. My own comment was to turn to Lord Gerald and hand him the purloined guide-book. I left him with a lively mental picture of his lordship descending upon the shell-stricken beaches of Sicily, Baedeker in hand. . . .

In October that year I was flying back from Naples to Algiers for a post-mortem on Salerno. We refuelled at Catania, and there Lord Gerald came aboard. He had recently succeeded his nephew who had been killed at Salerno, and as Duke of Wellington was returning to England to assume his new responsibilities. On the plane he restored the Baedeker to me, now with battle-honours to its credit. . . .

Eight years later, Creswell was my guest at a dining-club in London, and after dinner I formally handed the stolen Baedeker back to him. He received it with no little surprise; he had not missed it from his shelves.

(v) OPERATION AVALANCHE

Ten years afterwards. I have this morning been turning over my orders, reports, diary, technical analyses, and emergent memories of the most absorbing military operation within my immediate experience: the opposed landing on the Salerno beaches in September 1943, Operation Avalanche. The misery of Passchendaele, the intermittent strain and triumphant reaction of the two battles of El Alamein, linger vividly in the mind; but in these and other episodes the measure of one's participation was regimented and rationed at every turn. The air of Salerno was of a freer sort. In that minutely narrow strip of Italy which for days divided our crowded seaway from a bitter enemy, I walked with an unwonted sense of liberty and exhilaration. Surprise and accident thronged upon us from hour to hour, a constant stimulus; on all sides trained men responded with sureness to sudden orders of unaccustomed kinds. And through it all was a present sense of intimacy, an intimacy normal indeed to our desert warfare of the past years but here accentuated by the narrow confines of the scene. Light guns and heavy guns were packed in side by side, the heavy guns often enough in front of the light. Cockneys, Scots, swarthy Bechuanis and Swazis, gunners, privates, brigadiers, all alike dependent upon one another, spattered by the same high explosive, the same machine-guns, brewing up the same rich tea and scraping out the same meat-can. I remember reflecting one day, when my own brigade headquarters was under mortar-fire, that there was something of a grim Saturnalia about it all.

*   *   *

As commander of the 12th Anti-Aircraft Brigade, my own function in the landing was to organize and direct the anti-aircraft protection of the British 10th Corps, which in fact bore the brunt of the operation, on the left flank of the American Fifth Army.

This task was one of special interest because we were at the extreme limit of our own fighter protection and had to rely therefore on ground defence. The lists remind me that my brigade included three regiments of heavy artillery, three of light, two detached batteries of each category, two smoke companies for the purpose of laying smoke-screens, and the necessary operational units for inter-communication and pre-warning: in all, I suppose, some 8,000 men. To these a squadron of mobile captive balloons was shortly added. I have just described all these folk as 'trained men'; and so most of them were, but I recollect exceptions. Two or three of my units, which had been stagnating on the Egyptian Delta and had been posted to me only on the eve of embarkation, had very primitive ideas of speed and mobility. I remember that during my rounds on the day after the assault I was so painfully impressed with the inadequacy of one of these newly arrived batteries that I took it straight away out of the operational rôle, turned it into a field scarcely more than a thousand yards from the enemy, and put it through three long days of intensive training under my best available instructors. To do the battery full justice, both officers and men appreciated the situation and worked like slaves; so that at the end of the third day I was able to pass them out and send them back into action, with a new and mutual confidence in their capacity. Only our lack of progress, the crowded condition of the beaches, and the consequent redundancy of troops there made this fantastic interlude feasible, but the very anomaly of the situation cemented, I think, a rather special bond between myself and the neglected unit.

Then again, one of my smoke companies consisted of Swazi dock-labourers who, until a few days previously, had been unloading ships at Tripoli. Their conversion into front-line troops might have disturbed a more pliable and adaptable mentality. As it was, with the forbearance of their commanding officer, who understood them, they had held a solemn *indaba* at Tripoli on receiving news of the impending change, and after a continuous day's and night's meditation, had gravely indicated their assent. Now here they were, a long line of them standing grimly all night beside their little smoke-cans like bronze statuary; sleep neither permitted nor sought, for a sleeping Swazi is almost impossible to restore suddenly to active consciousness. Yet, in spite of their lack

of training and their incomplete understanding, they twice came
into action with the most beneficial effect during the battle and,
incidentally, suffered their share of casualties.

But the history of those critical days is matter for other pens and
occasions. Nor need the less advertised *minutiae* of an individual
brigade-commander's progress be thrust upon the reader, although
such minor histories may sometimes claim a certain scarcity value
with the passing of time. At the most, an occasional vignette may
be permitted to the present story, drawn without much consequence
from the miscellaneous material which at this moment lies in front
of me.

*   *   *

The LST (landing-ship for tanks) No. 402, Lieutenant-
Commander Sprigge, R.N.R., lay off the African coast at Bizerta,
carrying a naval crew of 50 and 243 army personnel, with heavy anti-
aircraft guns and vehicles packed tightly into its capacious hold, and
myself as brigade commander on the bridge beside the commander.
In front of us a long stream of smaller landing-craft, laden with
infantry, passed out of the harbour line-ahead and made for the
open sea under naval escort, with the precision of a drill manœuvre.
Our engines had given trouble, and night found us still at anchor
in a blackness that was impenetrable and a silence that was almost
eerie. Then suddenly the bombers were all about us. The sky was
aflame, starred by bursting shells and tracer and criss-crossed by
searchlights, in two of which the tiny moth-like form of an attacker
swayed and darted and tumbled about the sky. Fires began to glow
from the environs of the town, and in slowly mounting streaks
across the kaleidoscope a smoke barrage added undertones to the
scene. It was a noisy and spectacular farewell to Africa.

The next day, 7 September 1943, the western coast of Sicily lay
low down in the mist to starboard, and two massive 130-ton
pontoons (to bridge the landing) wallowed in our wake. There
was a cool sun on this Sunday morning, and, in the absence of a
chaplain, the commander and I mustered all hands to the fore peak
for a short ship's service, with the usual adjunct of a Union Jack
spread precariously across a packing-case altar. For the lesson I
chose Joshua i. 6–9; and I can still hear my voice seemingly

disembodied and echoing strangely from the stark and alien steel-work and the skyward guns of the little ship as the solemn sentences followed one another into the gusty air.

'Be strong and of good courage: for unto this people shalt thou divide for an inheritance the land, which I sware unto their fathers to give them.

'Only be thou strong and very courageous, that thou mayest observe to do according to all the law. . . . Turn not from it to the right hand or to the left, that thou mayest prosper whithersoever thou goest. . . .'

The Union Jack rose in a sudden draught and subsided askew upon its box. The bare heads and blue and khaki forms in front of me stood rigid save for the slight swaying of the ship.

'. . . Have not I commanded thee? Be strong and of a good courage; be not afraid, neither be thou dismayed: for the Lord thy God is with thee whithersoever thou goest.'

The fine resonance of the Old Testament had ever the stuff of battle in it, with just that hint of the theatre which helps a man through the first impact.

* * *

Northwards we fared across the Tyrrhenian Sea, line upon line of LST's, with larger ships and cruisers between us and the invisible coast of Italy, and a busy screen of destroyers, anti-submarine trawlers and motor launches all about us. During the night there had been gunfire over Sardinia away to the west. From the bridge beside the commander, the scene was picturesque but quiet, ordered and intelligent. A signal was climbing the mast of the leading ship, and I put out my hand for the code-book. Spelling out the signal with unaccustomed eyes I wrote on the pad ITALY HAS SURREN-DERED, and turned to the commander. 'Do you see what I see?' I said to him. He took the book from me, glanced at it, and replied 'Yes, I expect so. Now what are we going to do?' I picked up the megaphone and ordered all hands aft. Army and Navy packed in below the bridge, and I told the news. There was a moment's pause, then a wild burst of cheering that was echoed from ship to ship as the word spread. The cheering died and I again put up the megaphone. 'Well, that's that. Now I am going to ask you to do a little thinking. What does Italy's surrender mean to you and me? It means just this. It means that, instead of a reception committee of a few half-hearted Italians on the beach at Salerno, we shall find a first-class German armoured corps with its back well up. We shall beat it, but tomorrow's battle will be a trifle tougher than it might have been. Each one of us . . .' They dissolved slowly into serious little discussion-groups.

*   *   *

In the gathering darkness we altered course and, leaving the commander on the bridge, I went down to his tiny cabin underneath, took off my boots and immediately fell asleep. . . . A penetrating jolt, as though the ship had struck a rock, nearly threw me from the bed and a second jolt brought me to my feet. We had been closely straddled by two bombs, and as I climbed to the bridge hell was let loose. Rocket-ships were hurling blazing salvoes at the unseen coast; monitors, cruisers and destroyers were blasting the blackness and intensifying it by their lightning flashes. The first landing-craft, including one of my light batteries, were groping shorewards. The flickering night was alive with hidden activity.

Dawn, after a sudden faint start, grew slowly amidst the mist and smoke. Detached fragments of mountain began to appear in the intermittent rifts; I remember the greedy delight with which my eyes, mountain-starved by two years on African desert, feasted momentarily upon a jagged crest of the Apennines. Now we were zigzagging towards the beaches, evading the black, sinister mines which, loosened from the sea-bed around us by our devoted minesweepers, clustered like fishes' eggs amongst the waves. And now we were under shell-fire. In front of us a landing-craft with tanks aboard slowly rolled over and sank. A destroyer coming inshore to the rescue, was likewise hit. Then the Navy closed in and gave the offending battery everything. (When I visited the spot later in the day, I found the German guns knocked to all points of the compass and their plucky crews splashed about them.) Meanwhile, another German battery, four 88-millimetres, had got the range of our craft over open sights as we moved slowly in, awaiting our turn at the beach. The captain of the next landing-ship beside us was killed by a direct hit on the bridge. Another ship beyond was struck forward and received a number of casualties. Our turn was next. The rounds came over in sharp salvoes and bracketed us with perfect precision, sending showers of spray over us as we changed course cumbrously to vary range. The troops lay flat on deck or were mildly screened in the hold. The naval commander and the brigade commander on the bridge took it in turns, salvo by salvo, to stand and watch the beach ahead, making the usual fatuous and self-conscious jokes which are appropriate to such an occasion and taking turns ceremoniously also with the single tin-hat which we shared. At length the awaited sign flashed to us from the beach; the commander signalled 'full speed ahead' and we struck the beach fairly and squarely. Sprigge, R.N.R., had brought us in to a nicety.

*   *   *

My first recollection, when we came up to breathe, is that of a raging thirst. For the moment the battle had settled down quietly, as battles do during mutual readjustment, and beside us, impinging on the shore, was a field of those luscious elongated Italian tomatoes, ripe to perfection. We ate our fill of them, and their delicious savour is with me still. Our guns, some of them, were adequately dug in along the beach. Others were pushing forward to support the infantry as medium field-guns, or as an additional anti-tank screen. In a field nearby an artillery observation 'plane was being unpacked and put together, rather like an out-size toy. Beyond, a landing-ground was partially in our hands, and a fighter-strip was being prepared. Infantry and a few tanks were moving forward, a little uncertainly. There was intermittent machine-gun fire in front, and daring low-level attacks were made from time to time by enemy fighters. One of these was brought down on the beach, and its black smoke stood out in sharp contrast to the white fountains which enemy shells were still sending up off-shore. That night the enemy filtered back towards us and reoccupied one of the beaches, but for the most part the position was held, with mounting but not disproportionate casualties.

It was a long, fidgety but interesting battle. It had one rather particularly uneasy moment on the seventh day (15th September)

I remember, when an expected infantry brigade failed to arrive from Tripoli and left our line very thin on the ground. The right flank of 10th Corps was in fact penetrated by the enemy and an ugly situation was in the making. At midnight I was called up by the corps commander and ordered to collect an emergency force of all available gunners to fill the gap as infantry. In the course of half an hour some four hundred of my artillery-men, armed with an assortment of Bren-guns, Tommy-guns and rifles, were assembled from all quarters in the vivid moonlight, formed into a hollow square for a rapid appreciation of the situation from their brigadier, and marched off in groups to the broken front line. One group, under Major Sir Basil McFarland, redoubtable ex-mayor of London-derry, came quickly into action; the gap was sealed, and next day 'Gunnerforce' was creditably relieved for its proper duties by reinforcements brought in by air and sea. The incident, trivial enough in itself, was of the kind that varies routine and, by inter-change of experience, makes an army something more than a mere aggregation of specialists.

*   *   *

But enough of these *minutiae*. They are capable of indefinite but thankless extension. Those days were full of incident; let them remain the secret memories of old age. I pass on (with some casualties as my records show) over the coastwise ridge whence we looked first upon the promised plain of Naples, past Pompeii where, in a moment's respite in the Amphitheatre Gate, I wrote to Cyril Fox a letter quoted above, to Naples itself, into which I drove on 1st October as the Germans left northwards. There memory for a moment breaks the bounds of privacy.

Leaving my cumbrous armoured-car to follow, I threaded rapidly in a jeep along the broad street beside the docks, which were clogged with the capsized hulls of Italian warships and merchant-men. There was still intermittent firing in the further outskirts of the city, but all Naples was afoot to welcome us with flowers and strange varieties of Union Jack. At one point, where the Germans had overturned a number of tramcars across the road, I slowed down to negotiate the obstacle. The crowd surged forward and a man thrust a leaflet into my hands. It had been printed, manifestly at the risk of his life, when the Germans were still in occupation, and is one of my more treasured relics. It reads thus:

Brothers,

After thirtynine months of war, pains and grieves; after twenty years of tiranny and inhumanity, after have the innocent victims of the most perverce gang at the Government; today, September 8. 1943, we can cry at full voice our joys our enthusiasm for your coming.

We can't express with words our pleasure, but only we kneel ourself to the ground to thank Good, who have permit us to see this day.

With you we have divided the sorrow of the war, with you we wish to divide the day of the big victory.

We wish to march with you, until the last days against the enemy N.1,

We will be worth of your expectation, we will be your allied of twentyfive years ago

Hurra the allied

Hurra the free Italy

The committee of antifascist
ex
fighters of the big war

There spoke the general and genuine voice of Italy. That there were also others of a different sort in the recesses of the city was equally clear from the sniping and bomb-throwing which broke regularly upon the night air for another week or two in the higher part of the town. But for the most part there was no doubt about our welcome. On this first day, I drove on straight through the city and up the hill to the Aosta Palace of Capo di Monti, which I had marked down for my brigade headquarters. As I drove into the grounds towards the massive sandstone buildings, the old Dowager Duchess of Aosta, erect as a guardsman and lightly supported by a tall ivory-topped stick, was walking back across the lawn in the rain. She had been to the burial of five neighbouring townsfolk, for whom my advance-party had just dug graves a hundred yards away, and as we entered the palace together she told me the story, to the following effect.

The Hermann Goering armoured division, she said, had been there the previous day and, shortly before it pulled out, two of its Panzer Grenadiers had been shot—their new graves were likewise on the lawn. They had probably been picked off by American snipers at the head of our advance, but the German commander accused the Italian populace, sent a squad to the nearest house by the palace gates, pulled out the first five civilians, lined them up on the lawn and shot them, leaving them for us to bury. He then said that he would show those . . . . Italians what his tanks could do. He brought a tank up to the front of the palace (the tracks were still there) and fired a round at the palace itself. It made, however, almost no impression on the thick walls, so he swung his gun round and blew the inside out of the house from which the unhappy hostages had been collected. He then moved out—and we moved in.

The old duchess was utterly charming and bravely sad. Had I seen her younger son, the admiral? He had been in command of the little ships of the Italian fleet and had written to her two or three weeks earlier to ask her whether she thought that he ought to surrender or fight on. 'I am only a woman,' she had replied, 'and I know nothing of these matters. You must write to the King and ask him.' Since then, she had heard nothing. Had he surrendered? Where was he? I could not tell her, but ten days later her son himself answered her question by walking into the palace. He and his fleet had participated in that disciplined and dignified surrender at Malta of which the rearmost units of my brigade had been admiring witnesses en route for Salerno.

The duchess took me round her palace, showed me her excellent French tapestries, her indifferent pictures (the best, including the Goyas, had gone), and her great armoury of muskets of which she was particularly proud, though the Germans had abstracted the choicest—together with her own treasured rifles, for she had been a great game-shooter in her day. Her rooms were full of the dismembered heads of her victims, and she knew the saga of each one of them. . . .

A fortnight later, during a lull whilst the Army was fanning out north of Naples, my brigade major (Dick Stratton) and I spent a dozen hours on Capri. But that, as written at the time, must be a separate chapter.

(VI) TWENTY-FOUR HOURS' LEAVE
(*October, 1943*)

The island rose and dipped as the schooner was thrust towards it by the labouring motor. The surging peak, the sudden green precipices, the scattering of little white houses, were pleasant to see again with the passing of years. Amidst so much chaos, Capri at least was little changed. Mine-sweepers were plying between the promontory of Tiberius and the mainland. An American landing-craft and a British destroyer shared the tiny harbour with a handful of smaller fry. Otherwise all was peace, and on the quay the blue-clad hotel-porter fussed forward as of old for our packs and coats. A 'special' train (fifteen lire) on the funicular hauled the pair of us up to the town past the clinging orange-trees and hill-side cottages. On the terraced threshold at the summit the decrepit taxis and the line of Rosinantes, upheld by the shafts of antique buggies, had altered not at all. The cafés in the little square were still busy with their wine-selling as of old, save that Nordic honeymooners had given place to a scattering of Yankee soldiers and British ratings. The porter hastened busily in front of us up the cavernous lane to the Hotel Morgano Tiberio.

Then war began to rear its ugly head. Across the door the notice 'Officers Only' boded no respite there from one's caste and kind. The uncarpeted hotel corridors echoed emptily to our tread. The urbane and polyglot staff survived in a spectral world of two dimensions. Rather shyly, we handed over our rations. They were received deprecatingly, and transmitted avidly to the voided kitchens. Upstairs, only a thin trickle of cold water could be enticed into the ample bath; but from the balcony opened the scented vista of a blue sea and a sleepy and eventless town which no music-hall song or songster can vulgarize.

*   *   *

In the piazza, the Duke, with the aspect of Balbo and the piercing grey eye of Augustus John, sat possessively at the little table under the awning. Beside him, the monocled Marquis nodded a halo of grey hair, and beyond sat the Russian danseuse and her little daughter. On the other flank, the Duke was supported by a picturesque blonde, who punctuated the conversation with an occasional smile of modest intelligence. A thin brandy sustained the company, but no stimulus was needed for the flow of talk. The Marquis was rallying little Thaïs on her dancing, for she too was to become a great danseuse. The blonde, in a casual undertone, reassured us that after eighteen years in gaol her father, the assassin, was strong in the cause of Italy, but a trifle weak in the digestion and too occupied to indulge in the *apéritif.* The danseuse sparkled alternatively in French, Italian, Russian and Estonian, and explained that her Thaïs was the namesake of the saint, not the sinner. The Duke burst occasionally into song, irrelevant save in the private context of his own mind, but accepted without remark as a part of the *mise en scène.* Of a sudden he issued a *pronunciamento*: there would be a party, it would be that very night, it would be held in the café round the corner, the danseuse would dance, little Thaïs would dance, there would be singing. The time would be after dinner, ten o'clock. The assembly was purposefully adjourned.

*   *   *

It was five minutes to ten. The café was still exposed in all its internal gauntness by electric light, which at 10.30 would cease. An American subaltern lurched through the door, strode up to the coy but middle-aged woman at the booking-table, leaned confidentially over her and, without the formality of removing his steel helmet, kissed her experienced cheek. She thrust away the assaulting lips, though with no great determination. The dalliance was interrupted by the arrival of the Duke and the Blonde.

The staff—the imperilled booking-lady, the boots and a weedy waiter—bustled hastily about the noble guest, who left them to their preparations. Shortly he returned to find a funereal table surrounded by chairs like tombstones in a darksome corner. 'This is not a meeting of the League of Nations,' protested the Duke. 'It is a *Party.*' A fresh table and white linen were brought forward into the full glare of the electric bulb, sofas were placed about it, champagne glasses were set upon it. Guests and bottles appropriate to champagne appeared simultaneously upon the scene. Only the danseuse and her daughter had gone astray, and search failed to reveal them. Introductions, and the party was under way.

Here it is fitting to introduce the assembly.

Dramatis personae

THE PRINCE (a redoubtable old warrior who had fought against the Senussi in 1911, the Germans in 1915, and in the Spanish Civil War. A defender of Italy and liberty, but chiefly a fighting man).

THE DUKE (seven years in gaol as an anti-Fascist: forceful, cultivated, and intelligent).

THE BLONDE (daughter of T. Z., who, eighteen years ago, made a half-baked attempt to assassinate Mussolini, and was thereafter imprisoned until the surrender of Italy. Z. is a protagonist of the party which seeks to rehabilitate the Italian Army in the cause of liberation).

THE MARQUIS (many diplomatic and other friends in London).

A GIRL.

THE CONTESSA, of the Villa ——, Capri (middle-aged but doesn't believe it, formerly wife of a count in the diplomatic service, who divorced her 'because she was anti-Fascist'; a dominating charmer with penetrating and slightly Mongolian eyes.

THE YOUTH (son of a Neapolitan poet).

MYSELF ('the General').

MAJOR DICK STRATTON (my brigade major).

A FISHERMAN FROM THE HARBOUR.

*   *   *

Small talk grew into bigger talk, and the party warmed up. A dry but sugared white wine trickled gently round the table. The diplomatic Contessa flitted from London to Pekin, touching lightly upon an uncomprehending husband, a lovely daughter far away near Venice, and her own ambition for a higher life. Also her dogs. Four of them were circulating amongst the assembled legs. 'Lie down, Wednesday, you naughty little dog. Monday, sit up and beg! . . . *There's* a good dog. I can never pass a dog in the street, General. And I always christen them by the name of the day on which I picked them up. Except for Friday . . . Friday's dog is an unlucky dog.' (Pause.) 'You know, General, I saw you this morning in the town. I looked back at you—when you looked back at me. I regret. . . . I have *never* picked up a General. It would have been a new experience!' She sighed, and paused. 'Consider, my dear Contessa,' muttered the General reflectively, 'that my name would have been Friday.'

The Prince had reached the Battle of the Piave, and the Girl was listening to him with polite inattention. The Duke waved a hand towards the shadows, and a bowing figure emerged with a fiddle. The Duke called for song, a Neapolitan song, 'One of your father's songs' (to the smirking Youth). The Fisherman stood up, the fiddler waved his bow, and a flood of melody submerged the 'Battle of Madrid.' I know not whether a Neapolitan fisherman can fish. But song is his birthright, and no professor stood between the singer and his soul. The untutored loves of the Neapolitan shone from his eyes and sheltered beneath his clasping hands. His Italian listeners were taken to his bosom, and their hearts beat with his. A sudden and surprising explosion of soprano song from the Girl, four or five bars of a rich spontaneous baritone from the Duke, the party melted into ecstasy and flowed through the midnight hours into another day. 'Come to my villa,' murmured the Contessa. 'Yes,' replied the General; 'it is now Saturday.'

*   *   *

Half a waning moon blackened the tree-shadows across the little stone-paved lane above the sea. The scene had an easy loveliness that drugged and lulled the mind. A scattering of dogs flecked the alternating shine and shadow. The trousered Contessa with her captive on her arm and, behind them, the Duke, the Marquis, the Blonde and the Youth, formed a wraith-like procession, none the more substantial for its accompanying murmur of tongues. A mile or more, and then a hundred steps climbed to the ultimate arcaded terrace. The Youth produced the latch-key, and was dismissed to light the acetylene lamp whilst the guests sat out upon the parapet and spoke dangerously of politics in undertones which merged into the night. Through the window a light flickered reluctantly. The Contessa would show the General her pictures: portraits of herself in the flight of time, mostly as the Circe which was her 'Diplomatic self' but was clearly near enough to the truth to make one question the origin of her swarming menagerie. A bottle of brandy was produced and handed, with orders, to the waiting Youth. Around the glasses the company reassembled on chairs and a broad divan, with the uncertain lamp in their midst.

*　　　*　　　*

'This is the book of my friends,' the Contessa was saying. 'These written lines are their memorials.' 'You mean their grave-stones?' 'No. Most of them were dead before they arrived. A few, on the other hand, were re-born hereabouts. One or two of them are still alive'—and she indicated a flamboyant apostrophe from an Italian admirer. As he looked, the visitor's eye caught also the ingenuous entry which followed: 'I have had a wonderful time here. R. Smith, Sqn. Ldr., R.A.F.' 'Now it is your turn, General,' said the Contessa. The company pressed embarrassingly about him as he took her pen obediently and wrote his epitaph: 'Hic multi multa scripserunt; solus ego nihil scripsi. Thus the wise Pompeiian. I, less wise, will add my love.' 'That is the best of all,' purred the Contessa, clasping the book and glancing at the General with a witchery that sent him hastily for his hat. The Duke, the Blonde, and the voluble Marquis tripped gingerly after him from shadow to shadow down the long escalade. On the receding summit, Circe waved an arm across the moon, the while with the other she leaned carelessly upon the Youth as upon a walking-stick. Anon she turned back with him towards the house, and the homing guests stepped into the lane.

*　　　*　　　*

'I want your help.' The Duke had stopped suddenly beneath an orange-tree, and confronted the General like a Hounslow highway-man. 'Z. is the destined liberator of Italy. Four times he won the Medal of Valour with the silver palm. Twice he was recommended for the golden palm, but he had the misfortune to be a Socialist. He held the rifle which would have freed Italy from the tyrant, but again misfortune dogged him. We follow Z. We will follow you. Will you lead us to General Montgomery?' For a moment the torrent ceased, and the General struggled vaguely to regain his poise. Then once more the flood engulfed him. Italy had been wrecked. Italy could be saved. Italy *must* be saved, and one thing only could rescue her. 'Could you take us to General Montgomery?' Without waiting for an answer, the Duke resumed. 'This General of ours, Pavone, of whom so much has been said, he is already discredited. He is a politician. We are not politicians, we are not revolutionaries. We are soldiers and include all parties, all worthy men, all sincere patriots. We have one purpose. Our task is to rescue and rehabilitate, under your British Command, some small part of the broken Italian Army—broken by the ineptitude of its own leaders. . . . Our broken Army is the symbol of our broken Italy. And a broken Italy is useless, dangerous, not only to itself but to the world. . . . Give us a corps, a few regiments, of our legionaries. Give us our self-respect. Send us out as guerrillas. Send us to the furthest limits of Italy. Send us beyond our frontiers, wherever the spectre of Nazism is a present or future peril. Send us to your General Montgomery and his Eighth Army.'

The little parliament melted for a moment, and quickly re-grouped in the shadows. 'These patriots—ces hommes verraient dans la personne de T. Z., grand décoré de la première guerre mondiale, député socialiste de droite au parlement pré-fasciste, auteur du premier et du plus sérieux attentat contre Mussolini en 1925—non seulement leur chef militaire mais bien aussi leur drapeau, le centre de ralliement. . . .' In English, French, Italian, the tide of eloquence streamed onward. Occasionally the Marquis took over whilst the Duke gathered new strength. The daughter of the hero-assassin stood patiently behind them; she had heard something like this before. 'We are not "Badogliani," we are not "Pavoniani," we are United Italy. . . . Tell your General Montgomery that we are ready. Ce ne sera pas la première fois non plus—comme le preuve la sanglante guerre combattue à côté de l'Angleterre par le génération qui nous a précédé—que les Italiens se seront sciemment engagés d'enthousiasme sur le chemin de l'honneur et pour la défense de la dignité humaine. . . .'

The Blonde yawned slightly and fidgeted on a tired foot. Over the sea the sky was silvering in the pre-dawn. The twin grey faces of United Italy looked up appealingly through the half-light. 'Mon Général, nous sommes ceux qui ont été persecutés par le fascisme, ceux qui ont souffert le "confino" et les poursuites de la police fasciste, qui connurent dans leurs biens et dans leurs affections le joug honteux du régime mussolinien. . . .'

* * *

The first shaft of the sun struck the shadows from the empty lane.

10. Archaeology in India

THE old Archaeological Survey of India, now the Archaeological Department of the Republican Government of India, was and probably still is the largest and most complex archaeological machine in the world. Prior to the partition of 1947 it administered, directly or indirectly, the archaeology of one and a half million square miles of Asia, much of it difficult of access. In that vast area, it dealt with the structural preservation of ancient sites and buildings ranging from a crude monolith to the Taj Mahal; it was almost the only body in India with the money and indeed the urge to carry out archaeological excavation; it was responsible for a series of museums, some in urban centres, one at least a six-hours' march through jungle from the nearest railway; it was charged with the collection of the epigraphs, Hindu and Muslim, upon which, in the deficiency of a systematic historical literature, much of the history of India must be based; and its duties included the publication of all this miscellaneous material in reports and monographs. Such was its explicit function, but implicitly its task was also to arouse in the growing Indian universities and ultimately amongst the educated public a new sense of values in matters relating to the material heritage of India. It had its hands full.

This great machine was essentially the creation of two men, Lord Curzon and Sir John Marshall, and it came into effective existence during Curzon's Viceroyalty in 1902. But already in the nineteenth century long phases of neglect and destruction had been varied by phases of inadequate though useful activity. As long ago as 1862 General (Sir) Alexander Cunningham was temporarily appointed Director of Archaeology 'to make an accurate description of such remains as most deserve notice.' By 1871 the dimensions of this mission had become more clearly appreciated, and Cunningham was made Director General of the Archaeological Survey of India with the duty of superintending 'a complete search over the whole country and a systematic record and description of all architectural and other remains that are remarkable alike for their antiquity or their beauty, or their historic interest.'[1] In fact, Cunningham confined his attentions to North India, where his personal survey-work, carried out and published between 1862 and 1885, was of an outstanding range and quality. Today a surveyor in Cunningham's boots would be expected to operate primarily by aeroplane, train and car. Save for a rare train, Cunningham had none of these advantages. He used his boots for the purpose for which they were made, with interludes of saddle and bullock-cart. In consequence he saw the countryside, not through gaps in the clouds or engine-smoke, but at close and familiar range, stopping awhile to commune and converse when the spirit moved him as it often did. His mind was full of the records of the Chinese Buddhist pilgrims, and he followed their footsteps, re-creating with argument and with something approaching intuition the course of their travels and the shrines and cities which they saw. His name ranks high in the select sodality of discoverers; there was genius in his composition.

Meanwhile, in 1874, the survey of South India was delegated to the able but uninspired Dr. James Burgess, who later, in 1885, succeeded Cunningham as Director General. After Burgess's retirement in 1889, however, the department became very largely inoperative, and it was to all intents and purposes dead when, a dozen years later, Lord Curzon, with characteristic vigour and sustained interest, revived and reshaped it in something like its present form.

Curzon's long-range appointment of John Marshall to the reconstituted office of Director General is the subject of an apocryphal story which may be no truer than many apocryphal stories. But whether the very young Marshall who, in response to a telegram, arrived in India with his bride in 1902 was or was not the Marshall actually intended for the new and responsible post, there can be no doubt that Fors Fortuna knew her business. Curzon instantly took to the shyly confident youth, full of the Greek lands in which he had

---

[1] An account of these beginnings and of subsequent developments may be found in *Revealing India's Past*, edited by Sir John Cumming (London, The India Society, 1939).

lately been a student of archaeology, and the combination of the Viceroy's whole-hearted backing with the Director General's whole-hearted enthusiasm quickly set the department upon its feet. The task which awaited it was a colossal one. With gathering experience and strength, Marshall tackled it upon a proper scale, and inspecting his work a generation later I found myself constantly marvelling at its scope. No contemporary of Marshall's known to me could have left anything like so deep an imprint upon the archaeology of a subcontinent.

Let me amplify this last statement for a moment, because I must then turn to the reverse of the medal. Outstanding amongst Marshall's achievements are the first comprehensive scheme for conserving India's superb legacy of medieval and Moghul architecture; the drafting of a basically sound Ancient Monuments Act; the building up of an epigraphical department of the highest quality; the examination for more than twenty years of a site, Taxila, famous in the protohistory of north-western India and meeting-place of East and West; and the discovery of the Indus Civilization, which he has shown us to have been one of the great civilizations of the pre-classical world. These are merely the highest peaks in a lofty mountain-range. The annual reports published by the survey during Marshall's tenure are full of lesser but still imposing heights.

What then went wrong after Marshall's retirement in 1929? Why in the 'thirties did his old department sink so rapidly into disrepute, as indeed it did? I need not here resuscitate a whole family of clanking ghosts, but, in justice to Marshall on the one hand and Woolley and myself on the other, two or three of them may be exhibited.

First, the retiring Director General had, it must be remembered, taken office at a very early age and at a period when modern archaeological technique (outside Cranborne Chase) was in a rudimentary stage. In Greece, it was certainly no less rudimentary than elsewhere, and such little practical experience as the young Marshall had had was in Greece. His immense task in India inevitably barred close or continuous contact with international development, and in excavation his technical standards remained to the end substantially those of Greece and the Near East in 1900.

The defect was aggravated by other factors. Several of his senior colleagues, mostly European, retired about the same time as himself; and in less than ten years after his retirement the department had no fewer than four successive Directors General (two European and two Indian), all of them men at the extreme end of their service and not likely therefore either to innovate or even to maintain with any special fervour. And there was yet another factor of a personal kind. I once heard a friend and admirer of Marshall describe him as 'a beech tree under which nothing grew.' That was well put. Marshall was of a temperament which hinders the confident delegation of responsibility, and hinders therefore the adequate training of subordinates to assume responsibility. It may be that something in the air of Edwardian India, some germ surviving from the India of the Moghuls, had entered early into Marshall's system. Certain it is that, when I reached India in 1944, Marshall was still a remote king-god of whom his worshippers had no intelligent comprehension, and sought none.

Then finally, in 1932 the Indian Government, like others in the universal stringency, applied drastic financial cuts with much haste and little understanding. The survey was left with an utterly unbalanced, ill-trained and un-led staff. It disintegrated. . . .

In March 1938 the Viceroy, through the India Office, summoned Sir Leonard Woolley to the rescue. Woolley's advice was sought on four points:

(1) The most promising sites or areas for exploration.

(2) The best methods and agencies for achieving the speedy and fruitful development of exploration activities in general; consideration, in this regard, being had not only to Government but to non-official agencies such as universities, learned societies, etc.

(3) The best method of training or selecting officers for exploration work, including such points as the most suitable age for recruitment.

(4) Any general points bearing on the field of exploration and excavation not covered by items 1–3.

Sir Leonard was quick to point out that the 'general points' mentioned in item 4 might well be of crucial importance. For example, it would be impossible to recommend excavation and the consequent amassing of antiquities if no sufficient means existed for their conservation and exhibition, so that the question of museums was intimately connected with the inquiry. Furthermore, it would be futile to recommend excavations if there were not sufficient funds for the work, so that the finances of the department would also have to come under review. Again, excavations if not properly conducted were worse than useless in that they involved the destruction of historic evidence, so that the capacities of the staff had to be adjudged. Thus any advice given under items 1–3 would be strictly conditioned by observations under item 4.

In the light of these comments the terms of reference were indefinitely enlarged, and during the very active three months which Woolley spent in India in 1938 he examined all the main aspects of Indian archaeology. The resultant report, dated 28 February 1939, and the unpublished notes which lie behind it, are a monument of quick and penetrating vision and of trenchant but judicious and constructive criticism. My more ample opportunities at a later date for observation in detail confirmed Woolley's views at every significant point.

It is not fitting here to reproduce 'Sir Woolley's' Report at any length, but a hint may be given of its trend. On the negative side he found the conservation of ancient structures hidebound and undiscriminating, often enough 'wasteful financially and scientifically deplorable.' The departmental policy in regard to museums had been 'radically wrong and detrimental to the real interests of archaeology.' Excavation had been 'haphazard, initiated for no good scientific reason on new sites or carrying on the clearing of old sites which had already yielded their essential information.' The vital study of pottery had been neglected; in particular 'for the historic periods no information was available and a pottery type could not be dated within a thousand years. . . . On almost every [excavation] site which I visited there was evidence of the work having been done in an amateur fashion by men anxious indeed to do well but not sufficiently trained and experienced to know what good work is.' For these and many other criticisms chapter and verse were given, interleaved with an occasional word of commendation where feasible. The conclusion was that in museum work, in excavation and in conservation in some of its aspects, 'the staff of the Archaeological Department are insufficiently trained by precept and by experience; they are not themselves adequate to their task and naturally they are unable to train up their successors to any higher standard than their own—indeed, as regards the students and junior members it is a case of the blind leading the blind, and the quality of the department is likely to deteriorate progressively. Outside help is necessary if any good is to come of the department's work.'

In short, Sir Leonard recommended that 'a European Adviser in Archaeology be appointed for a strictly limited term of years.' I subsequently found that he had privately associated my name with that recommendation.

With the fatal timidity and vacillation which characterized the last years of the British Raj in India, the Woolley Report was issued and immediately withdrawn. Accordingly, it created a storm which could not be allayed by a study of the reasoned and manifestly impartial terms in which it had been framed. Only gradually, as its contents became more widely known and appreciated, did it gain that acceptance amongst educated Indians which it had deserved from the outset. After all, although the staff of the Archaeological Department was now nearly 100 per cent Indian, it owed its inadequacy basically to its inheritance from British direction. Had the steps taken actually in 1944–47 been taken a dozen years earlier, they could have been taken at a more rational pace and the thorny crisis would not have arisen. As it was, the hypersensitive condition of Indian opinion in and after 1939 impeded progress and obscured the objective.

The war inevitably hindered the implementation of the report. But by 1943 even war could not longer defer some sort of action, particularly since the transfer of power was now assuming an increasing definition and immediacy. At the end of June 1943, Mr. Amery, then Secretary of State for India, received a code telegram from the Viceroy (Lord Wavell) which included the following sentences:

'Post of Director General of Archaeology falls vacant next year and the Member for Education, after discussion with me, is extremely anxious to get a man ... from home for succession. I fear that condition of department is quite lamentable. It contains no one of any quality and level of its work is low. . . . I do not know if Mortimer Wheeler who I understand is at present serving in the Army would be possible. . . .'

The result of this message was the invitation which I received in July at Algiers, as narrated elsewhere. My reply was that, whilst I was not prepared to leave the Army until the conclusion of the forthcoming operation (the Salerno landing), I would accept the Director-Generalship if still available in six months' time.

Accordingly, in February 1944 I found myself imprisoned in a tiny cabin of the *City of Exeter* amidst the sprawling lines of a seven-knot convoy of about a hundred ships. Slowly we steamed westward as though seeking India in the track of Columbus, rounded the Azores, and veered towards the African coast. The brilliant lights of neutral Tangier came up on the starboard bow as we groped darkly into the Mediterranean, and the trouble which it was easy to forebode broke upon us in daylight north of Algiers. For an hour successive waves of German torpedo-bombers came at us low over the water, and in the carefree way of maritime anti-aircraft gunners the air was filled dangerously with an infinitude of polychrome shells. With El Alamein and Salerno fresh in the memory, my inglorious task was now to amuse the large number of small children assembled below deck; where, by rationalizing the attack as a bang-game, we weathered the little storm successfully and almost regretted the succeeding calm. Thereafter an eventless voyage took us to Bombay, and I stepped ashore with a mind full of ill-digested Indian history but with a pretty clear plan of campaign. My impact with the East was hospitably softened by Sir John Colville (later Lord Clydesmuir), at that time Governor of Bombay, and two days afterwards I took my seat very comfortably in the Frontier Mail, bound for Delhi and Simla.

11. Indian Summer: I. The Promised Land

On the top floor of the gaunt Railway Board building where the Archaeological Survey was then housed at Simla, I stepped over the recumbent forms of peons, past office windows revealing little clusters of idle clerks and hangers-on, to the office which I had taken over that morning from my Indian predecessor. As I opened my door I turned and looked back. The sleepers had not stirred, and only a wavering murmur like the distant drone of bees indicated the presence of drowsy human organisms within. I emitted a bull-like roar, and the place leapt to anxious life. . . . One after another my headquarters staff was ushered in, and within an hour the purge was complete. Bowed shoulders and apprehensive glances showed an office working as it had not worked for many a long day. That evening one of the peons (who later became my most admirable Headquarters Jemadar) said tremulously to my deputy's Irish wife, 'Oh, memsahib, a terrible thing has happened to us this day. . . .'

Had Jemadar Bagh Singh known the Revelation of St. John he might aptly have recalled the prophetic words: 'The Devil is come down amongst you having great wrath, because he knoweth that he hath but a short time.' The Devil had in fact a four years' contract from the Viceroy in his pocket; though, as events shaped themselves, only three of those years were to be effective, the fourth being submerged in the turbulence and bloodshed of Partition. In that theoretical four years, nearly everything had to be done. The department had drifted to a standstill, encumbered by ignorant seniors and devoid of replacements. Nor was it merely a matter of reshaping, refinancing, revitalizing. The dead wood of obsolete and erroneous ideas had to be uprooted, without (for political reasons) too drastic an uprooting of their elderly exponents. The Devil had to fight with one arm tied to his side. With the other he proceeded to lay about him.

Looking back at this period, 1944–48, from the quietude of a Chelsea study, it is not difficult to count both the losses and the gains. You can't have omelettes without breaking eggs, and I have no doubt that the omelettes which eventually emerged justified the breaking of a good many eggs, especially at the outset. Opposition, both political and departmental, was not inconsiderable, and was not lessened by the circumstance that before my arrival the appointment had been announced in the Indian Press as that of a 'Brigadier Wheeler'—manifestly another of those ignorant red-hatted blimps for whom a job had to be found. Subsequently it emerged that I had dabbled in Roman Britain: but what had Roman Britain to do with India? The question was a not unreasonable one, and I can now only retaliate by saying, 'See below, p. 194.' More than once during that four years the old and largely fallacious advice, 'Don't try to hurry the East,' was quoted to me; without perverseness, it remained a stimulus to new and yet more urgent activity. 'Remember and respect the Indian climate: the impossible hot weather, the rains.' At the outset, my staff was told that for the four short years we should ignore the hot weather; whilst the importance of the rains was that they pointed vividly to us, on our continuing rounds, some of the technical weaknesses which underlay our work. My older staff groaned at the wilful and pernicious unconventionality of the newcomer. The younger staff which I proceeded to recruit responded with a high spirit that was my greatest reward. Now, years later, my youngsters are taking charge, and I am satisfied with their prowess.

My immediate tasks were threefold: to set my idling staff at headquarters to work, to see the problem on the ground throughout India, and above all to meet every member of my staff, from Peshawar to Madras. The first of these tasks occupied a preliminary ten days at Simla, and included a project which, as things turned out, was to bear astonishingly good and abundant fruit.

At this point I may return for a moment to my cabin in the *City of Exeter*. There, brooding upon a scheme for fieldwork and excavation in India, I had jotted down the following notes:

'In the immense field offered by India for archaeological exploration, many alternative plans of almost equal value are necessarily feasible. It may be desirable to divide our programme into two separate parts, corresponding to the two main geographical divisions of the sub-continent: on the one hand to the great plains of the north between the Vindhyas and the Himalaya, and on the other to the plateau and the coastal strips of the south.

'In the north the great hiatus between the end of the Indus Valley civilization, dated by Mesopotamian contacts to the 3rd millennium B.C., and the absorption of North-West India into the historical Achaemenid empire of the 6th century B.C.—the hiatus which must have coincided with the formative period of modern India—is a standing challenge to Indian research. What was the material background of the Vedic hymns? What part if any did the Indus cities, representing one of the great civilizations of the ancient world, play in the formation of the Indian civilization of later ages? Of what sort were the Aryan invaders? Whence and when? These are questions in which the problems of India are integral with those of greater Asia, but they are also questions to which Indian scholarship may be expected to provide an important part of the answer. And further substantive advance is unlikely until Indian field-exploration, carefully planned and executed, provides fresh material evidence.

'In the south of India the archaeological problem is, in a sense, vaster still. There we have no dated contact with ancient Mesopotamia, no intrusive Persian empire. Scraps of information approximating to an uncertain history begin in the time of Asoka, but it was not until the Graeco-Roman geographers of the 1st and 2nd centuries A.D. included Indian trade within their survey that the historical map assumed something approaching a coherent outline. Not indeed until the time of the Pallavas of the 6th and 7th century A.D. is South Indian history firmly established upon a basis of written record. For earlier periods material is abundant, its inter-relationship unknown. It is a jumble of words with no consecutive meaning. But here again, planned work can gradually bring order and significance into chaos. A potential datum-line is provided by the impact of Roman commerce upon central and southern India, with the consequent deposition of Roman coins and coin-hoards of known date. The careful correlation of these coins with the contemporary Indian cultures is an obvious starting-point for research. It has not yet been attempted.

'Here then are two great problems which demand attention. In tackling them, I propose to work on a restricted and economical scale, with a view to developing the technical side of our work and to training the younger generation who will succeed us. The work may not be immediately spectacular in the popular sense of the term, but, properly planned and controlled, it is capable of adding notably to our knowledge of the components of Indian civilization. And that is a basic function of the Archaeological Survey.'

In my room at the top of the Railway Board building, now and then snatching books and papers from the paws of an intrusive monkey, I sat down and drew up a list of the many Roman coins which, since 1775, have been recorded from the soil of South India. I then sent for two of my officers, went through the list with them, and despatched them on a four thousand miles' tour with instructions to select one or more of the named sites where significant association with an Indian culture seemed a fair gamble and where excavation might be feasible. Thereafter I hurried off to the North-West Frontier and the Indus Valley.

On the borders of the Punjab and the North-West Frontier provinces a little railway junction has, at the instance of Sir John Marshall, been rechristened *Taxila*. The name is that of a famous city which, on a series of successive sites hereabouts, flourished as a local capital and university town between the fifth centuries B.C. and A.D. Its fame, already secure in classical and ancient Indian writings, is further enhanced by the three massive volumes in which Marshall has displayed the results of twenty years of intensive excavation, and it is not my purpose here to review this accessible literature. But I cannot omit a passing word about the site. It lies at the foot of the Himalaya, in a terrain sufficiently reminiscent of Greece to have been an additional lure to its excavator, with a crescendo of hill and mountain to the east of it, rising upwards into the brief dawn with a dazzling Turneresque opalescence of tones and undertones. Then, or in the grey pre-dawn when the

February mustard-fields are a sea of dim yellow and, overhead, a lone vulture on dawn-patrol masks its obscene aspect by the majestic sweep of its wings, the picture is one of unforgettable beauty. But it was on a hot morning of early May that I first knew this place, and what most struck my calculating eye was the presence of a colony of useful buildings and a first-class site-museum which together provided the ideal setting for a future training-camp. Thus early in my tour a major problem had settled itself without effort.

Then onwards. Three hundred miles to the south lies Harappa, the little country town beside which rise the dusty mounds of one of the two greatest cities of the Indus Valley civilization. Here, in 1921, a member of Marshall's staff had discovered remains of a people who used both stone and copper (but not iron) and were therefore in what archaeologists call a 'chalcolithic' phase of culture. The date of this manifestly ancient culture was then unknown but has since, after much further exploration, been defined roughly as 2500–1500 B.C. The 'Harappa' or 'Indus' civilization has now taken its place amongst the great civilizations of the ancient world, and it was with a proper—though, in the event, inadequate—sense of things to come that, on a May night in 1944, a four miles' tonga-ride along a track deep in sand brought me with my local Muslim officer from the nearest railway station to the little bungalow beside the moonlit mounds. Warned by my anxious colleague that we must start our inspection at 5.30 next morning and finish by 7.30, 'after which it would be too hot,' we turned in, with the dark figure of the 'punka-walla' crouched patiently in the entrance, and the night air rent by the howling of innumerable jackals in the neighbouring wilderness.

Next morning, punctually at 5.30, our little procession started out towards the heaps. Within ten minutes, I stopped and rubbed my eyes as I gazed upon the tallest mound, scarcely trusting my vision. Six hours later my embarrassed staff and I were still toiling with picks and knives under the blazing sun, the mad sahib setting a relentless pace. To explain what had happened, I must deviate for a moment into Indus archaeology.

The sites of the Indus civilization spread along the rivers from the Himalaya to the Arabian Sea, a distance of one thousand miles, and it was thus by far the largest unitary civilization of pre-classical times.

Within that great area two cities were outstanding and presumably in some manner metropolitan: Harappa itself and, four hundred miles to the south-west, Mohenjo-daro, beside the main stream of the Indus. Both cities were something like three miles in circumference; both were thought to be devoid of fortifications. Accordingly, prior to 1944 there was a tendency to regard the Indus Civilization as something extraneous to the normal trend of the autocratic or bureaucratic king- and priest-ridden societies further west, in Mesopotamia, Anatolia and Egypt. This apparently heterogeneous character, strangely anachronistic in the chalcolithic age, was stressed by Professor Gordon Childe in his *New Light on the Most Ancient East*, 1934. 'No multiplication of weapons of war and battle-scenes,' he wrote, 'attests futile conflicts between city-states as in Babylonia nor yet the force whereby a single king, as in Egypt, achieved by conquest internal peace and warded off jealous nomads by constant preparedness. We cannot even define the nucleus round which accumulated the surplus wealth of capital involved in the conversion of the village into the city. . . . One can indeed distinguish between industrial and commercial quarters, between the lowly abodes of artisans and shopkeepers and the larger mansions of prosperous burghers. But no temple nor palace dominates the rest though the total areas excavated would compare favourably with those explored in Mesopotamia. The visitor inevitably gets an impression of a democratic bourgeois economy, as in Crete, in contrast to the obviously centralized theocracies and monarchies hitherto described.'

This Elysian polity, not altogether devoid perhaps of a Marxist flavour, seemed too good to be true but was not on that account false. There was little in the printed evidence to contradict it. But the printed evidence was in fact singularly incomplete.

As I approached the highest mound at Harappa on that May morning, the truth, or a part of the truth, of the matter stood suddenly revealed to me in the strong sloping light of the early sun. The mound was fringed with great piled masses of yellow mud which could scarcely be other than monsoon-riven brick. Here and there it rose to tower-like peaks; everywhere it contrasted with the interior of the mound, where brickbats and potsherds covered the surface with a red cloak. Nay more; close inspection and a little scraping of the peripheral mud showed up the actual joints in the brickwork, and doubt was out of the question. The mound, standing high above the adjacent heaps, had been barricaded by a great brick wall, long worn and melted by the summer rains. The city, so far from being an unarmed sanctuary of peace, was dominated by the towers and battlements of a lofty man-made acropolis of defiantly feudal aspect. A few minutes' observation had radically changed the social character of the Indus civilization and put it at last into an acceptable secular focus. There remained the task of demonstrating the structural make-up of the newly found acropolis by excavation, and this was in fact to be achieved with rewarding success two years later.

Meanwhile I hurried on to Harappa's opposite number, Mohenjo-daro, away down in Sind. There, as we drove through the heaps and scrub towards the heart of the site, a high mound rose suddenly in front of us, crowned with the tattered *stupa* or shrine which Buddhist monks had added to it in the second century A.D. And there at once the same phenomenon was clear to see: the floodworn remains of an acropolis of similar size, orientation and relative position to that of Harappa, and similarly showing the mud or mud-brick of which its cliff-like edges were composed. In the adjacent bungalow I sat down and wrote to Gordon Childe in London that the bourgeois complacency of the Indus civilization had dissolved into dust and that, instead, a thoroughly militaristic imperialism had raised its ugly head amongst the ruins. To his credit he accepted the retrogression with a good and unhesitating grace, and in due course rewrote his book.

Back in New Delhi, not displeased with my hurried western tour, I made official contacts and sped upon my way east and south. At Patna I found the vice-chancellors of the nineteen Indian universities assembled in conference and seized the opportunity of haranguing them with such eloquence as I could muster on India's urgent need for a younger generation of archaeological explorers. The subsequent response was more favourable than I could have hoped, and it is a pleasure here and now to record the constant co-operation of most of the universities in our work. Incidentally, at least three of them have become themselves the patrons of archaeological field-research.

INDIAN SURVEYORS AT WORK IN AN UNFINISHED CUTTING THROUGH
THE DEFENCES OF THE PREHISTORIC CITADEL, HARAPPA, 1946

WITH INDIAN STUDENTS AT HARAPPA, 1946

At Calcutta, in the damp oppressive heat of June, I cooled my brow for a moment in eighteenth-century England. Who 'Captain Charles Wyatt of the Bengal Engineers' may have been, is unknown to me, but in Calcutta's Palladian Government House, which he built in 1799, he faithfully reproduced the spirit of an age of cultivated luxury: different as might be from the theatrical and rather uneasy ostentation of New Delhi. With a strangely prophetic sense, be it added, Wyatt chose as his model Kedleston Hall in Derbyshire, the future home of Lord Curzon. Now at Calcutta the hospitable Caseys held court—old friends with time for everything and everybody in years of unparalleled stress. An example is relevant. Since Taxila, I had formulated in my mind a detailed scheme for a training-school in archaeological excavation. One thing was lacking: a qualified colleague to share the very considerable task. On my way down to breakfast at Government House, the solution suddenly flashed to my mind. Years previously, R. G. Casey's younger brother Dermot had, as I have related, helped me in the excavation of Roman sites in Gloucestershire and at St. Albans. His discernment as an excavator had been of a rare quality, and he was a master of patient exposition. I asked my host what Dermot was doing. 'Oh, he's G2 or something of the sort in a base-camp in Tasmania,' was the reply. 'Would it be robbing the war-effort at this late date to abstract him from the Australian army?' Dick Casey's response was characteristic. 'I'll wire to the Viceroy,' he said, 'and ask for him. When do you want him?' I said that we should open the school at Taxila on 1st October. Lord Wavell at New Delhi reacted immediately; he cabled to the Australian Prime Minister and on 15th September a slightly puzzled Dermot Casey arrived at Simla with a small hand-bag after a precipitate journey in a bomber across five thousand miles of Indian Ocean. But that is to anticipate.

Southwards from Calcutta, in the heat of an impending monsoon, I made Madras, to find most government offices closed. A Japanese bomber, having lost its way over the Bay of Bengal, had recently discharged its remaining small bomb upon one of the open spaces of the city, with a moral effect which might have made the pilot smile. However, with the ready co-operation of the superintendent, a Dr. Aiyappan who became a good friend of mine, I

G

penetrated into the Government Museum and at leisure explored its inmost recesses. The sequel may properly be described as dramatic.

In a workshop cupboard my hand closed upon the neck and long handle of a pottery vessel strangely alien to that tropical environment. As I looked upon it I remember recalling that provocative question in the Legislative Assembly at New Delhi: 'What has Roman Britain got to do with India?' Here was the complete answer. Here was indeed much more than the complete answer. In my hand I held the first key to the protohistoric archaeology of South India, of half a million square miles of Asia. Here was India's reply to those words which, three months previously, I had penned a trifle anxiously on the *City of Exeter* and have reproduced above. Roman coins as an index to an associated Indian culture would have been good enough and somewhere on the other side of the peninsula my two officers were even then searching along the coast and amongst the backwaters for a point of impact. But Roman pottery such as the amphora-handle which I was already sketching in my notebook opened up possibilities beyond the reach of coinage, with its incomputable survival-value and its facile transmission. A wine-jar from the Mediterranean had not arrived alone; its presence indicated almost infinite possibilities. It had been found, said Aiyappan, on a site some eighty miles south of Madras, near Pondicherry in French India, where he and others had been carrying out some trial excavations on an ancient town-site beside the coast. Two days later I reached Pondicherry in the dawn, after an all-night train journey.

The French governor was away, but his officials were hospitality itself. Breakfast was prolonged far into the morning, and concluded with an admirable cognac. Thereafter we made our way in loquacious procession through the straightly marshalled streets of the little town to the public library. The guidebook affirms that 'Pondicherry can hardly be described as a "live" town. There are no European shops. The grass grows in the streets. . . .' But, though its much-battered defences have long perished, the place has an air of dormant history about it, something of the aspect of a French provincial town gone to seed and to sleep. It was at the same time un-Indian and un-British, with that indefinable air and odour of the creole. In war-time its population had been enlarged by un-advertised immigrants: a French marquis engaged, with the best motives, upon a perennially frustrate manœuvre to install a suspect wireless sending-station; his flamboyantly blonde wife who never seemed quite to force the prickly and complicated entrenchments of local society; a subfusc woman from Malay in an upstairs flat on the sea-front; the shapely young wife of the manager of a casino at Shanghai, whereabouts of manager at present unknown. And in the background, a chorus of three mills produced cotton-cloth under French or British management, two or three colonial French families made an adequate subsistence somewhat mysteriously out of oil-seed, and a celebrated *ashram* or metaphysical establishment provided indiscriminately for the spiritual indulgence of jaded Indians or bored (elderly) Frenchwomen. The social focus was a rather shoddy little *Cercle* adjoining the Governor's Palace. In the background a British consul-general kept an observant eye on things and persons, with the aid of a large Union Jack and carefully adjusted tea-parties.

An inner room of the public library contained three or four museum-cases. I strode hopefully forward, and, removing the dust with an excessively sweaty arm, peered into them. For the second time within the month, my eyes started in their sockets. Crowded together were fragments of a dozen more Roman amphorae, part of a Roman lamp, a Roman intaglio, a mass of Indian material—potsherds, beads, terracottas—and several fragments of a red-glazed ware which no one trained in the school of classical archaeology could mistake. After much searching, the keys were discovered and I found myself handling the fragments of cups and dishes of the time of Augustus and Tiberius from the famous potteries of Roman Arezzo. My search was nearly over. . . .

Two miles away, down the coast, a devious journey brought us to journey's end. Here a fishing hamlet, Virampatnam by name, looks upon the Bay of Bengal across a litter of string-tied boats and crude outriggers, and near it a former outlet of the Gingee River is ponded back to form a broad lagoon worthy of the shade of Long John Silver. The flanks of the lagoon are crested by groves of waving coco-nut palms, and from its fishful depths long lines of dark-skinned men from the adjacent villages gather a gullible food-supply with primitive fishing-rods. The western shore of the lagoon is flat, little above the average water-level; the eastern shore for some four hundred yards rises sheer to a height of twenty feet, and from the eroded cliff project the broken ends of brick walls. It was quickly evident that the whole height of the eastern shore was the product of urban accumulation. Two craters showed where local French and Indian antiquaries during the previous three years had extracted the material now in the public library. And let it be made clear that, devoid of science though their work had been, without it the potentialities of the site would have remained hidden. The unskilled excoriator has on occasion an honourable place in the history of archaeology. In particular, the name of Père L. Faucheux of Pondicherry deserves inclusion in the roll of fame, for that he at least stumbled unknowingly upon 'Roman' Arikamedu (Pondicherry) when more knowledgeable men had passed it by. Our work there in 1945 and that of J. M. Casal for the French Government in 1948 owed everything to Faucheux's untutored curiosity. And that curiosity was in turn based upon the accident that in 1937 local Indian children had picked up on the site an intaglio bearing a classical head (allegedly 'of Augustus') and had purveyed it for baksheesh to another local French antiquary. My own share in the business—initiated by my accidental observation in the Madras museum—was the recognition of the dated Roman pottery[1] and the subsequent exploitation of the site on methodical lines in the interests of Indian chronology. Of that, more in due course.

Once again in New Delhi, I found there Stuart Piggott and Glyn Daniel, the former in the Army, the latter in the Royal Air Force and both engaged upon air-photograph interpretation. On the principle of 'Othere the old sea-captain' and his walrus-tooth, I casually produced an Arretine sherd from Pondicherry, and the effect was gratifying—how childishly rewarding is a comprehending audience! In his spare time, Piggott was already at work upon that series of books and articles which have made him our foremost authority on prehistoric India. But there was little time for gossip.

[1] The previous report on the Arikamedu pottery had been as follows: 'The type of pottery varies at the different levels, the most artistic designs occurring about the actual sea-level'!

With the shrewd assistance of the Secretary for Education (Sir) S. H. Y. Oulsnam, to whose co-operation during my first two years in India I owe more than I can say, I prepared a shattering budget for Government, to cover a preliminary reorganization of the survey. Then, having picked up Dermot Casey in Simla, I repaired to Taxila, where for six months he and I proceeded to conduct a training-school which, I like to think in retrospect, did something to reorientate Indian field-archaeology.

I look back on that six months from October 1944 to March 1945 as one of the happier periods of my life. Work was unceasing and strenuous, but was liberally shared by colleagues and students alike. It was our good fortune to be joined by Gerard Mackworth Young, son of a one-time governor of the Punjab and himself a fluent speaker of Punjabi. Gerard had formerly been Defence Secretary in the New Delhi Government, but had resigned before the war in order to realize an ambition to live and work in Greece. There he became a colleague of Humfry Payne, Director of the British School of Archaeology, and, on Payne's premature death, succeeded him as Director. Early in the war he disposed skilfully of his immediate responsibilities by handing the school to Switzerland, left Greece in front of the invaders, and returned to his old department in India. In 1943 a peculiarly virulent mosquito struck him down with his first bout of malaria, and on recovery he came to me as a volunteer. At Taxila he made my task tolerable by assuming the administration of the school, and he fulfilled his very miscellaneous duties with knowledge and imperturbability. Nor can I forget the brief but notable intervention of my old archaeological photographer in England, M. B. Cookson, then in India as an Air Force officer, who spent his Christmas leave with me in 1944 and, by a short spell of intensive training, set my photographic department upon its feet. His precept and example were remembered by my Indian staff long after he left India.

But above all I have in mind the sixty-one students who flocked to me from the universities of India and from the archaeological departments of the Indian States: swarthy Muslims from the North-West Frontier and the Punjab, little round-faced talkative Bengalis, quick-witted Madrasis, dark southerners from Cochin and Travancore. Alas, today—only a few years later—such an assemblage of races, tongues and creeds would no longer be feasible. Religious and political barriers have split asunder those who in 1944 worked together with single purpose and common understanding. . . . Together or in close succession they passed through the three classes into which the school was divided. The largest class was that of trainees in the actual technique of excavation and in the preparation of the necessary field-records. The other classes dealt with surveying, photography, draftsmanship and administration. Punctually at 8.45 each morning the students filed out to their work; at 6.0 p.m. fieldwork ceased; at 9.0 p.m. the school reassembled for a lecture given by the staff, by visitors or by the students themselves on historical, archaeological or anthropological topics. They were strenuous days, lightened by goodwill and cheerful incident. One night, I remember, snow fell upon us—the first in those parts for seventeen years. The next morning a student from tropical India was found filling his pockets with ice from the pools 'to send to his parents who had never seen ice or snow.' They were good-natured children, and a dozen or more of them are doing sound archaeological work in India and Pakistan today. . . . They taught me much.

By March 1945 the period of preparation was over. I was now sure of myself and my staff, and was content. With picked colleagues and the best of my students I left Taxila, stayed for a day or two in New Delhi, and then went straight on to Pondicherry and Arikamedu, a two-thousand mile journey into the tropics.

12. Indian Summer: II. Achievement

IT is not relevant here to follow in detail the archaeological field-programme which for three years developed the results of the 1944 reconnaissance in North and South India. The reports of that work are to be found in the periodical *Ancient India*, of which the first number was issued in January 1946. The function of the new publication was to set a standard of prompt and adequate presentation such as had not been hitherto available in India; to reflect, in other words, the new standards which we were trying to establish in the field, and to encourage also systematic and purposeful indoor research. Looking back on our efforts I think that we can claim an appreciable measure of success. But it was not easy.

Indolence had brought the dwindling annual reports of the survey to a final standstill in 1936. The Government prohibition of departmental publication after the beginning of the war thus merely gave the virtuous impress of authority to a long-standing negligence. At the same time the prohibition made it very difficult for me in 1945 to obtain sanction from Government for the launching of a new type of publication on a fairly ambitious scale, and many months in that year were spent by Oulsnam and myself in argument and cajolery before the ban was broken. For broken it had to be. From the outset the work of reorganization would have been largely frustrate without *immediate* publication, with its attendant discipline and encouragement. From the outset I had laid down 'the absolute necessity for completing the written report of one season's work before resuming fieldwork in the next. If need be, a whole season's digging must be postponed to enable this essential task to be accomplished. Unrecorded excavation is destruction, and prompt and full publication must be regarded by the excavator as a point of honour. If he once allows his reporting to fall into arrears, the situation rapidly out-runs his control, and unfortunately the resultant loss is not to himself or his department but to science. Complete and punctual publication must be the invariable rule; no excuse whatsoever can condone deferment. . . .' And so on. All that trumpeting was well enough, but it could only be justified by instant and effective action. And this action had to be fitted into the interstices of a peculiarly crowded routine. It meant not merely the reversal of a Government decision but also something approaching a technical revolution, and the latter process was at least as formidable as the former. In one of my memoranda of the period I find the following paragraph:

'Printing is at present a bottle-neck in India. This is due in part to the war and to shortage of good paper. But it is due also to the technical inadequacy of a majority of the Indian presses, not excluding the Central Government press. Good half-tone blocks, which are essential for archaeological publication, are almost impossible to obtain and, when obtained, they are commonly spoiled by bad inking. Type-founts are generally antiquated and below the modern international standard. Printers assure me that their machinery is out-of-date and that properly trained technicians cannot be obtained in the market. There can be no worse advertisement of national effort than bad printing, since it is necessarily through this vehicle that the greater part of the world receives the national intellectual output. An improvement of printing facilities and printing standards is a primary necessity if Indian archaeology—and indeed Indian scholarship generally—is to receive adequate recognition. Good and prompt publication is the life-blood of research.'

Desperate hunting led me eventually to a high compound-wall in Lower Circular Road on the outskirts of Calcutta. Behind the wall stood, and stands, the charming little Regency building put up about 1830 by a Baptist mission, which proceeded to establish a small press there for propagandist and other purposes. In 1945 the standard of this little press was easily the highest in India, and it was to the personal co-operation of successive managers that the satisfactory technical quality of the early numbers of *Ancient India* was due. But the employment of an efficient and reasonably expensive British-controlled concern rather than a cheap and shoddy native one was a recurrent *casus belli* with Government.

On 1st April in that year I sat in a small bungalow amidst the palm-trees, a mile from the scene of my forthcoming excavation at Arikamedu, and wrote to Cyril Fox. 'Sheets of rain are descending into the jungle outside my verandah—all wrong for the tropics at this time of year and particularly inopportune for one who is about to dig below sea-level. . . . Here I'm living in solitary state about three miles from the small wall-less *bastide* that is Pondicherry, with my servant and jemadar and my posse of Ghurka guards, who protect me very amiably from God-knows-what wherever my headquarters be. In addition there is a varying number of naked gentlemen who somehow appoint themselves to my staff and appear unexpectedly on the bill at the end of the month as "sweeper," "water-carrier," "gardener," and what-not. Today my South Indian students, twenty or thirty of them in addition to those I brought with me from the north, are expected, and this evangelist mission of mine recommences. . . . This is the place, by the way, where last year I noticed Arretine pottery amongst the previous finds and where therefore, *for the first time*, we can hope to find an ancient South Indian culture objectively dated by association. Arikamedu can scarcely help becoming a classic site in the annals of Indian archaeology. The archaeology is in fact easy enough—it's the remote-control between here and Delhi and my H.Q. at Simla, 7,000 ft. up and 2,000 miles away, that makes things a trifle difficult in a phase of intrigue and reorganization. . . . But I must go and see about those students. I'll light a South Indian cigar and sample the rain.'

There may have been forty of them, all told, in the thatched hut, swarthy, volatile, speaking a variety of natal languages—Tamil, Telegu, Malayalam, Hindi, Urdu—but all recurring constantly to the only tongue common to us all. The impending operation was set before them. They were to be the pioneers of protohistoric archaeology in South India. Their own literature had pointed the way. Had not the *Silappadikaram*, 'The Lay of the Anklet,' told them long ago of the ancient city of Puhar, only sixty miles away down the coast? How 'the sun shone there over the open terraces, over the warehouses near the harbour . . . where were the abodes of Yavanas, men from the Graeco-Roman world, sailors from distant lands?' And now here at Arikamedu, the ancient Pondicherry or Puduchcheri, the Podoukē of the Greek geographers, they were about to find the wine-jars and table-wares brought thither from the Mediterranean in the first century A.D. by those same Yavanas. Nor was that all. Beside these wine-jars and table-wares they would find Indian things, an Indian culture, even an Indian civilization, which would share the known date of the imports and thus form a firm base for the systematization of South Indian archaeology. . . . *Only*, they must not expect *immediate* success. They would have to work for it. They might have to work for a fortnight before the first hint of success came their way.

I have never ceased to congratulate myself upon the inspiration of that last warning. We started badly, in an area which had been wrecked by brick-robbers from top to bottom. Spirits fell, and only the blessed word 'fortnight' staved off the utter despair which comes all too easily to the tropical mentality. It was in fact on the afternoon of the twelfth day that one of my students emerged from the water-logged depths, covered with slime but waving exultantly the base of a red dish, bearing upon it the name of its Italian maker. The Yavanas had been found, and the situation was saved. Thereafter the excavation became a triumph. By return of post the whole history of the potter and his family, the Vibieni of Arezzo, was in our hands, thanks to the prompt and liberal knowledge of Miss M. V. Taylor at Oxford. Other Italic wares and fragments of a hundred wine-jars, with a wide range of associated Indian products, sealed our success.

A little later, on 8th May, I was in a Royal Air Force 'plane over central India, heading for Madras from Delhi, to which I had repaired from Arikamedu for a committee-meeting. The pilot came through to us from the cockpit with the wirelessed news that the war had ended in Europe; he proposed to turn back to Delhi to celebrate and was with difficulty overborne, by numbers rather than by argument. At the Madras airport I found the car of the governor of Pondicherry awaiting an absent guest, so I boarded it and drove straight back to the palace in the French capital. There the victory celebrations were already in full blast. In the fierce sunshine stood the small, rotund form of His Excellency Monsieur Bonvin, in cocked hat and heavy gold-braided serge, the sweat streaming down his gracious, friendly countenance. He was receiving the French Colony, distinguished Indians, an inebriate Australian soldier; everyone who came his way was greeted with a welcoming smile. All that night the palace was open for drinks and dancing. The enterprising Australian soldier was there, he was still there when I left in the small hours, and he had by that time had many intimate conversations with the governor. As I drove to my bungalow in the moonlight I too determined to celebrate: by giving all my workpeople—men, women and children—extra pay on the morrow.

At pay-parade my praiseworthy proposal was explained to the waiting files by an interpreter. It was received by blank or inquiring looks, then a murmur. *What* victory? *What* war? What was it all about? The interpreter persevered. There had been a war, far away, a very great war. But now it was all over, and the sahib was pleased, and wanted them to be pleased too, so he was giving them all an extra rupee, in addition to their wages. The puzzled look remained. I intervened and told the interpreter to say no more about it but to ensure that each labourer received the bonus as a gift, if not from me, then from God.

Two days later, a small deputation waited upon me. My workers wanted to give me a party under the moon. Private inquiry revealed that every recipient of the extra rupee had put a quarter of it into a bag for the purpose of this party. Never have I been more touched than by this gesture of the humblest of folk; folk known to me well enough indeed individually by sight and prowess but barred by every barrier of language and custom.

The appointed evening arrived, and I was driving punctually from my bungalow to my headquarters down the intervening mile of dusty track between the cactus-bushes, when suddenly a great crowd of laughing and chattering villagers swept across my path and engulfed the car. Simultaneously, as though from ambush, two rival bands leapt out of opposite hedges and filled the air with a cacophony beyond belief. That on my left was disguised in battered *képis* and grubby red *pantalons*, and was armed with patinated brass instruments. It was in intent completely 'French,' though it bruised the night air with an astonishing noise which, after much repetition,

I vaguely recognized as an exotic version of 'Tipperary.' Its rivals were undisguisedly native, their uniform restricted to the loin-cloth, their orchestration based upon the drum and a sort of flute, their music unashamedly of the countryside. Ultimately the *képis* blew themselves to a standstill, and the drums and flutes held the field. A space was made in the crowd and into it stepped a circle of dancing youths, the rhythm of the dance emphasized by the beating of stick on stick. And so, with endless succession and reiteration, we moved forward a few yards at a time towards our goal—my headquarters. The flanking trees were full of adventurous villagers, who were now and then precipitated on to the crowd below by the breaking of an overladen branch. At last, within a furlong of our destination, the crowd paused and reluctantly opened up a vista. Lanterns on poles now rivalled the moonlight, and in the wavering beams two gaily bedecked forms were seen approaching from the further end of the avenue. They were hobby-horse dancers of a traditional local type, the one a crowned prince, the other a youth in the guise of a coy young maiden. They slowly gallivanted up to me, bowed low, and proceeded with much grace and vivacity to enact their dance—the prince strutting before the shy damozel, whose averted eyes gradually turned towards him as she slowly relented and finally, in an abandon of passion, touched him lightly on the arm and tripped away with him. . . . The dancers were the children and grandchildren of similar dancers, who for ages have peregrinated the countryside with a limited and familiar repertoire.

Thereafter the guest of honour, ensconced in a gilt baroque chair which had been conjured up at several removes from some French household, received the flowers and fruit appropriate to such occasions, was addressed in Tamil and Tamiloid French, and listened attentively to a Tamil ode, composed for the occasion and sung by a small boy in a piercing nasal voice. It was a party; a vivid memory, lit by unfading visions of a happy crowd of gentle folk and a moon-filled sky. . . .

To find, as we happily and abundantly did, firm equations between dated imports and a native culture was archaeologically useful, and indeed epoch-making, but was not itself enough. To complete the exercise, it remained to demonstrate how such an equation could be extended for the ordering of knowledge over a wide field—over a field in some measure proportionate to peninsular India. With that end in view, and the Arikamedu material freshly in my mind, I left Pondicherry on a rapid summer-tour of the South Indian museums. Of the results of that tour I have written elsewhere[1] and need say little here. Suffice it that, either in these more-or-less derelict museums or on the actual sites from which their material was derived, it was not difficult to identify salient features of the Arikamedu culture and so to transfer its dating for upwards of three hundred miles from the starting-point. In particular, on the arid inland plateau of northern Mysore, where the poorest peasants in the world comb the sand anxiously with their feeble fingers in case a ground-nut or two might have escaped their earlier harvesting, there were the sites of two ancient towns where Arikamedu pottery had come to light. And there the next practicable phase in the development of South Indian archaeology was instantly apparent. A word of explanation is necessary.

From the British Isles to the Caucasus and beyond are groups of tombs built often of large untrimmed stones and normally intended (it seems) for more than one ceremonial interment. The infinite variety of plan and circumstance from region to region or even tomb to tomb has long been a challenge to methodically-minded antiquaries, and the challenge has not remained unanswered. The possibility of some sort of relationship, however remote, between many of the groups is hinted both by their geographical distribution and by certain distinctive and recurrent features. Amongst the latter is a circular, or occasionally squarish, opening in the end-wall of the tomb or in an internal partition. These 'port-holes' occur in the British Isles, France, Spain, Sweden, North Africa, Syria, Palestine, Bulgaria, the Caucasus, Transcaucasia, and even in Iran; whilst in the innumerable large stone (megalithic) cists or graves of South India they are probably more often present than not. Does it follow that these far-flung monuments constitute a unitary problem, extending in space from Ireland to India and in time or culture from the Stone Age to the Age of Iron? The problem is one of more than academic interest. Any widespread affinity of this kind must, if proved, affect our pattern of human

[1] *Ancient India*, No. 4 (1948), pp. 308 ff.; *Archaeology from the Earth* (Oxford, 1954), pp. 121 ff.

achievement in vital fashion. But a first requisite in tracing or postulating any such pattern must be a precise chronology. And in 1945 the South Indian megaliths were still essentially undated.

Now one of the two ancient town-sites in northern Mysore to which my search for Arikamedu pottery brought me in 1945 was surrounded by the remains of a great cemetery of these port-hole tombs. The site itself, known as Brahmagiri from a neighbouring hill, had yielded to previous explorers a few pieces of pottery which we now knew, from our Arikamedu evidence, to be of the first century A.D. Here then was another potential equation: dig the tombs and the adjacent (and now partially dated) town-site simultaneously and equate the culture of the one with that (or those) of the other. With a mental resolution I hurried northwards to the hundred-and-one other matters that awaited me at headquarters.

Today I am glad to forget the tumultuous routine, significant enough at the time, which bent my back at this period. Once more in Simla, I wrote on 19th July to Fox. 'After ten months' absence from my headquarters (there's a model for you!) I'm back once more for a few weeks, preparing new demands on Government. I'm living at the United Service Club (Blimps and Blimps) and, in particular, sitting in my room after dinner and smoking a peculiarly pungent cheroot—you can probably smell it. My cigar and I are 7,000 feet above the sea, on the slope of an almost vertical hill-side. Facing me is the evening sun which streaks wanly through the rain-sodden sky at 7.5 p.m. precisely each day. It's the rains, and by rains I mean of course Rains—the sky just falls, and even the monkeys go and hide. . . . Both my excavations have turned out as they should, especially my Roman India at Pondicherry, which was an astonishing piece of luck for my first year. During the past few weeks I've been tracing its ramifications through central India to the far west coast. Given time and reasonable peace of mind (not predictable) we'll build a backbone and a few ribs into the jelloid mass which is South Indian archaeology. . . .'

Here I must interpolate that an absence from headquarters for ten whole months, however desirable (as indeed it was), would have been impossible but for the wise and devoted services of my deputy, Dr. N. P. Chakravarti. With a Cambridge doctorate behind him, Chakravarti had been Government Epigraphist for India under the

Survey, and seniority had brought him to Simla as Deputy Director General. We worked throughout my tenure with the closest mutual understanding, and in due course (1948) he succeeded me. My gratitude to him cannot be told.

I pass over much laborious administration, followed by an expedition to Iran on a 'cultural mission' in October, and arrive in 1946. On this mission I was accompanied by Margaret (we were married in Simla in 1945) and my senior Muslim officer, with an Indian retinue. Back in India, the time had come to abandon for the moment the lively problems of South India and to give North India its turn. There Harappa and the Indus civilization lay in wait, with the unexplored matter of the fortifications of which I have spoken on an earlier page, and much else. The weather was already warming up when, with the usual train of students, we shook off the polite dust of New Delhi and plunged into the bottomless sand of Harappa, out on the torrid Punjab plain. It was the end of June before our work there was finished—two months after fieldwork should legitimately have ceased—but we had no casualties and no grumbles. The heat was frequently 110 degrees in the shade and occasionally more. Daily from midday till 4.0 p.m. we knocked off, working in the mornings and in the cooling evenings. At 4.30 baskets of iced drink were carried round from group to group and were eagerly expected. Now and then a sand-storm would advance upon us like a solid moving cliff, penetrating to our inmost cupboards and smothering everything and everybody. But we were winning. At all points success dogged our steps. The great walls of the citadel emerged for the first time in their majesty as our picks cut through the encumbering debris. The historical character of the Indus civilization was changing and developing before our eyes. What mattered sweat and dust and a little cardiac overtime? Never have I had a team that, in so much discomfort, toiled more gamely, or with greater goodwill shared victory.

The full archaeological record of those days appeared punctually in *Ancient India* (January 1947), and, like other such records, lies outside this chronicle. More relevant is it to affirm here that by now, by the middle of 1946, I had at my call a trained and hardened junior staff and, behind and beyond that, young men in a dozen universities up and down the land with an understanding not merely of technique, but of the determination, persistence and over-all planning which alone can make technique significant. I like to think that some vestige of these virtues still remains in an India motivated by stimuli other than those which operated in 1946.

In September of that year Sir Olaf Caroe, then Secretary for External Affairs, sent us off on a second 'cultural mission,' this time to Afghanistan, with (Sir) Norman Edgley as President of the ancient Royal Asiatic Society of Bengal and M. A. Shakur as representing the North-West Frontier Province. A short account of this mission was published in *Antiquity* for 1947. Its most memorable moment was the spectacle of the vast sand-covered site on the Oxus plain where once stood Bactra, Mother of Cities. Of all places in the world, none is more likely to reward the excavator, and were this a chronicle of dreams there is much that I could write of Bactra. I pass it here with a backward glance and an urgent hope. Nineteen-forty-seven was to provide my last season of active fieldwork. On 15th August of that year the Union Jacks were pulled down outside the Secretariat at New Delhi. The blood-letting which had sporadi-cally preceded that event rose afterwards in a crescendo. Meanwhile, we had turned southwards again to Brahmagiri in northern Mysore and the problem of our megalithic tombs. Once more our deferred departure landed us in a tropical summer; but by that time my folk were used to the sight of their demented Director General un-ceasingly about them under the summer sun, and, to tell the truth, the D.G. was himself sufficiently inured to the trifling ordeal.

At Brahmagiri all went according to plan. The town-site revealed three successive cultures, the uppermost contemporary with Arikamedu (first century A.D.), the next below it that of the neigh-bouring megaliths, which were thus firmly planted in the last centuries B.C. All this has been told in detail elsewhere. But one small episode deserves the retelling.

Towards the end of our work at Brahmagiri I found myself wondering from time to time whether it was not all just a trifle too easy. Was there a catch in it after all? Were we absolutely certain that our Arikamedu dating was closely valid more than three hundred miles away in central India? I have mentioned that my wanderings in 1945 had taken me to *two* ancient urban sites in northern Mysore. One was of course Brahmagiri; the other, forty-five miles away, bore the picturesque name of Chandravalli, Moon-village. It lay in a valley adjoining the district-town of Chitaldrug, and had been slightly dug into at various times during the past half-century. This haphazard digging had produced pottery of Arikamedu and other types and five scattered Roman silver coins, of Augustus and Tiberius. If, by careful excavation, we could find yet more of these first-century coins in observed association with our Arikamedu wares, then the Arikamedu dating was proved for central India beyond shadow of doubt.

We therefore took over to Chandravalli a picked team, and laid out areas for excavation beside the former work. A few days later I went over again to inspect progress. The excellent young superintendent was rueful; our shot had missed the mark. He had found Arikamedu pottery, indeed, and the undated lead coins of the local dynasty, but not one of the essential Roman coins for which we were looking. In the evening sun we sat at a table and went through everything that had been found, bag by bag, envelope by envelope. My eye suddenly lighted upon a little lump of purple oxidization. Long familiarity with similar undistinguished vestiges on Romano-British sites left little doubt in my mind, and I sent for my chemist who was quartered in his field-laboratory nearby. Probability rapidly became certainty, and next day a *denarius* of Tiberius, minted between A.D. 26 and 37, was plain for all to see. The date of the coin and its associations in the soil could not more exactly have matched the evidence of our pottery at Arikamedu. I freely confess that as I stood there on the Indian plateau, far from any landfall for overseas traffic, with that crucial coin in my hand, I marvelled at the romantic chance that had brought me to it at the desired moment and in the desired setting. It was the crowning fortune of three years of steady planning and steadily attendant luck.

13. Indian Summer: III. Dissolution

OUR cross-country chase through South India after the 'new chronology' did not end at Brahmagiri. The considerable task remained of carrying our Arikamedu datum-line through to the great northern plains and thus of integrating the sub-continent from south to north. The central massif was geographically an unlikely line of advance, and my eyes turned to the coastal lowlands which fringe the hills or *ghats*, particularly on the east. There in Orissa, near the famous townlet of Bhubaneswar, where a multitude of medieval temples tower regally above the red earth, is a notable fortified site, Sisupalgarh, which may have been the Tosali of the Kalingas. Its manifest importance and its midway position between the Gangetic valley and the southern areas which we had been traversing singled it out as a likely focus, and a month before I left India my excavation branch, under my excellent pupil and colleague B. B. Lal, began work there. Once more, success attended us; on my final tour I called there and found that, on the one hand the long arm of Arikamedu had reached this northerly site, seven hundred miles from Pondicherry, and that, on the other hand, typical northern or Gangetic wares occurred in association. The twain had met in decent and orderly fashion. I felt unblushingly that the situation was almost worthy of the eulogy which had been addressed to me two days earlier at my previous halt. A deputation of charming elderly Brahmans, the sweetest and kindliest of old gentlemen, had placed flowers round my neck and then addressed to me their thanks and good wishes on my impending departure from India, with the following exordium: 'Honourable Sir, you found us in a Disorderly House; you are leaving us in an Orderly House....'

But in fact, when those benevolent words were spoken disorder of the deadliest kind had recently been reigning supreme at Delhi and throughout the Punjab. It is not my wish to recall at length the

time of trouble which ensued upon the Partition of India in August
1947. A year previously we had indeed had a foretaste of it at
Calcutta. There death and destruction had already walked abroad;
sewers had been blocked with human bodies, two harmless watch-
men had been killed in the compound of my headquarters at the
Indian Museum, across the road a vulture had been shot by a
passer-by and remained strangely upright, a ghastly sentinel over
the festering human corpse which it had been devouring. (On
hearing of the outbreak I had hurried to Calcutta to assure the
safety of the new and as yet unissued number of *Ancient India* from
the very real risk of fire, and had found the Baptist Mission Press
in something like a state of siege.) Yet all this was nothing to the
scenes enacted in the Hindu-Muslim war (for it was nothing less)
which laid low a million men, women and children in September
1947. At that time the roads, and the flanks of the roads, into the
East Punjab from the new Muslim state of Pakistan were choked
with a slow-moving river of misery: starving, panic-stricken Hindu
refugees, many of them dying by the wayside, ignored by their
dazed fellows as they died. And it was death for death. In the
heart of Delhi, Muslims and their families were at the same time
being butchered pitilessly overnight. To Cyril Fox, 8 September
1947: 'Well, Cyril, it's truly a merry world. When I drew up my
jeep at Delhi Station last night, I found I had parked beside a
bleeding body. I got out on the other side and walked into the
station, to see another body, newly stabbed by a passing Sikh under
the eyes of my servant, being rolled off the edge of the platform on
to the track. Of course there were armed police and soldiers on the
platform, but why should they interfere? My Muslim driver came
into my room yesterday, leaned against a pillar, and gasped out that
his wife, mother and whole family had been slaughtered. Three
other Muslim members of my staff with homes in the Punjab have
lost, literally lost, their families, and their homes have been burnt.
My second driver is in hospital with a knife-wound received in an
affray in which his brother was killed. At night I wake to the
nostalgic rattle of machine-guns in Connaught Place (New Delhi's
Piccadilly Circus). My Delhi staff is in a state of helpless terror, not
unjustifiable of course, poor fellows, but just *abject*, and I sometimes think that they almost *ask* to be knifed. . . .' And so on. The

Indian Government temporarily solved the problem by impounding the surviving Delhi Muslims in an old sixteenth-century fortress, the Purana Qila, where they continued to die of their own volition but at a retarded rate. I used to drive into the fortress with milk and vegetables for the members of my own Muslim staff, herded there like cattle without resource and without hope. They were tragic, tragic times and, as a European and therefore immune from deliberate attack, I saw much of the tragedy. To Fox again, 26 September 1947: 'In this civil war I am become a sort of general go-between. For example, two days ago the wife of one of my former Muslim colleagues besought me to evacuate her husband's sister from one of the principal Delhi hospitals, the British staff of which had been threatened with murder unless all Muslim patients were thrown out. I drove up to the hospital in my jeep but found the great iron gates locked. Outside them was a military guard (always untrustworthy in these times) and a crowd of rag-tags including several armed Sikhs, who are the No. 1 throat-cutters. Peering through the bars of the gate I attracted the attention of an English nurse, who came forward, put her finger to her lips, and opened the gates just enough to enable me to slip through. She said quickly, 'Don't speak here, they'll hear you,' and led me inside. I explained my mission; she replied that it was impossible—already that day two Muslim families in process of evacuation had been shot by the crowd as their cars left the gates, and it had been decided only to evacuate by night. I saw the English matron and persisted: there must be a side-gate to which I could take my jeep. She admitted that there was, but added: 'You know of course that there are three others with the patient?' As usual in India, the family had rallied immovably round the invalid. The matron and I proceeded to inspect the family. They consisted of the convalescent herself, another woman, a youth and an old man. The last was unalterably Muslim in appearance, but the others we arranged to have disguised as Hindus, the women shamelessly removing their *birkas* (shrouds) for the first time in their adult out-door lives. We were then introduced to a mountainous pile of luggage, from which I told them to select four pieces whilst I went out and casually brought round the jeep without attracting un-necessary attention, the nurse admitting me through the side gate.

When all was ready the cargo—the tin trunks and five human beings—piled into the jeep, the old man lying prone on the floor under a blanket, where he remained without stirring throughout the operation. The nurse then went down to the gate, peered out, and in due course waved us on. In second gear we darted through the gate, turned sharply away from the crowd (which was concentrating on the main entrance) and drove at full speed through the neighbouring Muslim quarter, now only too literally as quiet as the grave. Thence we proceeded through Connaught Place, where enthusiasts were happily burning a motor-car, and eventually landed outside the compound wall of Hyderabad House, which is a guarded Muslim refuge. I helped my charges over the wall, pushed the trunks after them and, much relieved, made my way back to my office. There I rang up the anxious wife and reported "all safe." Did she thank me? She merely expressed the hope that I would now go back to the hospital for the rest of the baggage! I reflectively replaced the receiver without reply.'

Yet, amidst all this dangerous and frustrating madness there were lucid moments. I find that to one of the letters which I have just quoted is the appended note: 'Now I must go to Lucknow and pay my respects to Her Excellency the lady Governor of the United Provinces—old Mrs. Naidu, who's a dear, but in her more poetic moods overrates the song of the bulbul. I'll try to tell her about the song of an honest blackbird in the English springtime.' Mrs. Sarojini Naidu, famous to an older generation, was a woman of some considerable genius, whether as a poetess, as a political orator or generally as the accepted Grande Dame of Congress India. She was a great friend of mine. Even in this time of stress her Province remained tolerably calm under her understanding eye, and the last of my many visits to her is still a robust and gracious memory.

By the end of the year the great blood-letting was over, though the misery and hate begotten of it have endured. Enough. From it I return to the relatively insignificant theme of departmental affairs. On looking through a bunch of my Indian letters which Sir Cyril Fox has unearthed from the back of his desk, I find in them a recurrent note of anger and despair, which jar a little upon my kindlier memory. Disloyalty, dishonesty and indolence were rife in almost every branch of the administration. As I landed at Bombay in 1944 I was handed an anonymous note written by some wretched member of my Indian staff against one of his colleagues, and others followed in steady succession until I broadcast a printed manifesto forbidding the practice in no uncertain terms—and even that did not completely stop it. From the Director General to the meanest clerk, no one was free from scandal of the most vindictive kind. My Indian predecessor, I was told deviously, had paid 15,000 rupees to the then (Indian) Secretary for Education (a man actually of irreproachable character) to secure his appointment as Director General, and I might expect my own bill in due course! Members of the Legislative Assembly, glad of any dirt however synthetic, recurrently concocted malicious questions in the Assembly against my staff or myself for political, anti-British ends. The gratuitous filth in which some considerable part of Indian politics wallowed in the 'forties is beyond belief and need not be further elaborated. My department was not of course the only objective by any means, but, since it was admittedly undergoing a purge at the hands of an Englishman, it offered special attractions to 'quit India' dialectic.

But there is another and far more important side to this picture. Those who worked closely with me—particularly the younger generation which we recruited—were on my side from the outset. They were my friends then, and are my friends now. We worked as a team for a common end, and none of us spared ourselves, whether draftsman, photographer, surveyor, assistant or officer. The disabilities with which these admirable young people had to contend were not those of disloyalty or indolence. They arose from social tradition and geographical environment.

To begin with, the conditions of family life in India militate largely against that spare-time research which is the backbone of Western scholarship. The large, sometimes immense, size of the Indian family-unit in a single crowded house, often including parents, brothers, sisters and even cousins as well as wife and children, is an inherited form of social insurance which at the same time insures very effectively against home-study. The young scholar, married off by his parents at an early age and expected to breed prolifically, finds it increasingly impossible even to maintain his professional reading, and thus gradually loses the ability and the urge to pursue his chosen subject save as a business routine. He loses, or fails to acquire, the *habit* of research.

And even where leisure can be snatched from these domestic embarrassments, the necessary literary apparatus is more often than not beyond the reach of the Indian scholar. I find a note that, 'save in Calcutta, with its Imperial Library and Royal Asiatic Society of Bengal, this difficulty is a serious handicap. The dearth of books dealing with the archaeology and history of Asia outside (but often related to) India is particularly noticeable, and this dearth, which is due in part to the fact that a considerable number of the books in question are in French or German, tends to emphasize the provincialism of Indian research.' The language problem remains indeed a formidable obstacle. At the outset, most Indian students are expected to know two languages, their local language and either Hindi or Urdu. To these must be added their classical language, Sanskrit or Persian. Further, if the results of their research are to reach a world-wide audience, the correct use of a European language (normally English) is a necessity which transcends political inhibitions but is nevertheless retarded by them. This is a formidable list, and the yet further addition of French and German exceeds the limits of a routine education. Thus astonishingly few Indians can today even spell their way through a French book, in spite of the high importance of the work done by French scholarship in South India, Gandhara, Afghanistan and Indo-China. For many reasons, the path of learning in modern India and Pakistan is not an easy one. It is a hard enough road for the keen and exceptional mind; for the second-raters, upon whom scholarship depends for much of its honest and necessary foot-slogging, it becomes an impassable tangle of conflicting urges and interests.

So far from exaggerating the difficulties which confront the Indian student, I have not in fact told their full tale. There are many contributory impediments to his progress. The vastness of his countryside affects him not only in the matter of library facilities; it isolates him also from his kind. Thus the average officer of the survey might be responsible for the archaeological administration of nearly a hundred thousand square miles of territory, much of it with indifferent communications. For a large part of his working life he is remote from his fellow-archaeologists and historians.

Contact is not merely the matter of an hour's journey between Oxford or Cambridge and London, or even a six-hours' journey from (or to) Edinburgh or Dublin. It may be a matter of days, and of a major grant of leave. Opportunities for discussion and informal mutual criticism are thus excessively rare. The essential stimulus provided by constant contact with co-workers and the interchange of ideas and methods is largely absent. In these circumstances the temptation to become a mere operative, climbing mechanically up a fixed salary-scale towards a timely pension, is only too present. Compared with his fellow-scholars in the smaller or more developed countries of the West, the average Indian archaeologist works *in vacuo*.

Nor is that all. The relatively small output of work, man for man, of the average educated Indian as compared with the output per man in the West is a matter of common knowledge. There are doubtless many causes, true or alleged: climate, a superabundant population, a disproportionate number of non-working days during the year, lack of incentive under alien rule. Of these factors, climate under modern conditions may largely be discounted; it has become rather a traditional excuse than a valid reason. With a properly organized working day, climate in India is far more favourable to archaeological work than is the climate of much of Europe. The pressure of a superabundant population is a more insidious source of demoralization: the instinct, still prevalent in India amongst all grades, to pass on jobs to others is largely a product of this factor. Out of it also has doubtless arisen the widespread notion that three inefficient men can do the work of one efficient man. The resultant accumulation of inefficiency was particularly manifest in the swollen office staffs which impeded administration during my Indian experience, and were incidentally a hot-bed of personal and political intrigue.

But, lastly, I must change the boot to the other foot. No educated man can be expected to work enthusiastically for a government which is not his own. In India that bar was removed on 15 August 1947. In future, the Indian will reap where he has sown, and I, for one, can only hope that, under the new stimulus, he will sow twice as hard and reap threefold. The watchword for the new India, counterpart to the Asokan lions which have been taken for an

Indian badge, might well be the old Asokan exhortation, 'Let small and great exert themselves.' During my four years in India I strove above all to preach (and practise) this principle of hard, honest work. If the British Raj has exhibited one unitary virtue in that complex sub-continent during two centuries of whole or partial rule, it has surely been of that fundamental, elementary kind: the importance of the job for its own sake, devoid of partiality, favour or affection—the sort of virtue which finds its ultimate apotheosis on the judicial bench. Unhappily, that virtue is not in itself enough. It works amongst dogs, it works also amongst barbarians; across the Brahmaputra in the jungles of Assam I saw in 1947 two lonely Englishmen happily ruling many thousands of happy tribesmen with undisputed authority and avuncular understanding. But, alas, that is not the whole story. In that same year I was in the club in the city of Madras, and invited a charming and cultivated Indian scholar, a man with a London doctorate, to lunch there with me. As we were sitting down, I became aware of a wildly gesticulating figure behind me and turned to find the club secretary anxiously beckoning me aside. 'You know, you can't bring *Indians* into the club!' he gibbered with starting eyes; 'It's against the rules!' Mark the year, 1947, the actual year of Partition! But had it been the year 1847 the moral would have been the same. Dogs and tribesmen, yes; but educated, sensitive fellow-creatures seem to need ultimately, if unreasonably, a vast deal more than laws and latrines— something more that we British just haven't got. The French have it, but then on the other hand they have neither laws nor latrines, so that their colonization is a little liable to be both inequitable and unsavoury. Speaking of which, I recall that I was in Madras again a few months after Partition, and, whilst travelling through the environs, came upon the perfect though unconscious comment on the Raj. Passing one of those delightful old colonnaded mansions, dignified relic of our best colonial architecture of a century or more ago and former residence of a judge, I observed that the place was already swarming with what must have been three families of Madrasis; ropes holding washing had been strung between the columns, and a gang of struggling workmen was just emerging with the sanitary convenience upon their shoulders! All concerned were a picture of happiness.

In 1943–44 two books appeared, from the pens of two men of the Indian Civil Service who knew India well, and loved India equally after their fashions. The titles of the two books adequately indicate how diverse those fashions were. The first book, written by the benevolent and successful brother of an English archbishop, was appropriately entitled *Friend of Friend*. The other, written by a critic whose critical faculty had been a sufficient bar to success, was *Strangers in India*. The archbishop's brother, nostalgic to the last K.C.I.E., concluded (autobiographically) that 'India does not really want to be quit of the type of men who used to serve her; India does not really want to be alone, separated from the Empire and its protecting power.' The critic wrote: 'No doubt there is much that could be said for a diehard policy—for retracing our steps and reverting to the old paternal rule. . . . But it is essentially a sterile policy. It affords no scope for change and growth. And it is not now a practicable policy. . . . It must be ruled out and banished altogether from the mind.' The Friend of Friend retired to his cabbages, the Stranger entered the service of the new India.

On 15 August 1947 I joined hands with Brigadier Thimayya (who later commanded the Indian armistice force in Korea) in an attempt to hold back the seething crowd that was threatening to overwhelm Jaharwalal Nehru on the *maidan* at New Delhi, whilst the Indian Air Force imprinted the triumphant word JAI upon the sky above us. Then I went back to my office and got on with my work.

14. Pakistan Postscript

PARTITION robbed my Indian Department of seven young Muslim officers, including three of my brightest recruits. Accordingly, when my tenure of office at New Delhi ended in 1948, I betook myself to the Pakistan capital, Karachi, to say good-bye and wish them well. Understandably, they were in a pretty poor pass. Muslims had necessarily been in a minority in the pre-Partition Survey, and their withdrawal to Pakistan had of course been dictated solely by the accident of creed, without any sort of regard to professional qualification. The resultant Archaeological Department of Pakistan was a peculiarly ill-assorted and ineffective assemblage. Nevertheless, I was considerably surprised when the Minister for Education (Fazlur Rahman), hearing that I was in Karachi, asked to see me, and invited me to return to Pakistan as a part-time Archaeological Adviser to the Government.

In New Delhi, the Muslim politicians had been my most persistent enemies: not because I had any antipathy to followers of the Prophet or any predisposition in favour of Siva or Vishnu, but for the simple reason that, shortly after my arrival, I had sacked a peculiarly incompetent and indolent Muslim officer who had friends in high places. The subsequent vendetta was of the unremitting oriental kind, pursued in season and out by the most devious and insidious paths. And now all was suddenly forgiven, and Medina, if not Mecca, was open to me. I paused before entering. Other plans were now afoot for me in England, and for most of seven years I had been away from home. It was time, if at all, to renew contacts there. I eventually temporized, and agreed, all being well, to return to Pakistan for three or four months annually for the next three years.

Accordingly, in 1949 and again in 1950 I spent the first part of the year in Pakistan, training, travelling, writing, excavating, and finally instituting the 'National Museum of Pakistan' at Karachi. Most of the details of this work, carried through with a willing but very unequal staff, may remain imprisoned in the Karachi files. To me, the experience was primarily of interest as an opportunity for seeing, in many aspects, a new and peculiarly bizarre political experiment in the first formative stage. It is easy to regret—and geographers must regret—the political fragmentation of so exceptionally tidy and seemly a slice of the map as the Indian subcontinent beneath its Himalayan frame. But the living contest of ideology *versus* geography on so vast a scale is enthralling and significant drama to any humanist, and a ring-side seat was a privilege of a memorable kind. Focused, as I saw it more than once, in the periodical battle of wits across the Indo-Pakistan conference-table, alternately at New Delhi and Karachi, the theme was not unworthy of an Eastern version of the *Dynasts*. Spread abroad, in the squalid, disease-ridden refugee-camps and in perennial and diabolical frontier outrages, it was a sordid commentary on the unredeemed bestiality of mankind. In this environment, the salvaging of the vestiges of past achievement was often enough a thankless and indeed irrelevant task. And yet, every now and then the fog broke for a moment and let through a faint ray of sensibility. Persistent attempts to make Pakistan aware of a past, to root its present hopes and sufferings in some sort of traditional and confident subsoil, were not altogether without effect.

In these attempts, one or two enlightened senior government servants came to my aid, both in the information branch and in the national railway service. I recall vividly how, when I was conducting a training-excavation at Mohenjo-daro in 1950 and was uncovering the vast brick podium of the third-millennium state granary on the citadel there, Railways came to me and suggested a popular excursion to the place from Karachi, some three hundred miles away. For those who may be inadequately instructed in the topography of Sind, the bare suggestion needs a little amplification. An excursion of the kind involved two long overnight journeys in a crowded train, arriving at a small wayside station about dawn. There the excursionists would have to wash and be fed, and thence in due course transported over eight miles of sand-track, the sand anchored intermittently by a fresh deposit of straw. Arrived at

Mohenjo-daro, they would have to be met, organized in separate detachments of manageable size, instructed in English and Urdu, and conducted on foot round the excavated streets and houses of the prehistoric city—a journey of two or three miles through thick, heavy sand. They would then have to be fed under an immense open-sided marquee by caterers brought from Karachi or Lahore with all equipment; and they would expect to be entertained by a lecture and perhaps by music after the repast. The whole project was without precedent, a complete gamble in cultural vulgarization.

The excursion was duly advertised in Karachi. The season was already advanced and the days were warming up, but the response was immediate. The train was packed from end to end with men, women and children, some of them infants-in-arms. At Mohenjo-daro, the vast marquee sprang up in the night, with adjacent kitchens and a mass of easy chairs, tables and tableware. My colleagues and myself, stationed in open order like markers on a review parade, received and marshalled the swarming multitude. I ran my eye over the motley, noisy crowd as it arrived. It consisted of shop-keepers, money-lenders, clerks, agents of various kinds— the little lay-folk of the capital, with their trailing families. Many of the visitors came armed for the adventure; I remember, in particular, a peculiarly repulsive small boy, about twelve years old and always in the forefront of the crowd, with a full-sized revolver and a fully charged bandolier strapped about him, and I made a mental note that, if there should be any trouble, my first act would be to brain him. Another figure that recurs to me is that of a bushy-bearded frontiersman girt waggishly with a revolver in a bright pink leather case, with cartridge-belt to match. Many brought shot-guns wherewith to alleviate the tedium of instruction. At one point I was haranguing my group in a main street of the old city, my eye fixed sternly upon the repulsive small boy in front of me, when there was a bang immediately behind me and a mangled dove fell into our midst. No one present paid the slightest attention to the incident, and I continued my harangue with scarcely a pause. But with half my mind I remember comparing the scene with an outing of the Royal Archaeological Institute.

After a prolonged *tiffin* of curries and *pilaus* and sweetmeats, I addressed the assembly under the open-sided marquee. 'They had seen that morning something of the famous Indus civilization, one of the great civilizations of the ancient world. . . . Four thousand years ago it occupied almost exactly the same area as their own great West Pakistan occupied today. . . . Here was their prototype, the shape of things to come. Here was a challenge from the past to the present! . . . The Indus civilization! Mohenjo-daro!' (Applause, the bushy gentleman with the decorative revolver leaping to his feet and echoing the salient words in Urdu, the repulsive small boy momentarily reducing his sinister scowl to a mere grimace.) As the hot sun rolled down the sky, the crowd dispersed, tired but irrepressible, a little more knowledgeable perhaps than when it arrived. The expedition was pronounced a success, and was repeated a fortnight later. The two episodes were at least an encouraging first attempt at the deliberate mass-education of a section of the semi-educated or uneducated public in the archaeology of their own country.

Indeed, whilst attempting to train the technicians of the Pakistan Archaeological Department in some part of their task, my constant aim was to create the hitherto non-existent public opinion which, in a self-governing State, was essential to their mission. I may recall one more example. Museums have never yet been the brightest jewels in the cultural crown of India, but sufficient interest had been aroused before 1947 to establish an all-India Museums Association which, on the model of the British one, met annually and produced an intermittent periodical of a sort. (I find that I was its president in 1948 but did not remain long enough to fill my term.) Now, in 1949, my energetic friend M. A. Shakur, curator of the Government Museum at Peshawar in the North-West Frontier Province, involved me, not altogether unwillingly, in the foundation of a Pakistan Museums Association, and had me installed as its first president at a remarkable open-air meeting at Peshawar. Somehow or other he had assembled under an awning a very considerable audience, rows of stalwart Afridis and other border-folk, magnificent-looking fellows, many of them luxuriantly bewhiskered. The Prime Minister of the Province presided, and eloquent addresses were delivered by all concerned. The highest ideals of museum-craft were expounded to an attentive if somewhat puzzled assembly, and then, like boys let out of school, we swarmed into a series of waiting buses. In long file, we left the town, crossed the plain and zig-zagged up the Khyber Pass—surely the most remarkable outing in the world-history of museums associations. Shortly before reaching the frontier we laboriously debussed, and streamed down the road towards the gate. It should be explained that at this time relations between Pakistan and Afghanistan were strained; it was not sur-prising therefore that the Afghan sentry, who, as we approached, was leaning over the gate in a coma, with a cigarette dangling vaguely from his lower lip, should suddenly leap to an anxious awareness of the advancing battalion and search hurriedly for his rifle. I hastened towards him with an open cigarette-case, and shortly both sides of the frontier relapsed into noisy merriment.

Thereafter we all of us adjourned to the summer bungalow of the political agent, on the hill-side above Landi Kotal, and there, at a long table laden to overflowing with massive *pilaus*, my picturesque Afridi hosts and their vastly overfed guest sat long and talked much in the cool, bright sunlight. The scene—the hurrying white clouds above the mountainous flanks of the pass, the sentries outside the compound, the lines of trembling poplars down below us beside the famous road—was not of the kind that customarily delights the eyes of presidents of museums associations. It would indeed be exaggeration to affirm that the underlying purpose of the function weighed unduly upon the thoughts of my fellow-diners.

Amidst all this very necessary propaganda, a little solid archaeo-logical work was intercalated in a somewhat spasmodic fashion. I have referred in passing to the excavation which I carried out at the famous Indus Valley capital, Mohenjo-daro, in March and April 1950 for the purpose of training my miscellaneous Pakistani staff. That episode deserves, perhaps, another word or two. From Bengal and the Punjab I assembled a dozen or more young officers and assistants, added a leavening of university students, and set them all to work with a gang of local peasants upon a few bricks which projected from one of the flanks of the citadel mound whereof I have spoken in an earlier chapter. With the gradual removal of the sand, the few bricks grew into many, until the stark walls of a huge platform began to emerge from the hill-side. The aspect was that of a fortress, towering grim and forbidding above the plain. And yet . . . I wondered.

The work proceeded at the deliberate pace of an orthodox excavation, with all the meticulous controls proper to the occasion. Stratified potsherds and other objects were recovered and recorded literally by the ton; four weeks after the beginning, twelve wagon-loads of *selected* pottery were sent back to base, and more followed. And day by day the sullen structure frowned upon us in growing immensity; day by day I became less certain what it signified. Something had to be done.

What was in fact done was rendered possible by a happy accident. A young Oxford graduate, Leslie Alcock, who had served awhile in the Indian Army, worked his way out to Karachi and presented himself as a volunteer. He had energy and a modicum of archaeo-logical experience. He now threw both into this recalcitrant task at Mohenjo-daro with a good will, and with his help we won through. During hot days we toiled at the mound. In the cooler evenings, in a tent lit with a pressure-lamp, we took it in turns to instruct the young idea. And, to do it justice, the young idea took the somewhat strenuous ordeal exceedingly well.

One of our tasks was to attempt what had not previously been seriously tried: to penetrate below the present water-table towards the foundations of the city far below it. For forty centuries or more, since (as before) man first built there, the swollen waters of the Indus, in the spring season when the snows melt in the high hills, had flooded the surrounding plain and left upon it fresh layers of fertile alluvium. Century by century, the land-surface had risen and, with it, the water-level below that surface. The earlier strata of Mohenjo-daro thus lie engulfed beneath many feet of water and mud, and have not been seen by modern eye. Our ambition was to reach them, in so far as limited time and materials allowed. The major part of this operation devolved upon Alcock.

The attempt was a brave one. Sixteen feet below the present surface we reached water. By pumping and baling, night and day, we descended ten feet further. The foundations of the citadel still lay below us when, in the last week of our work, the end came. The sides of our immense cuttings spurted a myriad jets of water and then, in the dark hours of the night, streamed noisily inwards like a mountain landslide. Fearing this, we had recorded our section to the last inch; but we were beaten, no time availed in which to

THE AUTHOR'S ARCHAEOLOGICAL EXCAVATION CAMP AT BRAHMAGIRI, SOUTH INDIA, 1947

WITH THE GOVERNOR-GENERAL OF PAKISTAN AT THE OPENING OF
THE PAKISTAN NATIONAL MUSEUM, APRIL 1950

redeem the disaster. The foundations of Mohenjo-daro are still to seek.

Above us, the pile of brickwork had all this time been growing in size and complexity. A grid of strange passages had appeared in it, signs of a one-time superstructure of timber, a curious platform alongside, with a carefully designed approach. In spite of its stark-ness, the structure became less and less like a fortress, but what was it?

Nothing short of complete excavation was now likely to unfold the secret. We took another village upon our strength and fairly hurled ourselves into the task amidst the hot brickwork, drawing, planning, recording as we went with something almost approaching desperation. As crisis and improvisation pursued each other across the scene, I remember thinking of Benvenuto Cellini and the casting of the *Perseus*. Then suddenly the problem answered itself.

I had paid a hurried visit to Karachi to see my Minister about the forthcoming State-opening of the National Museum which a part of my staff had been busily preparing there. It was 2 a.m. in bright moonlight when I returned to the little wayside station eight miles from Mohenjo-daro, to be met by Alcock in our jeep. 'Well,' I said, almost unthinkingly, 'how is the civic granary?' He looked a trifle startled, but by the end of the eight miles we had argued it backwards and forwards, and were of one mind. The high podium on the accessible flank of the citadel (away from the town), the grid of air-ducts to dry the floor of the great timber barn which had at one time crowned it, the loading-platform, the carefully planned approach for the wagons bringing in the tributary corn—every detail fell into place. Set prominently amidst the royal or municipal buildings, this had been the economic focus of the city, equivalent to the State Treasury of later times, register of the city's wealth and well-being. A new chapter had been added to the story of the ancient metropolis. Our work there was done, and we returned to its modern successor.

Karachi is one of the nodal points in trans-world traffic, and, as the capital of a new and needy state, was then (and maybe still is) the goal of high-level agents and touts of all kinds. Its social centre was the Palace Hotel, where on any evening one might observe a dozen nations in action. I call idly to mind that one day there I

H

passed a casual acquaintance in conversation with a strikingly flamboyant charmer, a woman manifestly of mature experience, bejewelled and arrayed in a superb *sari*, and was introduced to her as 'Princess.' Inquiry elicited the information that she was 'Turkish' (I suspected, Egyptian), that she had until very lately been a leading figure in the entourage of a certain maharaja, and that she was now trying to exchange the deserts of Pakistan for the more fruitful fields of Bombay. Exit permits were not always, however, an easy commodity, and I have come across a contemporary note of a conversation on the matter with the lady in question. It occurred the following morning on the staircase of the hotel, when, running up the stairs and turning a corner sharply, I nearly collided with the 'Princess.' She detained me.

'Ah, Monsieur, help me! That wicked passport man, he has taken away my passport and will not give it back to me unless I give HIM—how you say?—my Vir-tue.'

'Well, Princess, surely the quality of virtue is not strained?'

'Comment, Monsieur?'

'I said, what a *horrible* man.'

'Yes, *vairy* horrible. Mon Dieu! And I want *so much* my passport. It is terrible for a beautiful woman to travel about so alone. Everyone he want something. How *shall* I get my passport?'

'I am afraid, Princess, I have no alternative suggestion.'

'Oh, how you say?—Damnation!'

Two days later the helpless innocent had vanished successfully into the Bombay 'plane. . . .

The formal opening of the National Museum of Pakistan in April 1950 was a successful function, well reported in the Pakistan Press. The Governor-General, flanked by his Cabinet, made an imposing array on the platform, and in the body of the hall an abundance of flowers and the Corps Diplomatique concealed the scarcity of exhibits. In point of fact, in odd corners there lurked a sufficiently interesting nucleus of material from the pre-Aryan Indus cities, from Buddhist Taxila, from Buddhist shrines in Bengal, from the centres of modern Sindi craftsmanship, now dying rapidly owing to the flight of the essential Hindu middlemen. From the blackened ruins of Lahore, where flame and murder had penetrated into the old city during the Partition riots, I had rescued some fine fragments of ancient architectural woodcarving and now had them set up jauntily in the new museum. For the rest, a draped flag of Pakistan and an immense painted map of the largest Muslim state in the world reconciled the patriotic visitor to the spectacle of so many reminders of prophets before the Prophet and of the Godless who had bowed to other gods. In the evening sunlight we drank to the future in glasses of sweet orangeade and thought that on the whole we had done rather well.

And yet: a National Museum, universities or university colleges in Karachi, Lahore, Peshawar, Dacca, multitudes of jostling clerks of varying degrees of incompetence, a swarming illiterate peasantry —what a disparate complex from which to mould a new political unit of immense size and strategic world importance! One can but wish its leaders a clear vision and honest single-mindedness; they have a long and stony path in front of them. The following news-paragraph, from the *Pakistan Times* of 8 February 1949, hints at the jungle which lies at their doorstep.

THEY ALLOW PENS NOT PISTOLS

(By Our Special Representative)

'Are pens and pistols used by examinees of the Punjab University?'

An interesting side-light is thrown on this in a circular letter issued by the University of the Punjab to Heads of various educational institutions. It reads: 'It has been decided that candidates found possessing fire-arms or anything capable of being used as a weapon of offence in the examination hall shall be liable to punishment under "Unfair Means Regulation." '

Inquiries made by me show that quite a large number of examinees openly took help from the textbooks in answering questions in the University examinations in 1948. When the invigilators tried to stop them from doing so the examinees silenced them by showing loaded pistols.

The cultural veneer was indeed too thin for the part-time task which I had undertaken. In one's presence, with a finite programme and direct access to the Minister, advance was reasonably possible;

but as one's 'plane left Karachi each year for London, progress ceased and was replaced by sterile intrigue. In 1951 I refused the Minister's invitation to return yet again to this Sisyphean labour, and as I write these words in 1954 the Pakistan Department of Archaeology is numbered amongst the unburied dead. One can but hope.

15. Twenty Years Asleep

For me, I know nought; nothing I deny,
  Admit, reject, contemn; and what know *you*,
Except, perhaps, that you were born to die?
  And both may, after all, turn out untrue.
An age may come, Font of Eternity,
  When nothing shall be either old or new.
Death, so call'd, is a thing which makes men weep:
And yet a third of life is pass'd in sleep.

THE reflection that we—most of us—spend over twenty years of our miserable little lives asleep struck me sharply as a curious and rather shocking piece of celestial improvidence long before *Don Juan* came into my youthful hands, and has never ceased to depress me. Combined with the necessity for learning irregular Greek verbs before breakfast, it early inflicted upon me the anti-social habit of leaping from my bed at untimely hours, and it is not entirely due to the accidents of two wars that I am an authority on dawns. Whilst adoring luxury I abhor waste, and am firmly of the view that most of us are unconscionably wasteful in this matter of sleep. It must at the same time be added that I have been made aware of other opinions.

In the background, then, of the simple story comprised by this book has throughout lurked a certain anxiety to make the most active use of waking hours. Of what profit to others or even to myself that anxious precipitancy may have been is another matter, beyond my proper judgment. But from time to time we all sit back, whatever our occupation, and ask ourselves the question: 'Is what I am doing worth while? Whither am I going? Is my journey really necessary?' More often than not, we muff the answer with comfortable sophistry, with evasion, self-flattery and facile rationalization. As scientists, for example, we may justify our puny endeavours with the affirmation that *all* scientific knowledge, *all* scientific discovery, is worth while, and whatever we may be doing or have done as scientists is *ipso facto* justified. Science is an end in itself. What fools we are! We fastidiously select our boots and neckties, but are content to live by opportunity.

Yet not, I hope, entirely. Amidst a fair show of this folly I have sought with a measure of obstinacy to work to a plan or pattern and to create the occasion for fulfilment. In the field-archaeology and digging to which I have devoted much of my time, the period 1914–54 has been one of violent transition; so much so that the present generation, with its assumed techniques, its fluorine, nitrogen and radiocarbon tests and others in prospect, can only by a deliberate act of the imagination re-create the conditions of 1913–14. The crude sections, if any, upon which were based the pioneer excavations of Corbridge in 1908 or Hengistbury Head in 1911—enterprises with many virtues but strangely obliquitous to the achievement of Pitt Rivers twenty years before—constituted almost the only material training available to my generation. But in science, not least in archaeology, a generation is no more than fifteen years. Between 1922 and 1930 those who had been school-boys in 1914–18 were already knocking impatiently at the door. Forerunners of the brilliant group which is now (1954) in its prime—Ian Richmond, Christopher Hawkes, Nowell Myres, Grahame Clark and others—were demanding instruction from those who, with the five-year war-gap behind them, were themselves still *in statu pupillari*. Looking back over thirty years, I am less surprised at the many inadequacies of the situation than at the considerable body of useful work which was nevertheless produced.

Above all, within the limited horizons of my chosen province I was deeply conscious at this time of the responsibility which a deadly war had bequeathed to me. I do not want to over-emphasize my solitariness in those early 'twenties, but it was instant to my thoughts at the time and a recurrent stimulus to action. O. G. S. Crawford had a few years' start of me, and just before the 1914 war had begun to set the stage for that geographical interpretation of prehistory that Cyril Fox, also slightly my senior, was to establish on a classic footing in his studies of the Cambridge region and beyond. Crawford, too, was opening up new worlds through the

TODAY

medium of air-photography. Bushe-Fox indeed in 1922 returned to excavation at Richborough; but I was still essentially alone. To Crawford and Fox excavation was a minor incidental, and Bushe-Fox himself, for all his astuteness in the field, never fully developed the academic side of his work. For some years, until the new generation was ready to take over, I held the field, always with an appreciation of the hard fact that my position was the outcome of circumstance, not merit.

And then, alongside this missionary aspect of my work, which found expression eventually in the creation of the Institute of Archaeology in London, there were two other factors. First, it was my conviction at the outset that our work should be broadly based in public opinion. That may sound a strange and unnecessary ambition in an age when the Press and the B.B.C. are clamouring for archaeological news. But it is necessary to remember that that clamour is a relatively recent phenomenon, due in part (I like to think) to the very effort of which I am speaking. With archaeology in his mind, Pitt Rivers could write at the end of the last century that 'if ever a time should come when our illustrated newspapers take to recording interesting and sensible things, a new era will have arrived in the usefulness of these journals. . . . Let us hope for evolution in this as in all other things.' Looking backwards from 1954 it is legitimate to say that evolution has not been idle in this matter. But it has not been unprompted.

Secondly, it was equally my conviction that research should proceed, not fortuitously, but on a rigidly selective scale of values. Those values necessarily change from age to age and mind to mind; the prime point at issue is not their individual character but the necessity for their presence. Put simply, I would say to the young archaeologist, *Have a plan.* And, having a plan, see that the plan is worth while, is likely to add significantly to our knowledge of the human mind and human achievement. Let our work be creative to the maximum extent of which, in a reasonably limited space, it is capable. My experience is that far too large a proportion of our effort is expended with inadequate planning; and economic duress is by no means solely to blame. Planning on any liberal scale implies a contest with providence and reflects therefore a certain sense of adventure. And how astonishingly rare that sense of adventure is—how nearly universal the complacent philosophy of 'Easy live and quiet die!'

As I write those words, I recall how in 1945 it was my task to lead a small 'cultural mission' from the Government of India to the Government of Iran, and how for the first stage of the journey through the border country we were saddled with a British military escort under the command of a peculiarly solemn corporal. Early in the evening, as we emerged from the hills on to the great desert, we found that one of the three escort trucks had dropped back in the dust with a mechanical defect, and it soon became clear that progress for the day was at an end. Under a fine starlit sky of vast expanse, beside one of the lonely towers built in the eighteenth century by Nadir Shah on his way to purloin the Peacock Throne of Delhi, we lay upon the cool surface of the desert and smoked and talked. The conversation went as follows.

'Well, Corporal, how long have you been out here?'

'Near two years, Sir.'

'Seen much of the country?'

'Oh yes, Sir, up and down and round about. I seen most of it.'

'What fun. You must have had a grand time.'

'No, Sir.'

'What?'

'No, Sir. I 'ates it.'

'You'd rather be elsewhere?'

'Yes. I'd rather be doin' me proper job. I'd a good job before they put me in the army.'

'Oh, what was that?'

'I was a funeral specialist and embalmer in Tooting. A nice little business.'

Mentally at least he handed me his business card, and the conversation languished. Of life he demanded only death, and that vicariously. He was an honest realist, and I can only hope that he flourishes once more upon the mortality of Tooting.

Not for my corporal were the adventures of inquiry. He had found his balance, and questioned nought save the upsetting of it. He will, on the whole, have enjoyed his twenty years asleep, exempt from the malaise that is the penalty of those who—like all good archaeologists—must live and plan adventurously for the future.

Index